Benjamin Pitzer

Automatic Reconstruction of Textured 3D Models

Schriftenreihe
Institut für Mess- und Regelungstechnik,
Karlsruher Institut für Technologie (KIT)

Band 020

Eine Übersicht über alle bisher in dieser Schriftenreihe erschienenen Bände finden Sie am Ende des Buchs.

Automatic Reconstruction of Textured 3D Models

by
Benjamin Pitzer

KIT Scientific Publishing

Dissertation, Karlsruher Institut für Technologie (KIT)
Fakultät für Maschinenbau
Tag der mündlichen Prüfung: 22. Februar 2011
Referenten: Prof. Dr.-Ing. C. Stiller, Adj. Prof. Dr.-Ing. M. Brünig

Impressum

KIT Scientific Publishing

Karlsruher Institut für Technologie (KIT)
KIT Scientific Publishing
Straße am Forum 2
D-76131 Karlsruhe

KIT Scientific Publishing is a registered trademark of Karlsruhe Institute of Technology. Reprint using the book cover is not allowed.

www.ksp.kit.edu

Print on Demand 2014

ISSN 1613-4214
ISBN 978-3-86644-805-6
DOI: 10.5445/KSP/1000025619

Automatic Reconstruction of Textured 3D Models

Zur Erlangung des akademischen Grades eines

Doktors der Ingenieurwissenschaften

von der Fakultät für Maschinenbau
der Universität Karlsruhe (TH)
genehmigte

Dissertation

von

DIPL.-ING. BENJAMIN PITZER

aus Menlo Park, CA

Hauptreferent:	Prof. Dr.-Ing. C. Stiller
Korreferent:	Adj. Prof. Dr.-Ing. M. Brünig
Tag der mündlichen Prüfung:	22.02.2011

Abstract

3D reconstruction and visualization of environments is increasingly important and there is a wide range of application areas where 3D models are required. Reconstructing 3D models has therefore been a major research focus in academia and industry. For example, large scale efforts for the reconstruction of city models at a global scale are currently underway. A major limitation in those efforts is that creating realistic 3D models of environments is a tedious and time consuming task. In particular, two major issues persist which prevent a broader adoption of 3D modeling techniques: a lack of affordable 3D scanning devices that enable an easy acquisition of 3D data and algorithms capable of automatically processing this data into 3D models. We believe that autonomous technologies, which are capable of generating textured 3D models of real environments, will make the modeling process affordable and enable a wide variety of new applications. This thesis addresses the problem of automatic 3D reconstruction and we present a system for unsupervised reconstruction of textured 3D models in the context of modeling indoor environments. The contributions are solutions to all aspects of the modeling process and an integrated system for the automatic creation of large scale 3D models. We first present a robotic data acquisition system which allows us to automatically scan large environments in a short amount of time. We also propose a calibration procedure for this system that determines the internal and external calibration which is necessary to transform data from one sensor into the coordinate system of another sensor. Next, we present solutions for the multi-view data registration problem, which is essentially the problem of aligning the data of multiple 3D scans into a common coordinate system. We propose a novel non-rigid registration method based on a probabilistic SLAM framework. This method incorporates spatial correlation models as map priors to guide the optimization. Scans are aligned by optimizing robot pose estimates as well as scan points. We show that this non-rigid registration significantly improves the alignment. Next, we address the problem of reconstructing a consistent 3D surface representation from the registered point clouds. We propose a volumetric surface reconstruction method based on a Poisson framework. In a second step, we improve the accuracy of this reconstruction by optimizing the mesh vertices to achieve a better approximation of the true surface. We demonstrate that this method is very suitable for the reconstruction of indoor environments. Finally, we present a solution to the reconstruction of texture maps from multiple scans. Our texture reconstruction approach partitions the surface into segments, unfolds each segment onto a plane, and reconstructs a texture map by blending multiple views into a single composite. This technique results in a very realistic reconstruction of the surface appearance and greatly enhances the visual impression by adding more realism.

Contents

List of Symbols and Abbreviations

General Notation

$\mathbf{A}$	A matrix with *m* rows and *n* columns. $\mathbf{A} = \begin{pmatrix} a_{11} & a_{12} & \cdots & a_{1n} \\ a_{21} & a_{22} & \cdots & a_{2n} \\ \vdots & \vdots & \ddots & \vdots \\ a_{m1} & a_{m2} & \cdots & a_{mn} \end{pmatrix}$
$\mathbf{A}^{-1}$	The inverse of $\mathbf{A}$.
$\mathbf{A}^{\mathsf{T}}$	The transpose of $\mathbf{A}$.
$\Vert\mathbf{A}\Vert$	Matrix norm (subscript if any denotes what norm).
$\det(\mathbf{A})$	The determinant of $\mathbf{A}$.
	The null matrix. Zero in all entries.
$\mathbf{I}$	The identity matrix.
$\mathbf{x}$	A n-dimensional vector. $\mathbf{x} = \begin{pmatrix} x_1 & x_2 & \cdots & x_n \end{pmatrix}^{\mathsf{T}} = \begin{pmatrix} x_1 \\ x_2 \\ \vdots \\ x_n \end{pmatrix}$
$\mathbf{a} \cdot \mathbf{b}$	The dot product of two equal-length vectors $\mathbf{a} \cdot \mathbf{b} = \mathbf{a}^{\mathsf{T}}\mathbf{b}$.
$\mathbf{a} \times \mathbf{b}$	The cross product of two equal-length vectors.
$\mathcal{M}$	A set with *n* elements $\mathcal{M} = \{\mathbf{m}_1, \ldots, \mathbf{m}_n\}$.
s	A scalar.

Statistical Notation

$P(\cdot)$	Probability.
$P(\cdot \mid \cdot)$	Conditional probability.
$p(\cdot)$	Probability density.
$N(\mu, \sigma^2)$	A univariate normal distribution where the parameters μ and σ^2 are the mean and the variance.
$N_k(\boldsymbol{\mu}, \boldsymbol{\Sigma})$	A multivariate normal distribution where the parameters $\boldsymbol{\mu} \in \mathbb{R}^k$ and $\boldsymbol{\Sigma} \in \mathbb{R}^{k \times k}$ are the mean and the covariance matrix.

Acronyms

ADC	Analog-to-Digital Converter
AR	Augmented Reality
AUV	Autonomous Underwater Vehicles
BRDF	Bidirectional Reflectance Distribution Function
BSSRDF	Bidirectional Scattering-Surface Reflection Distribution Function
CAD	Computer-Aided Design
CCD	Charge-Coupled Device
CG	Conjugate Gradient
CLM	Concurrent Localization and Mapping
DoF	Degree of Freedom
EIF	Extended Information Filter
EKF	Extended Kalman Filter
HDR	High Dynamic Range
ICP	Iterative Closest Point
LIDAR	Light Detection And Ranging
MAP	Maximum A-Posteriori
MVS	Multi-View Stereo
NURBS	Non-Uniform Rational B-Spline
OPP	Orthogonal Procrustes Problem
RAG	Region Adjacency Graphs
RBF	Radial Basis Functions
RMS	Root Mean Square
SfM	Structure from Motion

SGD Stochastic Gradient Descent

SIFT Scale Invariant Feature Transform

SLAM Simultaneous Localization and Mapping

SVBRDF Spatial Varying Bidirectional Reflectance Distribution Function

1 Introduction

Realistic 3D representations of environments are becoming increasingly important to a wide variety of current and future applications: content creation for computer games and geospatial applications, 3D walkthroughs of real estates, digital preservation of cultural heritage and crime sites, and many more. In particular, 3D models of indoor environments are important for emergency planning, facility management, and surveillance applications. Creating such models from blueprints is a tedious task and hard to automate since many buildings do not comply with the blueprints created by their architects. Even accurate blueprints do not contain objects added after the building construction such as appliances and furniture.

Methods to digitize and reconstruct the shapes of complex three dimensional objects have evolved rapidly in recent years. The speed and accuracy of digitizing technologies owe much to advances in the areas of physics and electrical engineering, including the development of laser, Charge-Coupled Device (CCD), and high speed sampling Analog-to-Digital Converter (ADC) technology. Such technologies allow us to take detailed shape measurements with a resolution better than 0.1 mm[1] at rates exceeding 1 million samples per second[2].

Digital photography has also significantly evolved in the past decades and is likely to see further advances in the near future. The pixel count is only one of the major factors, though it is the most heavily marketed figure of merit. High-resolution digital cameras with sensors exceeding 12 megapixels[3] are available as a commodity and are even put into cellphones[4]. Other factors include the lens quality and image post-processing capabilities. Some cameras[5] have the function to combine multiple images shot with different exposures into one High Dynamic Range (HDR) image.

With all of the upcoming range finding and imaging technologies available at our disposal, it still remains very challenging to digitize environments such as building interiors. To capture a complete environment, many millions of range samples and many hundreds of images must be acquired. The resulting mass of data requires

---

[1] Cyberware Large Statue 3D Scanner (Model LSS) used in the Digital Michelangelo Project

[2] Velodyne HDL-64E used by many successful teams at the 2007 DARPA Urban Challenge

[3] Nikon D700 full-frame digital single-lens reflex camera

[4] Apple's iPhone 4 comes with a 5 megapixel camera

[5] Pentax K-7 camera with in-camera high dynamic range imaging function

algorithms that can efficiently and reliably generate computer models from these samples. The environment needs to be scanned from different viewpoints in order to completely reconstruct it leading to the question of where the best viewpoints are and how many are required for a complete scene coverage. Because each range scan and each camera image has its own local coordinate system, all data must be transformed into a common coordinate frame. This procedure is usually referred to as *registration*.

Raw range measurements obtained from scanning devices are often not a very suitable format for later use in applications. Parametric representations are typically more appropriate since they allow for the definition of surface attributes (normals, gradients) and are more suitable for rendering, efficient reduction, and collision testing. One fundamental question in digital geometry processing is how to represent a surface: What mathematical description should be chosen to represent the surface of a 3D object on a computer? Industrial design applications for car and airplane construction prefer Non-Uniform Rational B-Spline (NURBS) while the game and movie industries have focused on polygonal representations such as triangle meshes. In either case, the set of range samples has to be pre-processed into a set of point samples and then converted into a certain surface representation, e.g., a polygonal mesh or a collection of spline patches.

Often the purpose for scanning environments and reconstructing their surfaces is a visualization on a computer monitor. In this case, obtaining the surface geometry is not enough and we can get a much more realistic impression by reconstructing the surface appearance as well. A textured 3D model almost completely hides the polygonal nature of the underlying surface representation and results in a very natural appearance. Even the surface geometry appears to be more detailed which, in reality, is only an optical illusion that falsely represents the actual geometry.

Since the acquisition process merely samples the real environment, noise is inevitably introduced into the captured dataset. To minimize the negative effects of noise, post processing steps might be applied depending on the purpose of the data: for applications that aim at human perception, a pleasing visualization is emphasized whereas for others, such as autonomous navigation, an accurate and rich representation is preferred over attractiveness.

Today, the reconstruction and modeling process is still primarily done manually, ranging from a complete design from scratch to a semi-automated data acquisition with manual registration and reconstruction. Since human labor is expensive, these models usually lack details that might be vital for applications such as autonomous robot navigation.

1.1 Motivation

We are motivated to consider the 3D reconstruction problem by a number of application areas in science and engineering, including robotics, cultural heritage, video games, and city modeling. This section briefly discusses each of these applications.

Robotics

A robotic system must perceive the environment in which a task (navigation, manipulation) has to be executed. If a robot has to interact in an environment it must either be supplied with a sufficient model or it must build an internal representation of this environment from sensor data. So far, most approaches to mobile robot navigation assume that the robot operates in a plane. In this case, a 2D map marking drivable areas and obstacles may be sufficient for navigation. However, to navigate non-flat areas or to solve complex robotic tasks involving object manipulation a 3D representation becomes necessary. There is also a tendency to introduce high-level semantic information in several areas of robotics. Recent work in mapping and localization tries to extract semantically meaningful structures from sensor data during map building [Nüchter et al., 2005], or to use semantic knowledge for grasp planning and object manipulation [Xue et al., 2009]. This includes structure and high-level understanding of objects and their functions. A reconstructed 3D model can serve as rich source of information for semantic knowledge extraction and spatial reasoning.

Real Estate

A 3D walkthrough is the best way to visualize a property without actually going there. High-quality computer generated animations let you experience a home and get a realistic feel for its size and layout. Realtors already use this powerful tool to showcase a building while it is in the planning stages and to attract potential buyers through online presentations. Currently these models are crafted by artists and the process is tedious and time consuming. As the level of architectural realism increases so do the labor costs and creation time. For this reasons 3D walkthroughs are only generated for high-end real estate.

In recent years, there has been an increasing interest in the automatic generation of 3D models of entire cities. For example, GoogleEarth[6] and Microsoft Bing Maps[7] have started providing 3D models for a few cities and landmarks. This process not only results in high costs, which inhibits broad use of the models, but also makes it impossible to use them for applications where the goal is to monitor changes over time, such as detecting damage or possible danger zones after catastrophes.

Cultural Heritage

Monuments and buildings of outstanding universal value from the perspective of history, art, or science are often under threat from environmental conditions, structural instability, increased tourism and city development. 3D laser scanning, in combination with other digital documentation techniques and traditional survey methods, provides an extremely reliable and accurate way to document the spatial and visual characteristics of these sites. Digital representations not only provide an accurate record of these rapidly deteriorating sites, which can be saved for posterity, but also provide a comprehensive base dataset by which site managers, archaeologists, and conservators can monitor sites and perform necessary restoration work to ensure their physical integrity.

Entertainment Industry

The creation of compelling models is a crucial task in the development of successful movies and computer games. However, modeling large and realistic three-dimensional environments is a very time-consuming and expensive process, and it can require several person years of labor. For example, consider using a realistic 3D model of the Sistine Chapel in a 3D computer game. To create a realistic virtual reality of this famous place, a modeling process has to be performed, which includes taking numerous measurements and building a geometrically and photometrically correct representation. Today this process is primarily done by hand due to the high complexity of these environments. In the case of the Sistine Chapel, a computer graphics artist would have to spend many tedious hours of CAD-modeling while often facing the problem of a lack of photo-realism once the objects are rendered. The result may look visually correct, but lacks in architectural details, such as interior decoration and photo-realistic textures. This process could be drastically simplified by having an automatic 3D reconstruction system.

[6]http://earth.google.com/
[7]http://www.microsoft.com/maps/

1.2 Problem Statement

In engineering, building construction, manufacturing and many other industries, we create physical objects from digital models on a daily basis. However, the reverse problem, inferring a digital description from an existing physical object or environment, has received much less attention. We refer to this problem as *reverse-engineering* or *3D reconstruction*. Specifically, the reconstruction of indoor and outdoor environments received interest only recently as companies began to recognize that using reconstructed models is a way to generate revenue through location based services and advertisements. There are various properties of a 3D environment that one may be interested in recovering, including its shape, its color, its material properties, and even its functional properties. This thesis addresses the problem of recovering 3D shape, also called *surface reconstruction*, and the problem of recovering surface appearance, also called *texture reconstruction*. We present a complete system for automatic reconstruction of textured 3D models. The tasks required to fulfill our goal can be organized into a sequence of stages that process the input data. Each of these stages confronts us with its specific problems. From those, the questions addressed in this thesis are:

- How can we scan the environment's surface geometry using laser range-finders and color cameras?
- How can we accurately express all the data in a single coordinate system?
- How can we convert separate scans into a single surface description?
- How can we combine the color information from the different views to reconstruct a high quality texture?

1.3 Taxonomy of 3D Reconstruction Systems

Four main criteria define the taxonomy of a 3D reconstruction system: first, the architecture of the computational system itself; second, the nature of the target that is to be reconstructed; third, the type of sensors being used; and forth, the representation acting as an output of the modeling procedure.

1.3.1 System Architecture

The process of digitally reconstructing an environment can be decomposed into several modules, each performing a distinct part of the complex task. A general

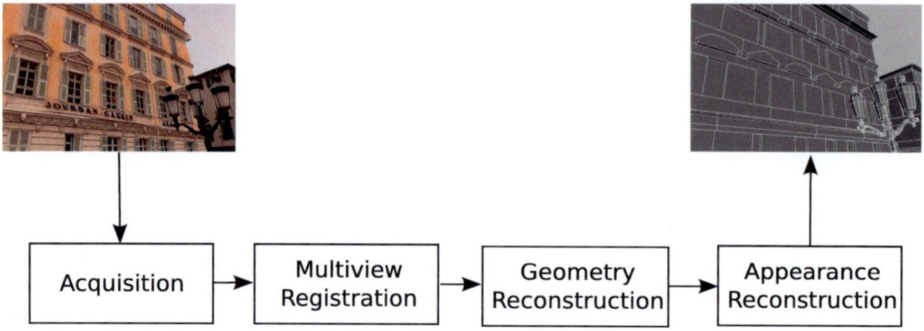

Figure 1.1: Generic structure of a system for 3D reconstruction.

framework embracing the modules is shown in Figure 1.1.

The function of each module is as follows:

- *Acquisition:* This module contains all functionality related to the acquisition of data relevant to the reconstruction process. This may include controlling a camera to take pictures, using a lidar for distance measurements, and even controling a mobile robot to position the sensors. The results of this module are raw measurements, such as images, distance measurements, and robot wheel odometry.

- *Multi-view Registration:* Typically, multiple data acquisitions from different view-points are necessary to digitize scenes without occlusions. The task of this module is to merge data from different views into a common coordinate system. This is a difficult problem to resolve since an externally referenced position estimate of the sensors is usually not available.

- *Geometry Reconstruction:* The efficient processing of geometric objects requires suitable data structures. In many applications, the use of polygonal meshes as surface representation is advantageous because of a good support in modern graphics cards and a well-defined spatial connectivity within the data structure. In this context, the registered data has to undergo post-processing in order to extract a consistent surface representation. This is referred to as *surface reconstruction*. Due to the enormous complexity of meshes acquired by 3D scanning, mesh decimation techniques are mandatory for error-controlled simplification.

- *Appearance Reconstruction:* In order to obtain photo-realistic models, the surface appearance is reconstructed and applied to the geometric model in the last step. The appearance of a material is a function of how that material interacts with light which includes simple reflectance or it may exhibit more complex phenomena such as sub-surface scattering. Specifically, for applications that aim to visualize for human observers, correctly reconstructing and reproducing the surface appearance greatly enhances the visual impression by adding more realism.

The inherent structure of this architecture suggests an implementation as a set of modules, each performing one or more of the subtask discussed above.

1.3.2 Object Type

An import criterion that defines a 3D reconstruction system is the type of object or environment that is supposed to be reconstructed. An obvious aspect to take into account is the object's size. Small objects, such as the mechanical parts depicted in Figure 1.2(a), can be held in one hand or put on a turntable to measure them from all sides keeping the sensors stationary. The reconstruction of large objects, such as statues (see Figure 1.2(c)), requires measurements from various different view-points to correctly capture all the details. When it comes to the reconstruction of environments, such as buildings and historical sites, such as the Taj Mahal (see Figure 1.2(b)), the data acquisition and modeling process can be extremely difficult. Thousands of scans may be necessary to capture the entire environment in a satisfactory resolution.

Not only the size, but also the complexity of three-dimensional objects is relevant for the design of a 3D reconstruction system. Specifically, non-convex objects may cause self-occlusions in the measuring process requiring more scans and a more complex sensor system.

The material of an object is another important aspect to be considered. Dark texture absorbs most of the light and makes geometry reconstruction with active light sources difficult. For the same reason, specular and transparent surfaces are extremely difficult to reconstruct.

1.3.3 Sensor Type

The nature of the sensor technology used in the reconstruction system affects the design of the acquisition module of the system. In the past, different kinds of 3D scanners were used for reconstruction. Focussing on non-contact sensors, 3D scanners can be divided into two main categories:

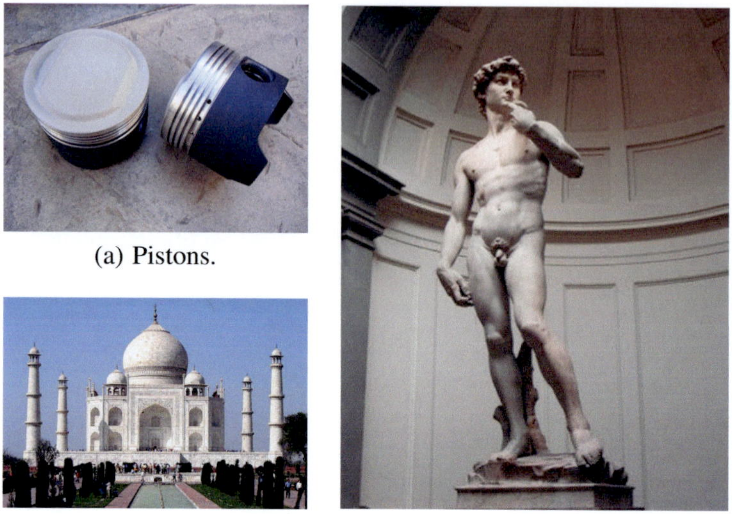

(a) Pistons.

(b) Taj Mahal.

(c) Michelangelo's David.

Figure 1.2: Examples of reconstruction objects: (a) mechanical parts, (b) historical sites, and (c) statues

Passive sensors do not emit any kind of light or other forms of radiation, but rather measure reflected ambient light. The most prominent technology in this category is *stereoscopic vision*, which uses two cameras observing the same scene from slightly different positions. The slight differences in the camera images are used to estimate depth by triangulation. Numerous other approaches exist exploiting different aspects of the image formation process typically referred as *shape-from-x*. Here x refers the underlying concept, e.g., shading, texture, defocus, and many more. The goal, however, is always the same: how to derive a 3D scene description from one or more 2D images. Passive sensors are typically cheap, because the cameras used in these sensors are built in mass-production and no other special hardware is required.

Active sensors emit some kind of radiation or light and detect its reflection in order to probe an object or environment. There are three sub-categories of active sensors which are widely used for reconstruction:

- *Time-of-flight* sensors measure the distance to a surface by timing the round-trip time of a pulse of light or sound. Examples include laser range finders and sonar sensors.

- *Active triangulation sensors* use the position of reflected light dots or stripes in a camera image to determine the distance of the underlying surface.
- *Structured light sensors* project a pattern of light on an object and look at the deformation of the pattern on the surface in order to determine depth and orientation.

Mobile robotics have relied heavily on active ranging sensors because most provide direct distance measurements. Active sensors also tend to provide more robust and accurate measurements since the technology does not rely on external illumination. In this thesis, we focus on active sensors for geometry reconstruction (in particular actuated laser range finders) and passive sensors (cameras) for appearance reconstruction.

1.3.4 Data Representation

The point clouds produced by 3D scanners are usually not used directly, although for simple visualization and measurement in the architecture and construction world, points may suffice. The process of converting a point cloud into a usable 3D model is called *reconstruction* or *modeling*. The following representations are commonly used:

In a polygonal representation of a shape, a curved surface is modeled as many small faceted planar surfaces. Polygon models, also called *mesh models*, are useful for visualization since polygons can be efficiently rendered on graphics cards. Reconstruction of a polygonal model from point cloud data involves finding and connecting adjacent points with straight lines in order to create a continuous surface.

A more sophisticated type of modeling surfaces involves using curved instead of planar surface patches to model a shape. These might be NURBS, Bézier patches or other curved representations of curved topology. Curved surface models have the advantage of modeling smooth surfaces more accurately and are more manipulable when used in Computer-Aided Design (CAD).

A third class of data representations are *volumetric representations*. In the simplest case, the space containing the object or scene to be reconstructed is equidistantly divided into small cubical volume elements called *voxels*. If a particular voxel does not belong to the object it is set transparent, whereas voxels within the object remain opaque and can additionally be colored according to material properties. Thus, the entire scene is composed of small cubes approximating the volume of the objects. In particular, medical applications make frequent use of this implicit representation because it is often necessary to visualize various tissue layers and the internal aspects of the human body.

1.4 State of the Art / Related Work

Several efforts have been made in the past regarding the creation of environment maps out of 3D range data. Since the creation of such maps involves the combination of several algorithms, we will address the most relevant publications for our work below. Related work on particular parts of the reconstruction pipeline will be addressed in their respective sections.

1.4.1 Automatic 3D Modeling Robots

One of the first projects that was concerned with an automatic system to reconstruct textured 3D models of building interiors is RESOLV (REconstruction using Scanned Laser and Video) [Sequeira et al., 1999]. A portable unit known as an EST (Environmental Sensor for Telepresence) is a push trolley that is moved around in the environment that shall be captured. The EST includes a scanning laser range finder for capturing the 3D structure of the surroundings and a video camera for adding the textures. A picture of EST is presented in Figure 1.3(a). The researchers developed software that performs several functions, including meshing of the range data, registration of video texture, and registration and integration of data acquired from different capture points. The RESOLV project aimed at modeling interiors for virtual reality and tele-presence which is part of our motivation. However, their approach was designed to reconstruct small (single-room sized) environments. Operating on the scale of a full office floor poses a major challenge.

The AVENUE (Autonomous Vehicle for Exploration and Navigation in Urban Environments) project [Allen et al., 2001] at Columbia University targeted the automation of urban site modeling. The research group around Peter K. Allen built a mobile robot based on iRobot's ATRV-2 plattform (see Figure 1.3(b)). The system is equipped with real-time kinematics (GPS, compass, tilt-sensors) and a camera for navigation. The main sensor for 3D reconstruction is a Cyrax laser range scanner that delivers high quality distance measurements at up to 100 m operating range. The focus of this work was on building a mobile data acquisition platform, including the design of a software architecture, localization components, and path planning.

Many research groups use 2D laser range finders to build 3D volumetric representations of the environment. Several approaches [Thrun et al., 2000,

(a) EST. (b) AVENUE. (c) Waegele.

Figure 1.3: Automatic 3D Modeling Robots.

Früh and Zakhor, 2003, Zhao and Shibasaki, 2001] use two 2D laser range finders to acquire 3D data. One scanner is mounted horizontally while the other one is mounted vertically. The latter one acquires a vertical scan line and transforms it into 3D points using the current robot pose, which is estimated from the range scans of the horizontal scanner. By accumulating the vertical scans, the system generates accurate three-dimensional models. An application of this was presented by [Thrun et al., 2004] to obtain 3D models of underground mines. The same setup with two scanners has been used by [Hähnel et al., 2003b] in indoor and outdoor applications. Along the same line as the approaches described above, the Wägele robot comprises two vertical laser range finders to obtain 3D information and a third one is used for localization. In this robot, an additional omnidirectional stereo camera provides texture information as well as additional range measurements [Biber et al., 2006]. See Figure 1.3(c) for a picture of the Wägele robot.

1.4.2 3D Mapping for Navigation

The reconstruction of 3D maps for robot navigation gained significant interest in robotics research over the past years. Nearly all state-of-the-art methods for mobile robot navigation assume robot operation in a two-dimensional environment and therefore three parameters, two for position and one for heading, are sufficient to describe the robot's state. Just recently, researchers have been extending solutions to full 6 DoF poses [Nüchter et al., 2004], and mapping of 3D environments [Howard et al., 2004, Hähnel et al., 2003b, Borrmann et al., 2008].

The mobile robot Kurt3D, developed by Hartmut Surmann and colleagues [Surmann et al., 2003], digitalizes environments in 3D. It uses a 3D laser range finder that is built on the basis of a 2D range which is actuated with a custom tilt unit. Self localization is a major issue for 3D map building, therefore the team developed a fast registration approach [Nüchter et al., 2003a, Nüchter et al., 2004] which extends the well known ICP (Iterative Closest Point) [Besl and McKay, 1992] algorithm. The data is further processed by extracting 3D planes and labeling those into the four categories: Wall, Floor, Ceiling, and Door. This is achieved by enforcing semantic constraints [Nüchter et al., 2003b] like: "A wall is orthogonal to the floor" or "A door is under the ceiling and above the floor".

At the 2007 Urban Challenge, a race for autonomous vehicles, many of the successful teams [Urmson et al., 2008, Miller et al., 2008, Montemerlo et al., 2008, Bohren et al., 2008, Kammel et al., 2008] made use of a novel 3D laser range finder. The Velodyne HDL-64E laser[8] has a spinning unit that includes 64 lasers collecting approximately one-million 3D points each second. This rich source of information was used for lane-precise localization, obstacle avoidance, and tracking of other vehicles. For navigation, 2D occupancy grid maps were predominantly used. Occupancy maps define obstacles in a crude binary sense, which overly simplifies the complex interactions between the robot and the environment. No distinction can be made between a small object that the vehicle could drive over and a large object that must be avoided. In order to construct more detailed maps for a fully autonomous system, it is necessary to expand the occupancy grid to three dimensions. A major drawback of rigid grids in 3D is their large memory requirements. This issue was addressed by [Wurm et al., 2010] using octree data structures which allocate memory only for occupied regions.

1.4.3 3D Reconstruction from Multiple Images

In the robotics community laser range finders are predominant for accurate mapping tasks. However, in the computer-vision domain researchers have developed powerful algorithms to reconstruct 3D models from photographs. The algorithms can be roughly clustered into two areas addressing two distinct issues: the first key challenge is *registration*, i.e., finding correspondences between images, and how they relate to one another in a common 3D coordinate system. This is also called Structure from Motion (SfM). Robust features, such as Lowe's Scale Invariant Feature Transform (SIFT) [Lowe, 2004] and techniques from photogrammetry such as bundle adjustment [Triggs et al., 2000] are now regarded

[8] http://www.velodyne.com/lidar/

as the gold standard for performing optimal 3D reconstruction from correspondences [Hartley and Zisserman, 2004]. The result of common SfM algorithms is a sparse 3D point cloud and the 6 DoF poses. The second key challenge is the reconstruction of a dense 3D model given the known camera poses. Multi-View Stereo (MVS) [Seitz et al., 2006] is one of the most successful approaches for producing dense models. The Middleburry dataset [Seitz et al., 2006] provides an extensive benchmark and evaluation suite for multi-view stereo reconstruction algorithms. Each dataset in the benchmark is registered with a ground-truth 3D model acquired via a laser scanning process. A notable example of a state-of-the-art multi-view stereo algorithm is [Furukawa et al., 2009], who presented a fully automated 3D reconstruction and visualization system for architectural scenes based on camera images. Although significant progress to improve the robustness of computer-vision reconstruction approaches has been made in the past decade, the approaches cannot yet compete with the accuracy of laser range finders. Specifically, textureless scenes which are often found in indoor environments remain very challenging.

1.4.4 3D Reconstruction of Objects

In addition to the approaches mentioned above, which are mainly used in the context of robot navigation of reconstruction of large environments, several researchers have studied the problem of creating high-resolution models of scientifically interesting objects. For example, in the Michelangelo project presented in [Levoy et al., 2000], historic statues were scanned with a high-resolution 3D scanning system. Techniques like this require significant manual assistance or make assumptions about the scene characteristics or data collection procedure. A more automated approach was presented in [Huber et al., 2000]. With their system, it is possible to take a collection of range images of a scene and automatically produce a realistic, geometrically accurate digital 3D model. In both approaches the major focus lies on data acquisition and registration of the individual scans. Color information is typically mapped onto the resulting models after creating the three-dimensional structures.

1.4.5 Commercial Products

While numerous operational sensors for 3D data acquisition are readily available on the market (optical, laser scanning, radar, thermal, acoustic, etc.), 3D reconstruction software offers predominantly manual and semi-automatic tools (e.g., Cyclone[9], PhotoModeler[10], and Google's Sketch-up[11]).

1.5 Goal and Structure

Until now, creating textured 3D models of environments was a tedious and time-consuming task that was mainly performed manually. This restricted the use of such models to a limited number of applications. The main issues preventing a broader adoption of 3D modeling techniques are: 1) A lack of affordable 3D scanning devices which allow for an easy acquisition of range data, and 2) algorithms capable of automatically processing range data into 3D models, in particular, algorithms for data registration, surface reconstruction, and texture reconstruction. The goal of this thesis is to address both issues by developing an affordable and capable system for unsupervised reconstruction of textured 3D models in the context of modeling indoor environments. The main contributions are:

- a robotic data acquisition system that enable an automatic acquisition of large amounts of textured 3D scans in a short amount of time;
- probabilistic algorithms for non-rigid registration which incorporate statistical sensor models and surface prior distributions to optimize alignment and the reconstructed surface at the same time;
- algorithms for reconstruction of a consistent 3D surface representation from registered point clouds and for the optimization of the resulting mesh to closely approximate the true surface;
- and methods to automatically generate blended textures from multiple images and multiple scans which are mapped onto the 3D model for photo-realistic visualization.

A significant contribution of this research is a functional system that covers all steps required to automatically reconstruct textured 3D models of large indoor environments. In the remainder of this thesis, we define this system and its components. Figure 1.4 depicts an overview on the complete reconstruction process which is divided into four distinct steps: *data acquisition*, *global registration*, *surface reconstruction*, and *texture reconstruction*.

[9]http://www.leica-geosystems.com
[10]http://www.photomodeler.com
[11]http://sketchup.google.com

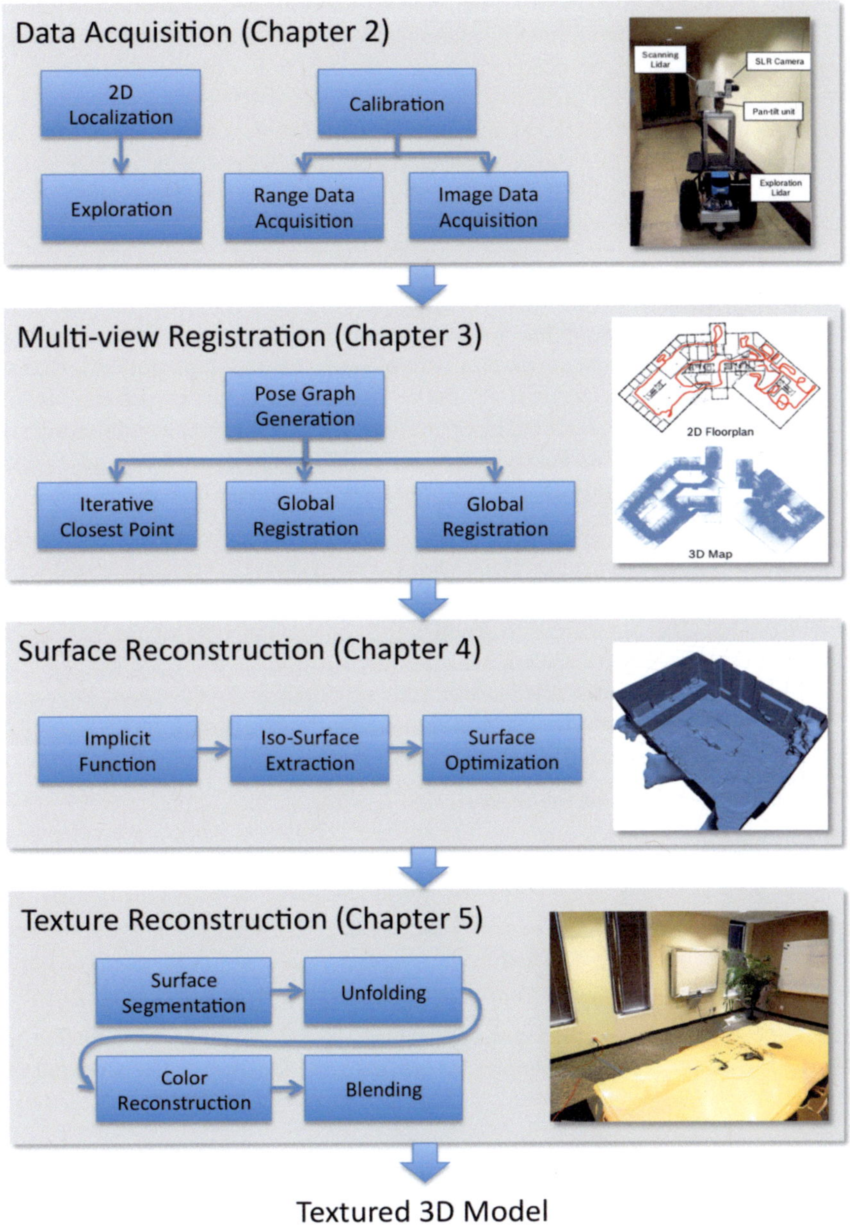

Figure 1.4: Overview of the reconstruction and modeling process.

Chapter 2 is dedicated to the first step, data acquisition. In this chapter, we describe a hardware setup which allows for automatic 3D scanning. In order to fuse data from multiple sensors, we need to represent the data in a common reference frame. We present a calibration procedure that first calibrates the sensors internal parameters and then determines the external calibration, which is necessary to transform data from one sensor into the coordinate system of another sensor. In this chapter, we further address the navigation algorithms used for automatic exploration and scanning large environments.

In Chapter 3, we are concerned with the problem of multi-view data registration, which is essentially the problem of aligning the data of multiple 3D scans into a common coordinate system. We first give an introduction in multi-view registration, followed by an analysis of a widely used pairwise registration technique. We then present a new method for multi-view registration that directly uses information obtained from pairwise registration, yet distributes the registration error evenly over all views. We also present a novel probabilistic and non-rigid registration method which incorporates sensor uncertainties and surface priors.

In Chapter 4 we investigate the problem of reconstructing a consistent 3D surface representation from registered point clouds. We propose a volumetric surface reconstruction method based on a Poisson framework in combination with surface optimization. The algorithm determines the topological type of the surface and produces a mesh which approximates the true surface. In a second step, we seek to improve the accuracy of this reconstruction by optimizing the mesh. We present an algorithm that adjusts the location of the mesh vertices to optimize the surface in order to achieve a better approximation of the true surface.

Chapter 5 is dedicated to the reconstruction of the surface appearance from multiple scans. We will demonstrate that reconstructing and adding a texture to the surface model results in a drastically more realistic 3D model. Our texture reconstruction approach consists of the following steps: surface partitioning (segmentation and slicing), surface unfolding, mesh re-parameterization, color reconstruction, and blending. The texture reconstruction is a key component of our 3D modeling system to create photo-realistic 3D models.

In Chapter 6, we present several applications of the reconstruction system presented in Chapters 2 to 5. Chapter 7 concludes the thesis and discusses possible future directions.

2 Data Acquisition

2.1 Introduction

An automated data acquisition system is the foundation for our 3D reconstruction system. Currently, robots suitable for this task are only available in research. For our experiments, a system was designed to match the requirements for scanning indoor environments and gives ample control over the data acquisition process. This scanning robot is put in a previously unmodeled environment and has the task to acquire the data necessary to reconstruct a 3D model. The data acquisition task can be decomposed into three subproblems: *exploration*, *navigation*, *scanning*.

Before continuing this chapter, some basic concepts have to be specified. A fundamental quantity to describe the position and orientation of data relative to some coordinate system is the *pose*:

Definition 2.1.1 (Pose). *The pose of a rigid body is defined as six dimensional vector* $\mathbf{x}_F = \begin{pmatrix} x & y & z & \phi & \theta & \psi \end{pmatrix}^{\mathsf{T}}$ *consisting of a three Cartesian coordinates and the orientation expressed as rotations about the three coordinate axes relative to the coordinate system F.*

In our case, all poses are expressed in the same global coordinate system and the frame designator is omitted for a compact notation. Note that the pose can also be expressed as a translation vector and a rotation matrix; refer to Appendix 8.1 for more details.

Definition 2.1.2 (Scan). *A scan* $\mathcal{S} = \{\mathcal{P}, \mathcal{C}, \mathbf{x}\}$ *is defined as the union of a set of 3D points:* $\mathcal{P} = \{\mathbf{p}_{1:M}\}$ *with* $\mathbf{p}_i \in \mathbb{R}^3$*; and a set of color images* $\mathcal{C} = \{\mathbf{G}_{1:N}\}$ *along with a robot pose* $\mathbf{x}$.

In the context of scans, the robot pose is also denoted as *viewpoint* or just *view*. The definition of an image $\mathbf{G}$ as a mathematical matrix is arbitrary, and it can be argued that a definition as a two-dimensional finite grid of image elements (pixels) or a functional representation is more appropriate. However, in our context, no specific definition is required.

The remainder of the chapter is structured as follows. In Section 2.2 we propose the hardware configuration of a scanning system and in Section 2.3 we present

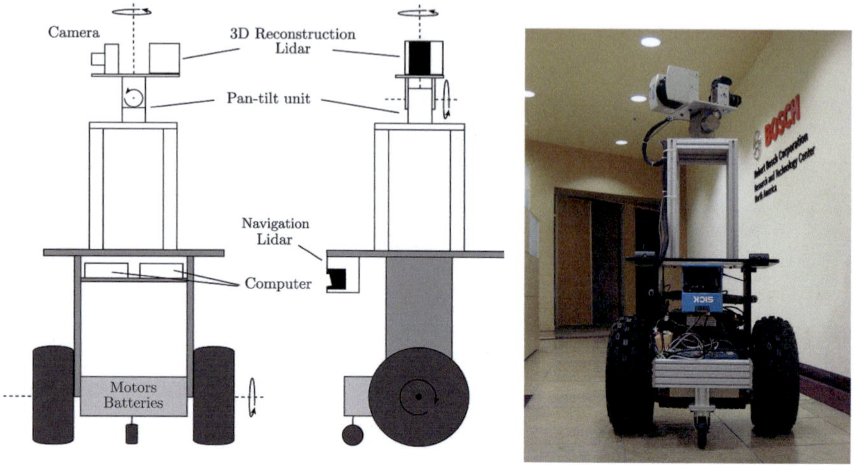

(a) Simplified model. (b) 3D Reconstruction Robot.

Figure 2.1: Hardware setup of our data acquisition system.

the calibration of such a system. In Section 2.4, we address the subproblem of exploration and present an algorithm using active exploration which allows the robot to select optimal viewpoints for 3D scans.

2.2 Physical Setup

The stated goal of this thesis is to study a system for unsupervised model generation. This implies a data acquisition system which is capable of performing all required measurements automatically. Our system for data acquisition consists of the following main parts. For our robotic platform we use a Segway RMP 200. The RMP can carry loads up to 91 kg over a range of up to 24 km. For the purpose of high-quality measurements, we equipped the RMP with an additional castor-wheel and disabled the dynamic stabilization. To collect data and perform online mapping and exploration, two on-board Mac Mini computers (2.0GHz Core 2 Duo processor, 1GB RAM) are mounted under the base plate. The computers use the open-source Robot Operating System (ROS) [Quigley et al., 2009] which provides a structured communications layer on top of the host operating system (linux in our case). Figure 2.1 depicts the hardware setup of our scanning robot.

3D scans are obtained by a laser range finder (SICK LMS200) and a digital SLR camera (Nikon D90) mounted rigidly on a pan-tilt unit. The laser range finder is

Figure 2.2: Example scan: panoramic range image (top) and texture image (bottom) with 1/2 degree resolution. Invalid cells are marked red.

mounted on a pan-tilt unit such that the plane of the laser's sweep is aligned with the vertical axis. Panning the laser about the vertical axis yields a panoramic range scan of the environment covering the full sphere. A range image created by our 3D scanner is shown in Figure 2.2. The camera is equipped with a fish-eye lens and mounted on the same rotation unit opposite of the laser. This setup allows us to capture high-resolution, wide angle still images of the scene while panning the laser. Because of the camera's wide field-of-view, it only requires six pictures to cover the scanned space. Stitching the captured images into a composite yields a full cylinder panorama similar to the range image (see Figure 2.2). A second laser range finder is mounted on the base and sweeps horizontally. This sensor is used for navigation and obstacle avoidance.

2.3 System Calibration

In order to fuse data from multiple sensors, namely lidar and camera, we need to represent the data in a common reference frame. On our platform, the camera provides intensity information in the form of an image and the 3D laser supplies depth information in form of a set of 3D points. The internal and external calibrations of this system enable the reprojection of the 3D points from the laser coordinate frame to the 2D coordinate frame of the image.

2.3.1 Internal Calibration

Camera Model

Cameras, or more general imaging devices which may or may not be equipped with lenses, have been studied well. The *pinhole perspective* projection model, first proposed by Brunelleschi at the beginning of the 15th century, is widely used to model the image formation processes in a camera since it provides a good approximation of most lenses and is mathematically convenient. According to [Tsai, 1987], a camera with lens distortions can be described by the following parameters:

- The **focal length** in pixels in the 2×1 vector $\mathbf{f}_c = \begin{pmatrix} f_x & f_y \end{pmatrix}^\mathsf{T}$.
- The **principal point** coordinates given by the 2×1 vector $\mathbf{c}_c = \begin{pmatrix} c_x & c_y \end{pmatrix}^\mathsf{T}$.
- The scalar **skew coefficient** defining the angle α_c between the x and y pixel axes.
- The image **distortion coefficients** (radial and tangential distortions) in the 5×1 vector $\mathbf{k}_c = \begin{pmatrix} k_1 & k_2 & k_3 & p_1 & p_2 \end{pmatrix}^\mathsf{T}$.

A projection from world coordinates $\mathbf{p} = \begin{pmatrix} x_c & y_c & z_c \end{pmatrix}^\mathsf{T}$ to image coordinates $\mathbf{p}' = \begin{pmatrix} u & v \end{pmatrix}^\mathsf{T}$ is described in the following. First, the normalized pinhole projection applied:

$$\mathbf{x}_n = \begin{pmatrix} x_c/z_c \\ y_c/z_c \end{pmatrix} = \begin{pmatrix} x_n \\ y_n \end{pmatrix} . \tag{2.1}$$

The normalized point after taking lens distortion into account:

$$\mathbf{x}_d = \begin{pmatrix} x_d \\ y_d \end{pmatrix} = \left(1 + k_1 r^2 + k_2 r^4 + k_3 r^6\right) \mathbf{x}_n + \mathbf{d}_x \text{ , with } r^2 = x_n^2 + y_n^2 \text{ ,} \tag{2.2}$$

where $\mathbf{d}_x$ is the tangential distortion vector:

$$\mathbf{d}_x = \begin{pmatrix} 2p_1 x_n y_n + p_2(r^2 + 2x_n^2) \\ p_1(r^2 + 2x_n^2) 2p_2 x_n y_n \end{pmatrix} . \tag{2.3}$$

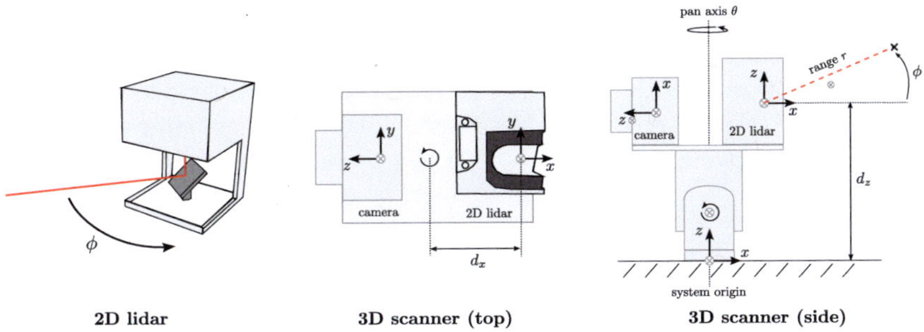

Figure 2.3: A 3D laser scanner is built by rotating a 2D lidar around its radial axis using a panning unit.

Once distortion is applied, the final pixel coordinates of the point are given by:

$$\mathbf{p}' = \begin{pmatrix} f_x & \alpha_c f_x & c_x \\ 0 & f_y & c_y \end{pmatrix} \begin{pmatrix} x_d \\ y_d \\ 1 \end{pmatrix} . \tag{2.4}$$

The estimation of the parameters $\mathbf{f}_c$, $\mathbf{c}_c$, $\mathbf{k}_c$, and α_c has been studied well [Heikkila and Silven, 1997, Zhang, 1999, Hartley and Zisserman, 2004]. In this work we employ the method of [Zhang, 1999]. This procedure requires observing a planar reference checkerboard calibration patterns, a scripted sequence of recorded camera views, and an off-line data processing. Recent years, however, have seen increasing interest in camera self-calibration methods. Continuous stereo self-calibration methods such as the one described in [Dang et al., 2009] could allow the recovery of camera parameters without a special calibration object and while the scanning robot is acquiring data.

Laser Model

A basic 2D laser range finder or Light Detection And Ranging (LIDAR) system consists of a 1D laser range finder rotating mirror deflecting the beam to different directions (see left side of Figure 2.3). The laser sweeps over the scene, gathering distance measurements at specified angle intervals. The motion of the mirror is restricted to a rotation around one axis resulting in 2D range measurements.

In order to enable 3D range measurements, our scanning system rotates a 2D scanner in a continuous manner around its radial axis. This 3D scanner is depicted in Figure 2.3. Combining the rotation of the mirror inside the 2D scanner by an angle ϕ with the external rotation by an angle θ of the scanner itself yields measured points conveniently described in spherical coordinates. However, since the two centers of rotation are not identical, offsets have to be added to the measured parameters. The 3D coordinates of a scanned point $\mathbf{p}$ corresponding to a measured range r in the coordinate frame of the 3D scanner are given by:

$$\mathbf{p} = \begin{pmatrix} x \\ y \\ z \end{pmatrix} = \begin{pmatrix} \cos(\theta)\left(\cos(\phi)\, r + d_x\right) \\ \sin(\theta)\left(\cos(\phi)\, r + d_x\right) \\ \sin(\phi)\, r + d_z \end{pmatrix} . \tag{2.5}$$

The rotation angles ϕ and θ are available at each measurement from the state of the 2D scanner and the panning unit respectively. The fixed parameters d_x and d_z are manually measured once for the hardware configuration.

In addition to the actual point data, we also want to estimate the statistical error inherent to the 3D measurements for later use in the registration and reconstruction algorithms. As pointed out by [Böhler et al., 2003], there are mainly two sources of errors disturbing the measurements of a 2D laser scanner: ranging and deflection errors.

In most laser range finders, range is computed using the time of flight or a phase comparison between the emitted and the returned signal. Ranging scanners for distances up to 100 m show about the same range accuracy for any range. Ranging errors mostly stem from distance and reflectivity of the scanned objects which directly affects range measurements along the laser beam. The distribution chosen to model these errors is Gaussian:

$$r = \hat{r} + e_r \,, \quad e_r \sim N\left(0, \sigma_r^2\right) \tag{2.6}$$

Through evaluating hundreds of scans of a flat surface, we determined our scanner's standard deviation σ_r was 5 mm.

Deflection errors arise from discrepancies between the actual deflection angles of the scanning laser beam and the measured angles of the mirror inside the scanner. Since the positions of single points are difficult to be verified, few investigations of this problem are known. Errors can be detected by measuring short horizontal and vertical distances between objects (e.g., spheres), which are located at the same distance from the scanner. Comparing those scans to measurements derived from more accurate surveying methods yields an error estimate. In practical applications, angular errors are negligible compared to ranging errors. For completeness we also model deflection errors as a Gaussian distribution:

$$\phi = \hat{\phi} + e_\phi \,, \quad e_\phi \sim N\left(0, \sigma_\phi^2\right) \tag{2.7}$$

and set $\sigma_\phi = 0\ 05\,^\circ$ which is a reasonable value according to the specification of our scanner. Since ranging and deflection errors stem from independent physical processes, we can justify to model the distributions to be independent as well. In Section 3.4.4, we will use this error model and its parameters to derive a probabilistic model of the measurement process used in a new registration algorithm.

2.3.2 Extrinsic Calibration

As a second calibration step, we seek to find the rotation $\mathbf{R}$ and the translation $\mathbf{t}$ – the external calibration – between the camera and the laser range finder. In photogrammetry, the function to minimize is usually the error of reprojecting a 3D point onto the image plane. This would require knowing the exact correspondence of a 3D lidar measurement and a 2D image point. These correspondences are difficult to establish and would require a calibration pattern exhibiting features visible in both sensors. Instead, we use a planar checkerboard calibration pattern, such as the one we employed to find the internal camera parameters in Section 2.3.1. More specifically, the procedure of [Zhang, 1999] estimates the location of the calibration plane in 3D. The shape of the same calibration pattern can also be observed by the laser range finder and one can robustly establish a correspondence between camera and lidar data.

For the region in the range image corresponding to the calibration pattern, a robust total least squares estimator is used to fit a plane to the set of points in 3D. The equation of a plane using a unit normal vector $\mathbf{n}$ and a scalar distance d from the origin is:

$$\mathbf{n} \cdot \mathbf{x} - d = 0\,, \tag{2.8}$$

where $\mathbf{x}$ denotes a 3D point in the plane. The least squares estimator results in an estimate of $\mathbf{n}_l$ and d_l in the laser coordinate frame, whereas the previously described camera calibration procedure results in an estimate of $\mathbf{n}_c$ and d_c in the camera coordinate frame. Figure 2.4 depicts a camera image of the employed calibration target and the corresponding laser range image. Estimating the rigid transformation between the laser and camera frame can now be achieved by finding the transform that minimizes the difference in observations of the calibration plane. While a distance metric for point features can be defined easily, it is not so obvious for planes. We separate the problem by estimating translation and rotation independently.

The translation $\mathbf{t}$ can be estimated by minimizing the difference in distance from the camera origin to the planes, represented in the camera coordinate system and

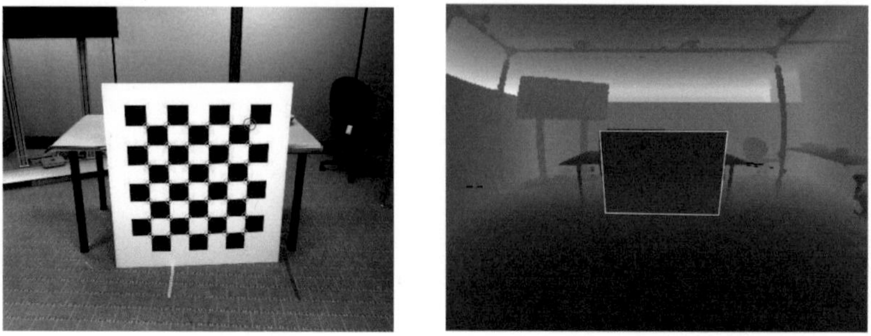

(a) Camera image. (b) Laser range image.

Figure 2.4: Camera and lidar are calibrated by aligning a planar calibration target. The checkerboard pattern is used to estimate a plane in camera coordinates while a least squares estimator finds the same plane in the range image (right). The estimated plane is marked in yellow.

the laser coordinate system. The distances are given by d_l and d_c and upon translation by $\mathbf{t}$, the new distance becomes $d_c - \mathbf{n}_c \cdot \mathbf{t}$. The squared difference for one camera image/range image observation pair becomes:

$$\Delta d^2 = \Big[d_l - (d_c - \mathbf{n}_c \cdot \mathbf{t})\Big]^2 . \tag{2.9}$$

Now, consider a multitude of such pairs generated by moving the calibration target to different locations. For this over-constrained estimation the translation $\mathbf{t}$ is estimated over all pairs with the following objective function:

$$\hat{\mathbf{t}} = \operatorname*{argmin}_{\mathbf{t}} \sum_i \Big[d_{l,i} - (d_{c,i} - \mathbf{n}_{c,i} \cdot \mathbf{t})\Big]^2 . \tag{2.10}$$

A closed form solution of this minimization problem can be found by concatenating the plane parameters into a matrix form, e.g., $\mathbf{D}_l = \big(d_{l,1}\ d_{l,2}\ \dots\ d_{l,n}\big)^{\mathsf{T}}$ for n camera image/range image observation pairs. Then the least squares objective function for $\mathbf{t}$ is equivalent to

$$\hat{\mathbf{t}} = \operatorname*{argmin}_{\mathbf{t}} \left\|\mathbf{D}_l - \big(\mathbf{D}_c - \mathbf{N}_c^{\mathsf{T}}\mathbf{t}\big)\right\|^2 , \tag{2.11}$$

which has a closed form solution given by:

$$\hat{\mathbf{t}} = \Big(\mathbf{N}_c\mathbf{N}_c^{\mathsf{T}}\Big)^{-1}\mathbf{N}_c\Big(\mathbf{D}_c - \mathbf{D}_l\Big) . \tag{2.12}$$

The rotation $\mathbf{R}$ can be estimated by minimizing the difference in the angular difference between the normals of the corresponding planes. The objective function may be written as the rotation that maximizes the sum of cosines of the respective angles, or

$$\hat{\mathbf{R}} = \underset{\mathbf{R}}{\operatorname{argmax}} \sum_i \mathbf{n}_{c,i}^\mathsf{T} \, \mathbf{R} \, \mathbf{n}_{l,i} \ . \tag{2.13}$$

To ensure the resulting solution $\hat{\mathbf{R}}$ is a member of the rotation group SO(3), we have to enforce the orthonormality condition $\mathbf{R}^\mathsf{T}\mathbf{R} = \mathbf{I}_3$ as well as the orientation preserving property $\det(\mathbf{R}) = 1$. This problem is an instance of the well-studied Orthogonal Procrustes Problem (OPP) [Schönemann, 1966] and has the closed form solution given by:

$$\hat{\mathbf{R}} = \mathbf{V}\mathbf{U}^\mathsf{T} \tag{2.14}$$

where $\mathbf{N}_l\mathbf{N}_c^\mathsf{T} = \mathbf{U}\mathbf{S}\mathbf{V}^\mathsf{T}$ is the associated singular value decomposition.

2.4 Exploration

In robotics terms, *exploration* is the task of controlling a robot so as to maximize its knowledge about its environment. In our case, the robot has to acquire a static 3D model of the environment; and therefore, the exploration means to maximize the cumulative information we have about each part of the environment. Since our robot has no prior knowledge, the information is zero in the beginning and the exploration is successful when enough measurements are taken to cover the whole environment. In other words, an exploration strategy is required to determine the next viewpoint the robot should move to in order to obtain more information about the environment.

Our exploration strategy is a two step procedure. First, we define the set of possible viewpoints or candidate viewpoints. Second, we evaluate those candidates to find the best one. To define a set of candidate viewpoints we use a *frontier heuristic* [Yamauchi, 1997] yielding a small set of viewpoints $\mathcal{V} = \{\mathbf{x}_1, \ldots, \mathbf{x}_n\}$. The exploration algorithm maintains a 2D occupancy grid map [Elfes, 1989] to record which parts of the environment have been observed. Obstacle free boundaries between observed and unobserved regions, so called frontiers (see Figure 2.5), define candidate viewpoints. A grid cell is considered as observed if it has eight neighbors and its uncertainty, measured by the entropy in the patch, is below a threshold. The entropy of the i-th grid cell $\mathbf{m}_i$ is defined as:

$$h_i = h(\mathbf{m}_i) = -p_i \ \log p_i - (1 - p_i) \ \log(1 - p_i) \ , \tag{2.15}$$

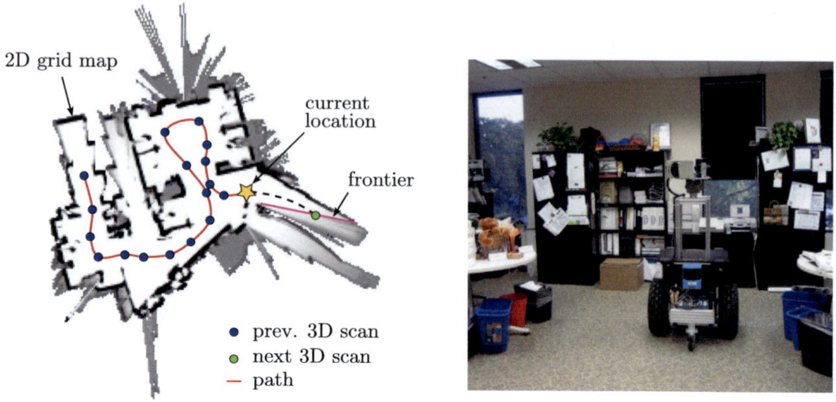

Figure 2.5: The robot maintains a 2D grid map for exploration. The next viewpoint for a 3D scan is determined by the boundary between observed and unobserved regions (frontiers).

with $p_i = p(\mathbf{m}_i)$ denotes the cell's occupancy probability. A location is considered a candidate viewpoint if it is reachable by the robot, and there is at least one frontier cell that is likely to be observable from that viewpoint. The utility of a candidate viewpoint $\mathbf{x}_i$ is the expected information gain which is approximated using its entropy $h(\mathbf{x}_i)$ [Thrun et al., 2004]. The cost for the candidate is defined by the travel distance from the current viewpoint $\mathbf{x}_j$ to the candidate $t(\mathbf{x}_i, \mathbf{x}_j) = \text{dist}(\mathbf{x}_i, \mathbf{x}_j)$. Now we select the candidate viewpoint as our next viewpoint to perform a 3D scan that maximizes the following equation:

$$\hat{\mathbf{x}}_i = \underset{i}{\text{argmax}}\, h(\mathbf{x}_i) - \beta\, t(\mathbf{x}_i, \mathbf{x}_j)\ , \tag{2.16}$$

with $\beta \geq 0$ being a quantity that determines the relative importance of utility versus cost. The next viewpoint is used as goal point for the robot's navigation system. Upon arriving at a goal point, the robot will perform a full 3D scan of its environment and update its exploration map. New boundaries and a new goal point will then be calculated. This process repeats until no reachable frontiers remain.

2.5 Conclusion

In this chapter, we described methods for automatic data acquisition. We proposed, a 3D scanning robot which allows for autonomous exploration and scanning of large environments. This hardware configuration was specifically designed to match our requirements for scanning indoor environments with a mobile robot. This configuration, however, represents a much larger group of scanning devices that combine distance sensors, such as laser range finders, stereo-cameras, with imaging sensors, such as cameras. In fact, the algorithms for processing the data acquired by our system described in the subsequent chapters are hardware agnostic and can be applied to any other system using range and color sensing. Furthermore, we presented a novel calibration procedure to calculate the extrinsic calibration between camera and laser range finder. Our method extracts the plane of a calibration target in the camera image and in the laser range image. Estimating the rigid transformation between the laser and camera frame was then performed by finding the rotation and translation that minimizes the difference in observations of the calibration plane. This external calibration enables subsequent processing steps to transform data points between sensor coordinate systems and fuse color with range data. Lastly, we addressed the subproblem of exploration and view point selection for 3D scanning. The presented algorithm uses active exploration enabling the robot to select optimal viewpoints for 3D scans. This algorithm generates navigation targets that maximize the expected information gain based on a 2D map representation.

3 Multi-View Registration

In this chapter, we address the problem of *multi-view data registration*, which is essentially the problem of aligning multiple scans into a common coordinate system. This chapter presents new algorithms for aligning multiple scans. We first give an introduction to multi-view registration followed by a description of a widely used pairwise registration technique. We then present a new method for multi-view registration that directly uses information obtained from pairwise registration yet distributes the registration error evenly over all views. In the last part we present a novel probabilistic registration method which incorporates sensor uncertainties and surface priors. Our method performs a non-rigid registration and therefore not only estimates the rigid transformations that align the scans but also allows for deformations of the scans themselves. A short discussion concludes the chapter.

3.1 Introduction

Scans produced by 3D scanners, such as the one described in the previous chapter, are intrinsically limited by occlusions and range restrictions. This requires the

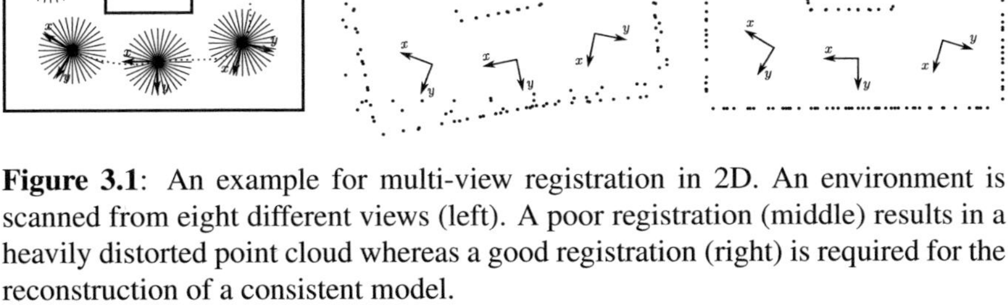

Figure 3.1: An example for multi-view registration in 2D. An environment is scanned from eight different views (left). A poor registration (middle) results in a heavily distorted point cloud whereas a good registration (right) is required for the reconstruction of a consistent model.

acquisition of multiple scans covering parts of an environment. In practice, the 3D scanner is moved to various locations within an environment and the surfaces visible to the scanner are captured. The scanner is then reoriented, so that other parts of the environment can be scanned, and this is repeated until most (ideally, all) of the environment is captured. Clearly, if we want to construct a complete and consistent model of an environment from the scans, we have to first align the scans and express all data in one common coordinate system. In order to align scans we have to find the *rigid body transform* that precisely aligns the overlapping parts of scans from different locations into a consistent model as shown in Figure 3.1 on the right. This process is called *registration* or *multi-view registration* since it typically involves many scans.

The registration problem would be easy to solve if we could precisely measure an externally referenced pose for each scan. Unfortunately, even very expensive pose estimation systems do not deliver enough accuracy to register scans purely based on their output. In practice, the accuracy of pose estimates is much less than that of a laser scanner. Figure 3.1 shows an example of the multi-view registration problem in 2D. Here, a 2D environment is scanned by a simulated scanner from eight different views (left). The figure in the middle depicts a registration based on a (noisy) external pose reference which results in a heavily distorted point cloud. Aligning the scans using multi-view registration techniques can achieve superior results and recover a consistent model of the simulated environment (right). Note, that approximate pose estimates such as an external pose reference or wheel odometry can serve as a good starting point for multi-view registration algorithms that are discussed in this chapter.

Exploration of metric maps while maintaining an accurate position estimate is a frequent issue in robot navigation. Specifically, problems in which the robot has no a priori map and no external position reference are particularly challenging. Such scenarios may arise for Autonomous Underwater Vehicles (AUV), mining applications, or planetary surface explorations. This problem has been referred to as Concurrent Localization and Mapping (CLM) and Simultaneous Localization and Mapping (SLAM). The CLM or SLAM problem can be posed as a multi-view registration problem: given a set of scans, find the rigid body transforms that will align the scans and form a globally consistent a map.

In this work we want to address the problem of reconstructing a map based on range measurements from a mobile platform. In recent years, building maps of physical environments with mobile robots has been a central problem for the robotics community. Research over the last decade has led to impressive results. Several successful algorithms emerged, among them Relaxation [Duckett et al., 2002], CEKF [Guivant and Nebot, 2002], SEIF [Thrun, 2002],

FastSLAM [Montemerlo et al., 2002], MLR [Frese and Duckett, 2003], TJTF [Paskin, 2003], and ATLAS [Bosse et al., 2003]. Nearly all state-of-the-art methods are probabilistic and most of them are robust to noise and small variations of the environment. Comprehensive surveys can be found in [Thrun, 2002] or more recently in [Bailey and Durrant-Whyte, 2006a, Bailey and Durrant-Whyte, 2006b, Bonin-Font et al., 2008].

3.2 Pairwise Rigid-Registration

The core of many multi-view registration schemes is a pairwise registration algoritm. Algorithms for the pairwise registration of points clouds can be roughly categorized into two classes: *voting methods* and *correspondence methods*.

Voting methods make use of the fact that the rigid transform is low-dimensional. Those methods exhaustively search for the small number of parameters required to specify the optimal transform. For example, the Generalized Hough transform [Hecker and Bolle, 1994], geometric hashing [Wolfson and Rigoutsos, 1997], and pose clustering [Stockman, 1987] quantize the transformation space into a six dimensional table. For each triplet of points in the model shape and each triplet in the data shape, the transformation between the triplets is computed and a vote is recorded in the corresponding cell of the table. The entry with the most votes gives the optimal aligning transform.

Correspondence methods solve the registration problem by finding the corresponding points in two scans. Given a set of point-pairs, a rigid transformation can be computed by minimizing the distance between corresponding points. The quasi-standard method for aligning two point clouds and also a classical example for correspondence methods is the Iterative Closest Point (ICP) algorithm [Besl and McKay, 1992]. We will briefly discuss the algorithm in the following section since it constitutes the base for our multi-view registration approach.

3.2.1 The Iterative Closest Point Algorithm (ICP)

The ICP algorithm is widely used for geometric alignment of three-dimensional models when an initial estimate of the relative pose is known. Many variants of ICP have been proposed [Rusinkiewicz and Levoy, 2001, Nüchter et al., 2004], affecting all phases of the algorithm. Given two independently acquired sets of 3D points $\mathcal{P} = \{\mathbf{p}_i\}$ with M points and $\mathcal{Q} = \{\mathbf{q}_i\}$ with N points, we want to find the rigid body transformation $\mathbf{T}$ consisting of a rotation $\mathbf{R}$ and a translation

Figure 3.2: The ICP algorithm iteratively finds point pairs and determines the rigid body transformation that minimizes the registration error. In this example, corresponding points (marked by green lines) are determined based on point distance, normal distance, and color similarity.

$\mathbf{t}$ which minimizes a given alignment error metric H. The outline of the original ICP algorithm is as follows:

1. Choose a subset of $\mathcal{P}$ consisting of $K \leq M$ points, and for each point $\mathbf{p}_i$ in this subset find the closest point $\mathbf{q}_i$. Those point pairs $(\mathbf{p}_i, \mathbf{q}_i)$ form the correspondence set $\mathcal{J}$.

2. Using the correspondence set, determine the rigid body transformation $\mathbf{T}$ that minimizes the alignment error by minimizing H.

3. Apply the transformation $\mathbf{T}$ to all points in $\mathcal{P}$: $\mathbf{p}_i \mapsto \mathbf{R}\mathbf{p}_i + \mathbf{t}$.

4. Repeat step 1 to 3 until convergence is reached.

Figure 3.2 shows an example for an ICP based registration. In the original formulation of ICP the alignment error is defined as:

$$H(\mathbf{R}, \mathbf{t}) = \sum_{(\mathbf{p}_i, \mathbf{q}_i) \in \mathcal{J}} \left\| \mathbf{R}\mathbf{p}_i + \mathbf{t} - \mathbf{q}_i \right\|^2 . \tag{3.1}$$

This formulation directly minimizes the sum of squared distances between the paired points. Ideally, $\mathbf{p}_i$ and its pair $\mathbf{q}_i$ should correspond to the same point on the object's surface. In this case the ICP algorithm converges to a perfect alignment in just one iteration. In practice, finding the correct correspondences of partially overlapping surfaces without a good initial alignment is very difficult. Therefore, the ICP algorithm estimates the registration transformation in small steps. [Besl and McKay, 1992] showed that the algorithm converges always monotonically to a local minimum. In other words, each iteration will improve the registration even if the pairings are not perfect. As the surfaces move closer, finding better point pairs becomes more likely. However, ICP is not guaranteed to reach a global minimum. Most often this occurs in situations when the initial alignment is very poor. In this case, ICP may converge to a local minimum of H and therefore a wrong alignment. In the following sections we will discuss all phases of ICP in more detail and present various improvements to the original algorithm.

3.2.2 Correspondence Search

In each iteration step, the ICP algorithm selects a set of corresponding points $(\mathbf{p}_i, \mathbf{q}_i)$. In traditional ICP [Besl and McKay, 1992] the Euclidean distance in 3D space is used to find corresponding points. For each point $\mathbf{p}_i \in \mathcal{P}$ the closest point $\mathbf{q}_i \in \mathcal{Q}$ is found by:

$$\mathbf{q}_i = \underset{\mathbf{q} \in \mathcal{Q}}{\operatorname{argmin}} \left\| \mathbf{R}\mathbf{p}_i + \mathbf{t} - \mathbf{q}_n \right\|^2 . \tag{3.2}$$

This means closest points are searched for in 3D Euclidean space. In many cases this pairing process is suboptimal as we can see from the example shown in Figure 3.3 on the left. In our case, we have color data available for each point hence better correspondences can be found by including this information in the correspondence search. We modify the distance metric of Equation 3.2 and add terms for color similarity as well as normal similarity:

$$\mathbf{q}_i = \underset{\mathbf{q} \in \mathcal{Q}}{\operatorname{argmin}} \left[\left\| \mathbf{R}\mathbf{p}_i + \mathbf{t} - \mathbf{q}_n \right\|^2 + \alpha \left\| \mathbf{R}\mathbf{n}_i - \mathbf{n}_n \right\|^2 + \beta \left\| \mathbf{c}_i - \mathbf{c}_n \right\|^2 \right] . \tag{3.3}$$

Here, $\mathbf{n}_i$ denotes the normal vector and $\mathbf{c}_i$ denotes the color triplets of the corresponding 3D point $\mathbf{p}_i$. The constants α and β are weighting factors that define the importance of the respective term for the search of the closest point. A similar metric has been previously suggested by [Johnson and Kang, 1997a]. An example of correspondences for this distance metric are presented in Figure 3.3 on the right.

In a brute force implementation, the search for correspondence is of the complexity $O\big((M+N)^2\big)$ with M being the number of points in $\mathcal{P}$ and N being the number

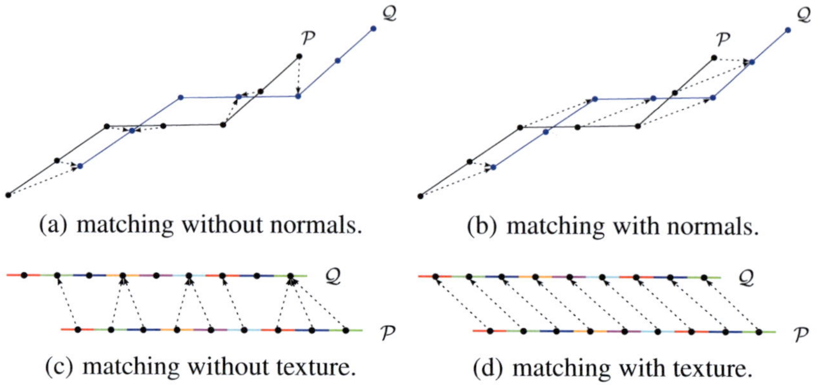

Figure 3.3: The traditional ICP algorithm proposed by [Besl and McKay, 1992] finds point pairs using the Euclidean distance in 3D (a). Including normal (b) and texture (d) information into this matching process improves the number of correct pairs.

of points in $\mathcal{Q}$ respectively. kD-trees (here $k = 9$) have been suggested by various authors [Zhang, 1994, Rusinkiewicz and Levoy, 2001] to speed up the data access. This ensures that a data correspondence can be selected in $O\big(\log(M + N)\big)$.

3.2.3 Error Metric

The next piece of the ICP algorithm is the error metric and the algorithm for minimizing it. The metric originally proposed by [Besl and McKay, 1992] minimizes the sum of squared distances between corresponding points and is therefore called *point-to-point error metric*. For an error metric of this form, there exist closed form solutions for determining the rigid-body transformation that minimizes the error. An evaluation of the numerical accuracy and stability of solutions using singular value decomposition, quaternions, and orthogonal matrices is available in [Eggert et al., 1997]. These evaluations conclude that differences among different solutions are small. [Chen and Medioni, 1992] considered the more specific problem of aligning range data for object modeling and their approach assumes the data to be locally planar. Their *point-to-plane error metric* minimizes the sum of squared distances from each source point to the plane containing the destination

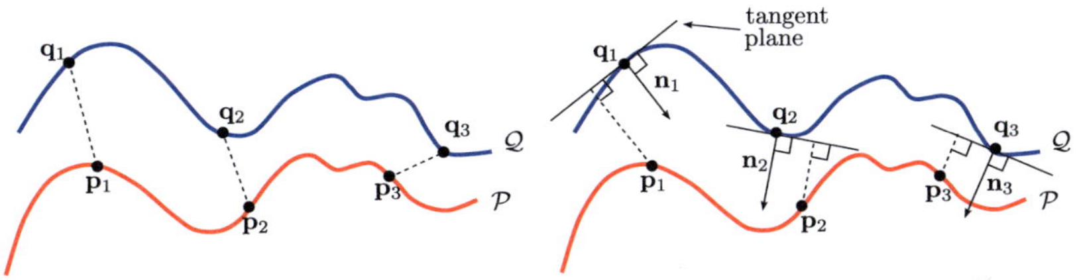

(a) point-to-point error metric. (b) point-to-plane error metric.

Figure 3.4: Using the *point-to-point error metric* (left) the sum of squared Euclidean distances of all point pairs $(\mathbf{p}_i, \mathbf{q}_i)$ is minimized. In contrast, the *point-to-plane error metric* [Chen and Medioni, 1992] minimizes the sum of the squared distance between each source point and the tangent plane at its corresponding destination point (right).

point and oriented perpendicular to the destination normal:

$$H(\mathbf{R}, \mathbf{t}) = \sum_{(\mathbf{p}_i, \mathbf{q}_i) \in \mathcal{J}} \left[(\mathbf{R}\mathbf{p}_i + \mathbf{t} - \mathbf{q}_i) \cdot \mathbf{n}_i \right]^2 \tag{3.4}$$

where $\mathbf{n}_i$ denotes the normal at the corresponding point $\mathbf{q}_i$ (see Figure 3.4). In this case, H minimizes the sum of squared distances for each $\mathbf{p}_i$ to the corresponding tangent plane at $\mathbf{q}_i$. Unfortunately, no closed-form solutions are available for this minimization. However, the least-squares equation may be solved using a generic non-linear method (e.g., Levenberg-Marquardt). In order to find the transformation which minimizes the alignment error, we assume that rotations are small and linearize Equation 3.4, approximating $\cos(\theta)$ by 1 and $\sin(\theta)$ by θ. We obtain a rotation matrix which is a linear function of the rotation angles:

$$\mathbf{R} = \begin{pmatrix} c_\psi c_\theta & c_\psi s_\theta s_\phi - s_\psi c_\phi & c_\psi s_\theta c_\phi + s_\psi s_\phi \\ s_\psi c_\theta & s_\psi s_\theta s_\phi + c_\psi c_\phi & s_\psi s_\theta c_\phi - c_\psi s_\phi \\ -s_\theta & c_\theta s_\phi & c_\theta c_\phi \end{pmatrix} \tag{3.5}$$

$$\approx \begin{pmatrix} 1 & -\psi & \theta \\ \psi & 1 & -\phi \\ -\theta & \phi & 1 \end{pmatrix} \approx \mathbf{I}_3 + \triangle\mathbf{R}\,. \tag{3.6}$$

Here ϕ, θ, and ψ are rotations about the x, y, and z axis, respectively. The expressions $c_\psi := \cos(\psi)$ and $s_\psi := \sin(\psi)$ are used for notational brevity. Inserting the linearized rotation matrix into Equation 3.4 leads to:

$$\begin{aligned} H(\mathbf{R},\mathbf{t}) &\approx \sum_{(\mathbf{p}_i,\mathbf{q}_i)\in\mathcal{J}} \left[\left((\mathbf{I}_3 + \triangle\mathbf{R})\,\mathbf{p}_i + \mathbf{t} - \mathbf{q}_i\right)\cdot\mathbf{n}_i\right]^2 \\ &= \sum_{i(\mathbf{p}_i,\mathbf{q}_i)\in\mathcal{J}} \left[(\triangle\mathbf{R}\mathbf{p}_i)\cdot\mathbf{n}_i + \mathbf{t}\cdot\mathbf{n}_i + (\mathbf{p}_i - \mathbf{q}_i)\cdot\mathbf{n}_i\right]^2 . \end{aligned} \tag{3.7}$$

Since $\triangle\mathbf{R}\mathbf{p}_i = \mathbf{r}\times\mathbf{p}_i$ where $\mathbf{r} = \begin{pmatrix}\phi & \theta & \psi\end{pmatrix}^\mathsf{T}$ is a vector of rotations, we can define

$$(\triangle\mathbf{R}\mathbf{p}_i)\cdot\mathbf{n}_i = (\mathbf{r}\times\mathbf{p}_i)\cdot\mathbf{n}_i = \mathbf{r}\cdot(\mathbf{p}_i\times\mathbf{n}_i)\ . \tag{3.8}$$

Setting $\mathbf{c}_i = \mathbf{p}_i \times \mathbf{n}_i$, the alignment error may be written as

$$H(\mathbf{R},\mathbf{t}) \approx \sum_{(\mathbf{p}_i,\mathbf{q}_i)\in\mathcal{J}} \left[(\mathbf{p}_i - \mathbf{q}_i)\cdot\mathbf{n}_i + \mathbf{t}\cdot\mathbf{n}_i + \mathbf{r}\cdot\mathbf{c}_i\right]^2 . \tag{3.9}$$

Now, we solve for the aligning transform by setting the partial derivatives of H in Equation 3.9 to zero w.r.t. $\mathbf{r}$ and $\mathbf{t}$. The form of the resulting linear system is

$$\underbrace{\mathbf{C}\mathbf{C}^\mathsf{T}}_{\mathbf{A}}\underbrace{\begin{pmatrix}\mathbf{r}\\ \mathbf{t}\end{pmatrix}}_{\mathbf{x}} = \underbrace{-\,\mathbf{C}\mathbf{d}}_{\mathbf{b}} \tag{3.10}$$

with

$$\mathbf{C} = \begin{pmatrix}\mathbf{c}_1 & \cdots & \mathbf{c}_K\\ \mathbf{n}_1 & \cdots & \mathbf{n}_K\end{pmatrix} \quad \text{, and} \quad \mathbf{d} = \begin{pmatrix}(\mathbf{p}_1 - \mathbf{q}_1)\cdot\mathbf{n}_1\\ \vdots \\ (\mathbf{p}_K - \mathbf{q}_K)\cdot\mathbf{n}_K\end{pmatrix} . \tag{3.11}$$

Equation 3.10 is of the form $\mathbf{A}\mathbf{x} = \mathbf{b}$ where $\mathbf{x}$ is the 6×1 vector of unknowns we want to retrieve. As $\mathbf{A}$ is symmetric and positive definite, we can solve $\mathbf{A}\mathbf{x} = \mathbf{b}$ by first computing the Cholesky decomposition $\mathbf{A} = \mathbf{L}\mathbf{L}^\mathsf{T}$ with $\mathbf{L}$ being a lower triangular matrix with strictly positive diagonal entries, then solving $\mathbf{L}\mathbf{y} = \mathbf{b}$ for $\mathbf{y}$, and finally solving $\mathbf{L}^\mathsf{T}\mathbf{x} = \mathbf{y}$ for $\mathbf{x}$.

3.2.4 Experiments

In the first experiment a dataset captured from a conference room with our scanning system is used to evaluate different variants of the pairwise ICP matching

(a) Two unregistered scans. (b) Registered scans.

Figure 3.5: A scanned conference room serves as input to the algorithms. The left picture shows two out of four scans coarsely aligned by wheel odometry. All methods converge to the same correct registration (right).

algorithm. Figure 3.5 depicts two out of four scans from this dataset. The scene is an easy case for most ICP variants, since it contains well defined coarse-scale geometry features which make an alignment easy. Yet it is very representative for the data acquired by our scanning system. The dataset is manually aligned to obtain ground truth robot poses. We then evaluate the performance of different ICP algorithms relative to this correct alignment. The metric we will use to compare the results is root-mean square point-to-point distance for the points in the test dataset and the corresponding points in the aligned reference dataset. This allows for a more objective comparisons of the performance of ICP variants than using the error metrics computed by the algorithms themselves.

We first look at the performance for different methods of the correspondence search. Figure 3.6(a) presents a comparison of convergence rates for different correspondence search methods. For the selected scene, our proposed method using a combination of point, normal, and color matching produces the best results. All methods converge to the same correct registration. However, incorporating additional clues, such as normal and color information, to the standard correspondence search leads to a faster convergence. We hypothesize that the reason for this is that more correct pairings are formed in early iterations. Secondly, we compare the performance of two error metrics: point-to-point and point-to-plane. Figure 3.6(b) depicts a comparison of convergence rates for both metrics. On the choosen dataset, we see that the point-to-plane error metric performs significantly better than the point-to-point metric. It takes the algorithm using a point-to-point metric more than 100 iterations to converge and the residual alignment error is 1.45 mm. The alignment error of the unregistered dataset is 0.48 m. The algorithm using a point-to-plane metric, however, converges to a simular residual alignment error within 5 iterations.

In the second experiment, we use ICP for a pairwise alignment of a larger dataset. This dataset maps the first floor of Stanford's Gates Building and it consists of 8 scans (see Figure 3.7). An initial registration of the data is performed by using the robot's wheel odometry. This aligns the scans only coarsely but serves as a good starting point for the ICP registration. Next, we perform a registration with our ICP variant using point, normal, and color similarity for the correspondence search as well as the point-to-plane error metric. The result of this registration is presented on the right side of Figure 3.7. One will note that each pair is seemingly aligned well. However, small residual errors in this pairwise registration process accumulate and cause inconsistencies in the data. In our case, the first and the last scan are not aligned well.

3.2.5 Conclusion

In this section, we presented a pairwise ICP alignment strategy for solving the multi-view registration problem. We have shown typical results that capture the significant differences in performance using variations of the standard ICP algorithm. We demonstrated that ICP-based registration techniques work well for a pairwise registration of point clouds.

There are three main sources of error for ICP. The first source of error is wrong convergence: ICP can converge to a local minimum out of the attraction area of the true solution. The reasons for this behavior are the iterative nature of the algorithm. A coarse initial alignment of the data is essential for ICP to converge to the correct alignment. In our case, a good starting point for the ICP registration is given by the robot's wheel odometry. The second source of error is underconstrained situations: in some environments there is not enough information to estimate the pose of the robot completely. Those situations occur when surfaces can slide in one or more directions without affecting the error function. Refer to [Gelfand et al., 2003] for a comprehensive analysis. Our strategy for finding correspondences by adding color and normals to the search not only leads to a better convergence but also alleviates the effect of underconstraint alignments. The third source of error is sensor noise: even though ICP arrives in the attraction area of the true solution, the outcome is different because of noise. Sensor noise is difficult to address in ICP since data points are assumed fixed and without error. Allowing

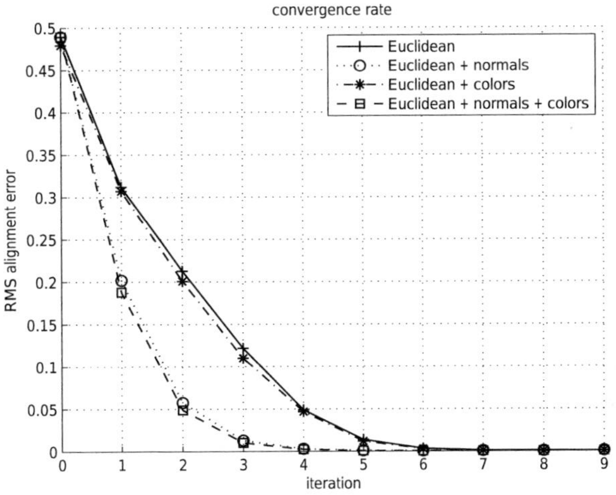

(a) Correspondence search.

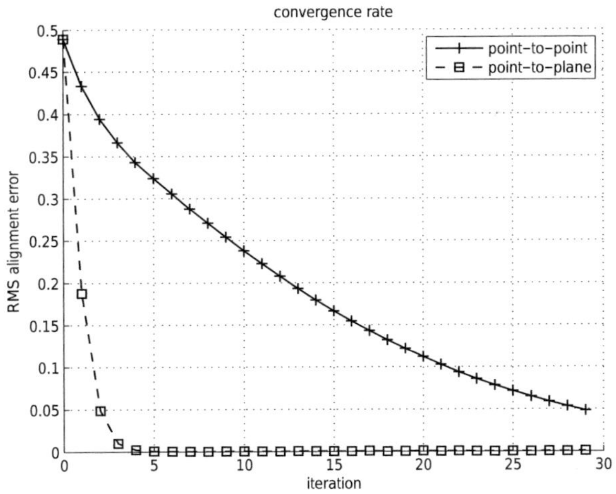

(b) Error metrics.

Figure 3.6: Comparison of different ICP variants on scanned data. We analyze the convergence rates using different methods of correspondence search (top) as well as different error metrics (bottom) on the conference room dataset.

(a) Registration using odometry. (b) Registration using ICP.

Figure 3.7: Results for the registration on 8 scans. Registration based on wheel odometry (left) retrieved from the scanner leads to a highly distorted model. Using the ICP algorithm with several modifications yields good results for registering textured 3D scans (right). However, residual errors in this registration process accumulate and cause inconsistencies when scanning large loops.

data points to adjust for noise implies a fundamentally different type of non-rigid registration which we will address in Section 3.4.

When applied to a larger number of scans, an incremental registration process may result in residual errors which accumulate over time. This leads to inconsistencies especially when scanning large loops such as depicted in Figure 3.7(b). Without a global registration technique even small errors accumulate while sequentially registering the scans of those loops. Specifically, errors in orientation may cause large displacements as they act like levers in a sequential registration process.

In the following sections we will use the ICP variant using point distance, normal distance, and color similarity for the correspondence search as well as the point-to-plane error metric for pairwise scan matching.

3.3 Global Registration

As discussed in the previous section, *pairwise matching* methods accumulate registration errors such that the registration of many scans leads to inconsistent maps. [Pulli, 1999] presented a method that minimizes the registration error by iteratively registering one scan to all neighboring scans. In this way the accumulated alignment error is spread over the whole set of acquired 3D scans. While in Pulli's method the pairwise alignment was interactive, [Nüchter et al., 2004] extended this idea to a totally automated procedure. However, neither one of these methods easily allows to incorporate additional information, such as sensor noise and the uncertainty of robot poses.

Our method belongs to the family of SLAM algorithms and is based on the concepts of *GraphSLAM* [Thrun and Montemerlo, 2005]. GraphSLAM models robot poses as nodes in a graph and edges correspond to constraints. An optimization over the nodes seeks to satisfy all constraints as good as possible. Our approach linearizes the optimization problem and solves the resulting equation system using the Conjugate Gradient (CG) method. This is similar to [Nieto et al., 2006] in the way that scan matching is used in a global optimization scheme. However, we explicitly incorporate uncertainties of the scan matching as well as the robot's position estimate.

[Olson et al., 2006] proposed Stochastic Gradient Descent (SGD) to optimize pose graphs. This approach has the advantage of being easy to implement and exceptionally robust to wrong initial guesses. Later, [Grisetti et al., 2007a] extended this approach by applying a tree based parameterization that significantly increases the convergence speed. The main problem of these approaches is that they assume the error in the graph to be more or less uniform, and thus they are difficult to apply to graphs where some constraints are under-specified. Also, because of the iterative nature of SGD a large number of iterations are required to reduce the residual error.

3.3.1 Pose Graphs

Our multi-view registration problem naturally forms a sparse graph (see Figure 3.8). Each node in this graph represents a pose of the scanner at which a scan was taken. The edges in the graph correspond to events: a *motion event* connects two consecutive scanner poses, and a *registration event* links two poses that were registered by aligning the corresponding scans using a registration algorithm such as the ICP algorithm described in the previous section. The edges form soft constraints and they carry information relating the relative position of two nodes, along with the uncertainty of that information.

A constraint can be thought of as a spring attached to two nodes trying to pull them into a certain configuration. The idle state of the spring corresponds to the relative pose distance as a result of a motion or registration event. Mathematically, a constraint is a set of simultaneous equations that relates the current estimate of two poses $\mathbf{x}_i$ and $\mathbf{x}_j$ to a measured or observed relative pose $\tilde{\mathbf{d}}_{ij}$. We write this

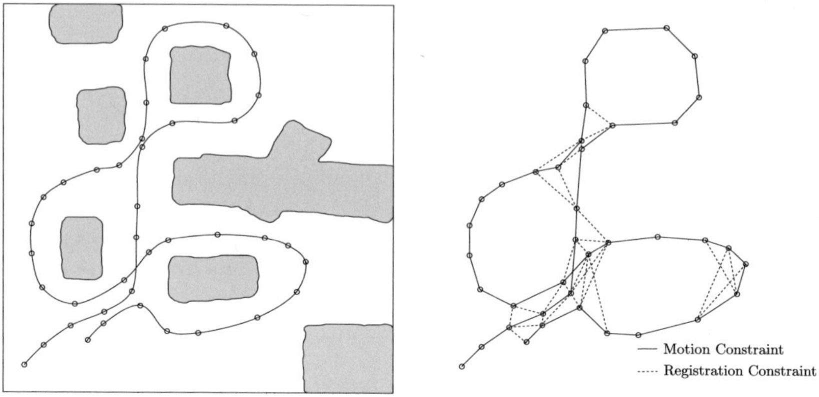

(a) Robot path. (b) Pose graph.

Figure 3.8: The multi-view registration problem forms a sparse graph. Nodes in this graph represent scan poses while edges are formed by motion and registration events. The left picture shows the path of a scanning robot in a simulated environment. The robot stops to create scans. The right picture shows the graph representation of the corresponding multi-view registration problem.

relation as Mahalanobis distance:

$$\chi_{ij}^2 = \left(\mathbf{d}_{ij} - \tilde{\mathbf{d}}_{ij}\right)^{\mathsf{T}} \mathbf{\Sigma}_{ij}^{-1} \left(\mathbf{d}_{ij} - \tilde{\mathbf{d}}_{ij}\right) \tag{3.12}$$

where the $\mathbf{d}_{ij} = \mathbf{x}_j \ominus \mathbf{x}_i$ corresponds to the relative pose between frames i and j. See Appendix 8.2 for a detailed description of the pose compounding operation and its properties. The difference between the current state and the observation is the residual

$$\mathbf{r}_{ij} = \mathbf{d}_{ij} - \tilde{\mathbf{d}}_{ij} \ , \tag{3.13}$$

which is scaled by the constraint's confidence $\mathbf{\Sigma}_{ij}^{-1}$. We assume that the constraints are uncertain quantities and that this uncertainty can be represented as a multivariate Gaussian distribution over the parameters of the rigid-body transformation. Maximizing the probability $P\left(\mathbf{d}_{ij}|\tilde{\mathbf{d}}_{ij}\right)$ for all $\left(i,j\right) \in \mathcal{J}$ simultaneously, where $\mathcal{J}$ is a set of indices of node pairs in the pose graph connected by either motion or registration edges, corresponds to finding the optimal estimate of all robot poses. Under the assumption that all errors in the observations are distributed independently, maximizing the probability $P\left(\mathbf{d}_{ij}|\tilde{\mathbf{d}}_{ij}\right)$ is equivalent to minimizing the following Mahalanobis distance:

$$E_{\mathcal{G}} = \sum_{(i,j)\in\mathcal{J}} \mathbf{r}_{ij}^{\mathsf{T}} \mathbf{\Sigma}_{ij}^{-1} \mathbf{r}_{ij} \ . \tag{3.14}$$

$E_{\mathcal{G}}$ represents a differentiable energy function that takes all motion constraints and all registration constraints and measures how consistent they are (low energy corresponds to high consistency).

Motion Constraints

Assume the scanner starts from a pose $\mathbf{x}_a$ and travels some distance before reaching a second pose $\mathbf{x}_b$. We denote the true difference in pose by $\mathbf{d}_{ab}$. The odometry of the scanning robot gives us an uncertain measurement $\tilde{\mathbf{d}}_{ab}$ of the true pose difference, and we can directly define a term for each *motion constraint* in the energy function Equation 3.14:

$$\chi^2_{\text{odo}} = \left(\mathbf{d}_{ab} - \tilde{\mathbf{d}}_{ab}\right)^{\mathsf{T}} \mathbf{\Sigma}_{\text{odo}}^{-1} \left(\mathbf{d}_{ab} - \tilde{\mathbf{d}}_{ab}\right) \ . \tag{3.15}$$

The covariance matrix $\mathbf{\Sigma}_{\text{odo}}$ captures the uncertainty of the odometry measurements. A detailed derivation of covariance matrices for robot motion based on odometry will be covered in Section 3.4.3. For now, we can assume that we have a good estimate of the covariance matrix.

ICP Matching Constraints

For each pair of overlapping scans (i, j), a *matching constraint* between the corresponding poses of these scans is added to the pose graph. The ICP registration algorithm described Section 3.2 is used to register one pair at a time into a common coordinate system. The result is a rigid transformation that aligns the points of one scan with the portions of a surface that it shares with another scan. This transform is another estimate of true difference between two poses, and we can define a term for each matching constraint:

$$\chi^2_{\text{icp}} = \left(\mathbf{d}_{ij} - \tilde{\mathbf{d}}_{ij}\right)^{\mathsf{T}} \mathbf{\Sigma}_{\text{icp}}^{-1} \left(\mathbf{d}_{ij} - \tilde{\mathbf{d}}_{ij}\right) \ . \tag{3.16}$$

The accuracy of ICP depends on the geometric information (e.g., local curvatures) contained in the point sets. If insufficient shape information is available, inaccurate or incorrect registration may occur. Several methods have been proposed for evaluating the stability of the registration [Stoddart et al., 1998,

Bengtsson and Baerveldt, 2003, Gelfand et al., 2003, Segal et al., 2009]. We use the method of [Bengtsson and Baerveldt, 2003] which estimates the covariance by examining the shape of the error function. The idea is that if the error function H is quadratic (which it is), then the optimal least-squares estimate would be $\mathbf{x} = \mathbf{A}^{-1}\mathbf{b}$ according to the linear system in Equation 3.10. The covariance of $\mathbf{x}$ equals to

$$\mathbf{C} = \left(\frac{1}{2} \frac{\partial^2}{\partial \mathbf{x}^2} H\left(\mathbf{R}, \mathbf{t}\right) \right)^{-1} \sigma^2 . \tag{3.17}$$

An unbiased estimate s^2 of σ^2 in Equation 3.17 would be $s^2 = H\left(\mathbf{R}, \mathbf{t}\right)/(K-3)$, where K is the number of correspondences.

3.3.2 Optimal Pose Estimation

Linear Estimation

One approach for determining the optimal pose according to Equation 3.14 was proposed by [Lu and Milios, 1997]. Their solution assumes the pose compounding operation can be linearized and solve the resulting linear system. For the linear case the compounding operation has the simple form

$$\mathbf{d}_{ij} = \mathbf{x}_j \ominus \mathbf{x}_i \equiv \mathbf{x}_j - \mathbf{x}_i . \tag{3.18}$$

The energy function can can now be written as:

$$E_{\text{lin}} = \sum_{(i,j)\in \mathcal{J}} \left(\mathbf{x}_j - \mathbf{x}_i - \tilde{\mathbf{d}}_{ij}\right)^{\mathsf{T}} \mathbf{\Sigma}_{ij}^{-1} \left(\mathbf{x}_j - \mathbf{x}_i - \tilde{\mathbf{d}}_{ij}\right) . \tag{3.19}$$

To minimize Equation 3.19, the equation is expressed in a matrix form:

$$E_{\text{lin}} = \left(\mathbf{HX} - \tilde{\mathbf{D}}\right)^{\mathsf{T}} \mathbf{\Sigma}^{-1} \left(\mathbf{HX} - \tilde{\mathbf{D}}\right) . \tag{3.20}$$

Here $\tilde{\mathbf{D}}$ is a matrix concatenating all observations, $\mathbf{X}$ a matrix concatenating all poses, and $\mathbf{H}$ an incidence matrix with all entries being $1, -1$, or 0. The matrix $\mathbf{\Sigma}$ is the new covariance matrix of $\tilde{\mathbf{D}}$ which consists of $\mathbf{\Sigma}_{ij}$ sub-matrices. Now, the solution for $\mathbf{X}$ which minimizes E_{lin} is given by:

$$\mathbf{X} = \left(\mathbf{H}^{\mathsf{T}}\mathbf{\Sigma}^{-1}\mathbf{H}\right)^{-1} \mathbf{H}^{\mathsf{T}}\mathbf{\Sigma}^{-1}\tilde{\mathbf{D}} , \tag{3.21}$$

with a covariance of $\mathbf{X}$:

$$\mathbf{\Sigma}_X = \left(\mathbf{H}^\mathsf{T}\mathbf{\Sigma}^{-1}\mathbf{H}\right)^{-1} . \tag{3.22}$$

As stated above, we assume the observations errors associated with each link to be independent. Therefore, $\mathbf{\Sigma}$ will be block-diagonal and the solution of $\mathbf{X}$ and $\mathbf{\Sigma}_X$ can be simplified to improve the performance for the typically occurring large number of observations. We set $\mathbf{G} = \mathbf{H}^\mathsf{T}\mathbf{\Sigma}^{-1}\mathbf{H}$ and $\mathbf{B} = \mathbf{H}^\mathsf{T}\mathbf{\Sigma}^{-1}\tilde{\mathbf{D}}$ and expand the matrix multiplications. The matrix $\mathbf{G}$ consists of the following sub-matrices:

$$\mathbf{G} = \begin{cases} \sum_{j=0}^{t} \mathbf{\Sigma}_{i,j}^{-1} & (i = j) \\ -\mathbf{\Sigma}_{i,j}^{-1} & (i \neq j) \end{cases} , \tag{3.23}$$

and the matrix $\mathbf{B}$ consists of the following sub-matrices:

$$\mathbf{B} = \sum_{j=0;\, i \neq j}^{t} \mathbf{\Sigma}_{i,j}^{-1}\tilde{\mathbf{D}}_{i,j} . \tag{3.24}$$

With this simplification, Equation 3.21 can be rewritten as:

$$\mathbf{G}\mathbf{X} = \mathbf{B} . \tag{3.25}$$

The proposed algorithm then requires $\mathbf{G}$ to be invertible. It has been shown that this holds true when all link covariance matrices are positive or negative definite, and the pose graph is connected, i.e., there exist no two separate subgraphs [Lu and Milios, 1997, Borrmann et al., 2008]. The second condition is met trivially in practice since at least all consecutive poses are linked by motion links.

Assuming the linear case holds for the compounding operation, the optimal pose estimation results in solving the sparse linear system of Equation 3.25. Refer to Appendix 8.3.2 for details on methods for solving systems of this type. In general, $\mathbf{x}_j - \mathbf{x}_i$ is not a good approximation of the compound operator $\mathbf{x}_j \ominus \mathbf{x}_i$ since it involves complex trigonometric operations. See Appendix 8.2 for more details.

Linearization of the Compound Operator

Instead of assuming the compound operation to be linear, a better approximation is a direct linearization of Equation 3.14 through Taylor expansion. Suppose each pose graph edge is a measurement $\tilde{\mathbf{d}}$ of the true relative pose $\mathbf{d} = \mathbf{x}_j \ominus \mathbf{x}_i$. The measurement covariance of $\tilde{\mathbf{d}}$ is denoted by $\tilde{\mathbf{\Sigma}}$. Let $\tilde{\mathbf{x}}_i$ and $\tilde{\mathbf{x}}_j$ be the measurements of $\mathbf{x}_i$ and $\mathbf{x}_j$. The observation error is denoted by $\triangle\mathbf{x}_i = \tilde{\mathbf{x}}_i - \mathbf{x}_i$ and $\triangle\mathbf{x}_j = \tilde{\mathbf{x}}_j - \mathbf{x}_j$. The residual becomes:

$$\begin{aligned}
\triangle\mathbf{d} &= \tilde{\mathbf{d}} - \mathbf{d} && (3.26)\\
&= \tilde{\mathbf{d}} - \mathbf{x}_j \ominus \mathbf{x}_i && (3.27)\\
&= \tilde{\mathbf{d}} - (\tilde{\mathbf{x}}_j - \triangle\mathbf{x}_j) \ominus (\tilde{\mathbf{x}}_i - \triangle\mathbf{x}_i) && (3.28)\\
&:= r(\mathbf{x}_i, \mathbf{x}_j) \ . && (3.29)
\end{aligned}$$

A Taylor expansion leads to:

$$\begin{aligned}
\triangle\mathbf{d} &\approx r(\tilde{\mathbf{x}}_i, \tilde{\mathbf{x}}_j) + \frac{\partial r(\tilde{\mathbf{x}}_i, \tilde{\mathbf{x}}_j)}{\partial \tilde{\mathbf{x}}_i}(\mathbf{x}_i - \tilde{\mathbf{x}}_i) + \frac{\partial r(\tilde{\mathbf{x}}_i, \tilde{\mathbf{x}}_j)}{\partial \tilde{\mathbf{x}}_j}(\mathbf{x}_j - \tilde{\mathbf{x}}_j) && (3.30)\\
&= \tilde{\mathbf{d}} - (\tilde{\mathbf{x}}_j \ominus \tilde{\mathbf{x}}_i) - \mathbf{J}_{\tilde{\mathbf{x}}_i \ominus}\{\tilde{\mathbf{x}}_j, \tilde{\mathbf{x}}_i\}\triangle\mathbf{x}_i - \mathbf{J}_{\tilde{\mathbf{x}}_j \ominus}\{\tilde{\mathbf{x}}_j, \tilde{\mathbf{x}}_i\}\triangle\mathbf{x}_j && (3.31)
\end{aligned}$$

Analytical expressions of the Jacobians $\mathbf{J}_{\tilde{\mathbf{x}}_j \ominus}\{\tilde{\mathbf{x}}_j, \tilde{\mathbf{x}}_i\}$ and $\mathbf{J}_{\tilde{\mathbf{x}}_i \ominus}\{\tilde{\mathbf{x}}_j, \tilde{\mathbf{x}}_i\}$ are straightforward though lengthy. We refer the reader to Appendix 8.2 for more details. Equation 3.31 is a linar equation but not in the right format to be processed in a linear system like in the previous section. However, Equation 3.31 can be written as:

$$\triangle\mathbf{d} \approx \tilde{\mathbf{d}} - (\tilde{\mathbf{x}}_j \ominus \tilde{\mathbf{x}}_i) + \tilde{\mathbf{K}}_j^{-1}\left(\triangle\mathbf{x}_j - \tilde{\mathbf{H}}_{ij}\triangle\mathbf{x}_i\right) \quad (3.32)$$

with

$$\begin{aligned}
\tilde{\mathbf{K}}_j^{-1} &= \begin{pmatrix} \tilde{\mathbf{R}}_j & \\ & \mathbf{I}_3 \end{pmatrix} \qquad \text{and} && (3.33)\\
\tilde{\mathbf{H}}_{ij} &= \tilde{\mathbf{H}}_j^{-1}\tilde{\mathbf{H}}_i \ . && (3.34)
\end{aligned}$$

Here $\tilde{\mathbf{R}}_j$ denotes the rotation matrix corresponding to the pose estimate $\tilde{\mathbf{x}}_j$. The matrix $\tilde{\mathbf{H}}_i$ is defined as:

$$\tilde{\mathbf{H}}_i = \begin{pmatrix}
1 & 0 & 0 & 0 & \tilde{z}_i c_{\tilde{\phi}_i} + \tilde{y}_i s_{\tilde{\phi}_i} & \tilde{y}_i c_{\tilde{\phi}_i} c_{\tilde{\theta}_i} - \tilde{z}_i c_{\tilde{\theta}_i} s_{\tilde{\phi}_i}\\
0 & 1 & 0 & -\tilde{z}_i & -\tilde{x}_i s_{\tilde{\phi}_i} & -\tilde{x}_i c_{\tilde{\phi}_i} c_{\tilde{\theta}_i} - \tilde{z}_i s_{\tilde{\theta}_i}\\
0 & 0 & 1 & \tilde{y}_i & -\tilde{x}_i c_{\tilde{\phi}_i} & \tilde{x}_i c_{\tilde{\theta}_i} s_{\tilde{\phi}_i} + \tilde{y}_i s_{\tilde{\theta}_i}\\
0 & 0 & 0 & 1 & 0 & s_{\tilde{\theta}_i}\\
0 & 0 & 0 & 0 & s_{\tilde{\phi}_i} & c_{\tilde{\phi}_i} c_{\tilde{\theta}_i}\\
0 & 0 & 0 & 0 & c_{\tilde{\phi}_i} & c_{\tilde{\theta}_i} s_{\tilde{\phi}_i}
\end{pmatrix} \quad (3.35)$$

using the expressions $c_{\tilde{\phi}_i} := \cos(\tilde{\phi}_i)$ and $s_{\tilde{\phi}_i} := \sin(\tilde{\phi}_i)$ for notational brevity. The matrix $\tilde{\mathbf{H}}_j$ is given analogously. If we now define a new residual to be $\triangle\mathbf{d}' = -\tilde{\mathbf{H}}_j\tilde{\mathbf{K}}_j\triangle\mathbf{d}$, then we can write:

$$\triangle\mathbf{d}' = \left(\tilde{\mathbf{H}}_j\triangle\mathbf{x}_j - \tilde{\mathbf{H}}_i\triangle\mathbf{x}_i\right) - \tilde{\mathbf{H}}_j\tilde{\mathbf{K}}_j\left((\tilde{\mathbf{x}}_j \ominus \tilde{\mathbf{x}}_i) - \tilde{\mathbf{d}}\right) \tag{3.36}$$

$$= \mathbf{d}' - \tilde{\mathbf{d}}' \tag{3.37}$$

where we denote

$$\tilde{\mathbf{d}}' = \tilde{\mathbf{H}}_j\tilde{\mathbf{K}}_j\left((\tilde{\mathbf{x}}_j \ominus \tilde{\mathbf{x}}_i) - \tilde{\mathbf{d}}\right) \tag{3.38}$$

$$\mathbf{d}' = \tilde{\mathbf{H}}_j\triangle\mathbf{x}_j - \tilde{\mathbf{H}}_i\triangle\mathbf{x}_i\ . \tag{3.39}$$

The reason for substitution is that we now have an expressions which is very similar to the linear case of the compound operation in Equation 3.18. Specifically, we have a measurement equation for $\mathbf{d}'$ where $\tilde{\mathbf{d}}'$ can be considered as an observation of $\mathbf{d}'$. The covariance $\tilde{\mathbf{\Sigma}}'$ of $\tilde{\mathbf{d}}'$ can be computed from the covariance $\tilde{\mathbf{\Sigma}}$ of $\tilde{\mathbf{d}}$:

$$\tilde{\mathbf{\Sigma}}'_{ij} = \tilde{\mathbf{H}}_j\tilde{\mathbf{K}}_j\tilde{\mathbf{\Sigma}}_{ij}\tilde{\mathbf{K}}_j^{\mathsf{T}}\tilde{\mathbf{H}}_j^{\mathsf{T}}\ . \tag{3.40}$$

Inserting the new expressions into our energy function of Equation 3.20 results in:

$$E \approx \sum_{(i,j)\in\mathcal{J}} \left(\mathbf{d}'_{ij} - \tilde{\mathbf{d}}'_{ij}\right)^{\mathsf{T}} \tilde{\mathbf{\Sigma}}'^{-1}_{ij} \left(\mathbf{d}'_{ij} - \tilde{\mathbf{d}}'_{ij}\right) \tag{3.41}$$

$$= \sum_{(i,j)\in\mathcal{J}} \left(\mathbf{v}_j - \mathbf{v}_i - \tilde{\mathbf{d}}'_{ij}\right)^{\mathsf{T}} \tilde{\mathbf{\Sigma}}'^{-1}_{ij} \left(\mathbf{v}_j - \mathbf{v}_i - \tilde{\mathbf{d}}'_{ij}\right) \tag{3.42}$$

with $\mathbf{v}_i = \tilde{\mathbf{H}}_i\triangle\mathbf{x}_i$ and $\mathbf{v}_j = \tilde{\mathbf{H}}_j\triangle\mathbf{x}_j$. Following the steps discussed above, we can minimize this function for $\mathbf{v}_i$ and $\mathbf{v}_j$ by solving the linear system in Equation 3.25. We recall that the system had the following form:

$$\mathbf{G}\mathbf{V} = \mathbf{B}\ . \tag{3.43}$$

The presented linearization of the compound operator $\ominus$ enables us to use the same linear estimation as in the previous section by setting

$$\mathbf{G} = \begin{cases} \displaystyle\sum_{j=0}^{t} \tilde{\mathbf{\Sigma}}'^{-1}_{ij} & (i = j) \\ -\tilde{\mathbf{\Sigma}}'^{-1}_{ij} & (i \neq j) \end{cases} \tag{3.44}$$

and

$$\mathbf{B} = \sum_{j=0;\, i \neq j}^{t} \tilde{\boldsymbol{\Sigma}}_{ij}^{\prime -1} \tilde{\mathbf{D}}_{ij}^{\prime} \,. \tag{3.45}$$

Once again, $\tilde{\mathbf{D}}'_{ij}$ is a matrix concatenating all observations $\tilde{\mathbf{d}}'_{ij}$. The matrix $\mathbf{V}$, in this case, concatenates all terms $\mathbf{v}_i$. Once we solve Equation 3.43 for all $\mathbf{v}_i$ the poses $\mathbf{x}_i$ are simply calculated by:

$$\mathbf{x}_i = \tilde{\mathbf{x}}_i - \tilde{\mathbf{H}}_i^{-1} \mathbf{v}_i \tag{3.46}$$

In practice, it takes several iterations for solving Equation 3.43 since linear approximations were made in deriving the optimization criterion. Solving for $\mathbf{V}$ repeatedly by re-evaluating $\mathbf{G}$ and $\mathbf{B}$ around the state estimate each time, improves the pose estimates until convergence is reached.

3.3.3 Experiments

First, we use a synthetically-generated scene to evaluate different variants of the global registration on pose graphs. The *sphere* scene (see Figure 3.9) is a simulated trajectory in which the scanning system was moved on the surface of a sphere. It consists of 2200 poses which are connected by 8647 constraints in a pose graph. Consecutive poses are connected by motion constraints, and each pose is connected to all its direct neighbors by matching constraints. The nodes of the pose graph as well as the constraints between the nodes were distorted with Gaussian noise. The resulting distorted graph (Figure 3.9(a)) serves as input to our algorithms. To provide quantitative results, Figure 3.9(b) depicts the evolution of the average error per constraint versus the iteration number. As expected, the linear estimation method converges in just one iteration of solving the linear system and additional iterations won't improve the results (Figure 3.9(b)). However, it won't find an appropriate configuration of the pose graph since the non-commutativity of the compound operation is simply ignored in this case. An optimization with linearization of the compound operation and linear estimation, as presented in the previous section, converges to a configuration with small errors in less than 10 iterations. In fact, from Figure 3.9(c) one can see that the structure of the sphere is already recovered within the first few iterations and more iterations merely transform the graph into the final configuration. For a comparison, we also applied the approach of [Grisetti et al., 2007a] to the dataset. This approach converts a posegraph into a tree structure and applies SGD optimization. It converges into a configuration with small residual errors within 1000 iterations. Our optimization

(a) Input pose graph.

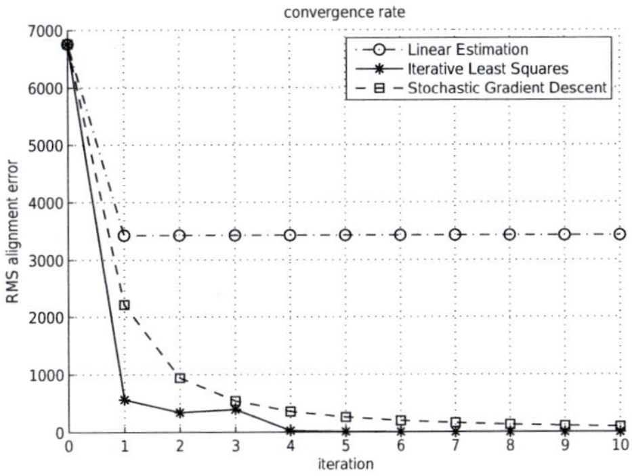

(b) Quantitative results.

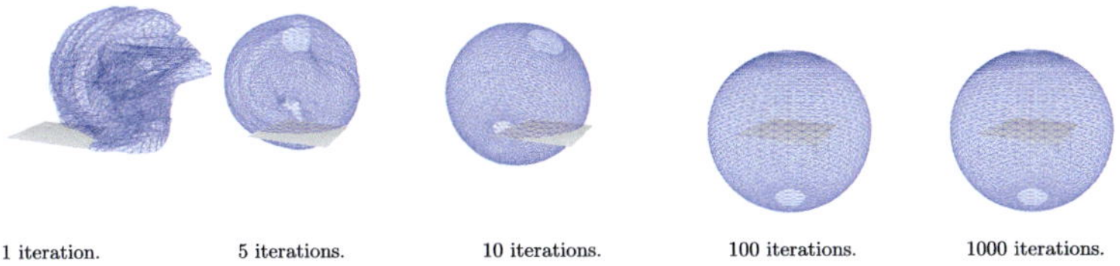

(c) Our optimization using Iterative Least Squares.

(d) Optimization using Stochastic Gradient Descent [Grisetti et al., 2007a].

Figure 3.9: Optimization of a simulated trajectory of a robot moving on the surface of a sphere. The top left image (a) shows the input trajectory which consists of 2,200 poses and 8,647 constraints.

requires only 10 iterations for the same residual errors. Each SGD iteration takes in the order of 1 s while solving the linear system in Equation 3.43 requires about 10 s per iteration. Therefore, our approach still is one order of magnitude faster than SGD.

As a second example, we evaluate our global registration algorithm with a real data acquired by our scanning system captured in an office environment. The dataset, as depicted in Figure 3.10, consists of 133 scans covering an area of 50 m by 140 m meter. Using the robot's odometry, 132 motion constraints were added to the pose graph. Applying a pairwise ICP registration on overlapping scans another 275 matching constraints were added to the pose graph. We compared the resulting registration to a 2D floor plan, which was manually created by an architect since ground truth for this dataset is not available. The total time for aligning the data is 532 s, while most time of the multi-view registration is spent on disk IO and the ICP scan matching. Once the pose graph is generated, our optimization algorithm converges with only a few iterations and in less than 1 second.

3.3.4 Conclusion

In this section, we presented a method for aligning scans globally. Our approach resembles the concept of GraphSLAM by using the poses of the scanner as graph nodes and observations (motion and ICP matching) as graph edges. The graph is optimized by linearizing the compound operator and minimizing the resulting least squares energy function. The linearized version of originally non-linear energy function is essentially the *information form* where the matrix $\mathbf{G}$ in Equation 3.43 is called the *information matrix* and the matrix $\mathbf{B}$ in the same equation is denoted as the *information vector*. If we solve Equation 3.43 for $\mathbf{V}$, we have an Extended Information Filter (EIF). With a different parameterization this estimation problem could also be formulated as an Extended Kalman Filter (EKF). The result would be the same since EIFs are computationally equivalent to EKFs, but they represent information differently: instead of maintaining a covariance matrix, the EIF maintains an inverse covariance matrix (the information matrix).

In our experiments, we showed that this method is capable of optimizing large datasets with hundreds of scans. Essentially, this method distributes the errors introduced by uncertain measurements over the graph as whole. At the core of our method, the ICP algorithm performs a pairwise rigid registration for overlapping scans. This registration may not be perfect and local errors are introduced. However, our proposed global registration optimizes all poses simultaneously, which effectively eliminates accumulations of local errors.

Our method assumes that pairs of scans can be aligned using a rigid registration, i.e., the motion between two scans is rigid. It cannot adequately handle non-rigid warps frequently present in real-world datasets. For example, imperfect sensor calibrations add systematic errors to the data requiring a non-rigid deformation between scans.

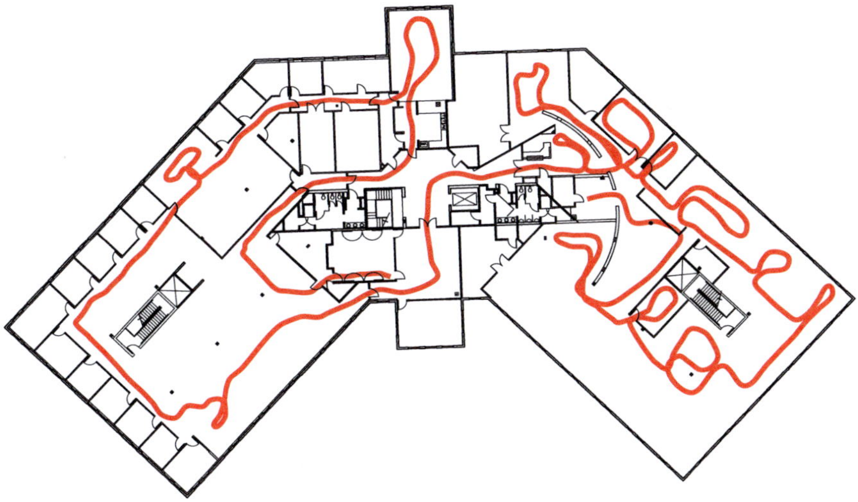

(a) Floor-plan with robot path.

(b) Registered point cloud.

Figure 3.10: The top figure shows a manually created floor plan and the path taken by our scanning robot. The bottom figure presents the 3D point cloud registered using our multi-view registration approach.

3.4 Probabilistic Non-Rigid Registration

In the previous section, we presented a least squares solution for the global registration problem. The formulation was based on the assumption that we can register pairs of scans and spread the residual error over the whole set of scans. A key limitation of this type of algorithm lies in the requirement to split the global registration into pairwise rigid registrations and a subsequent optimization. Typically the later step involves reducing the data to a more sparse representation such as a pose graph. Unfortunately, a lot of the originally retrieved information is discarded. For example, wrong data associations can be detected and repaired during the optimization process if the appropriate data is included in the optimization procedure. Non-linearities in the rigid registration as well as imperfect sensor calibrations add systematic errors into the data which are impossible to model in a rigid registration framework but they lead to artifacts, which drastically decrease the quality of subsequent processing steps, such as surface reconstruction.

To address this issue, this section investigates an approach for aligning scans in a probabilistic and non-rigid fashion. Our approach is an instance of a probabilistic SLAM algorithm used to simultaneously perform a registration and determine the most likely 3D map. Early work in SLAM assumed that a map used for mobile robots could be modeled as a discrete set of landmarks. Different kinds of representations or maps have been proposed in robotics and in the artificial intelligence literature, ranging from low-level metric maps such as landmark maps [Dissanayake et al., 2001] and occupancy grids [Elfes, 1989], to topological graphs that contain high-level qualitative information [Kuipers and Byun, 1993], and even to multi-hierarchies of successively higher level abstractions [Fernandez-Madrigal and Gonzalez, 2002].

Traditionally SLAM implementations based on Kalman filter data fusion rely on simple geometric models for defining landmarks. This limits landmark based algorithms to environments suited for such models and tends to discard much potentially useful data. Only more recently, the work in [Nieto et al., 2007] showed how to define landmarks composed of raw sensed data.

The occupancy grid framework, as proposed in [Elfes, 1989], is used in many practical SLAM implementations [Hähnel et al., 2003a, Grisetti et al., 2007b]. It employs a multidimensional (typically 2D or 3D) tessellation of space into cells, where each cell stores a probabilistic estimate of its occupancy state. For each grid cell, sensor measurements are integrated using, e.g., the Bayes rule to reduce the effect of sensor noise. This allows a variety of robotic tasks to be addressed through operations performed directly on the occupancy grid representation. The limited resolution of grid maps is the source for several problems. As pointed out in [Montemerlo and Thrun, 2004], a systematic error is introduced since the resolution of sensors typically used for perception varies with distance. Generally, the occupancy grid is modeled as a spatially uncorrelated random field. The individual cell states can be estimated as independent random variables. Again, a random structure is assumed for this model.

The assumption of line-based environments [Garulli et al., 2005] and orthogonality as a geometrical constraints [Harati and Siegwart, 2007] have been previously used by other researchers. Those approaches require features to be reliably extracted from the data as a preprocessing step which limits the performance of the subsequent SLAM algorithm.

From the discussion above we can identify some limitations of current SLAM approaches:

1. While much effort in robotic mapping is spent on large scale environments, little attention is put on the true accuracy of the resulting map.

2. Most map representations used in current SLAM approaches assume a random structure of the map or the features in the map. In reality, these assumptions rarely hold, since all man-made environments are highly structured. For example, the insides of buildings are a common workspace for mobile robots and are constructed with a well known methodology.

3. Information included in the sensor data is discarded at an early stage of processing: landmark maps discard much useful data while occupancy grid maps have an inherently limited resolution and suffer from discretization errors.

In this section, we propose a novel formulation of the SLAM problem which incorporates spatial correlation models and does not rely on the notion of discrete landmarks or pairwise scan matching. We demonstrate that this formulation can be used for a non-rigid multi-view registration of scans. This idea was first presented in [Pitzer and Stiller, 2010] for 2D SLAM and extended to 3D in [Pitzer et al., 2010].

3.4.1 Formulation of the Probabilistic SLAM Problem

We start with an outline of the original formulation of probabilistic SLAM. At at a time t the following quantities are defined:

- $\mathbf{x}_t$: A vector describing the robot pose (position and orientation). See Appendix 8.1 for more details.
- $\mathbf{u}_t$: The motion vector that carries information about the change of the robot's pose from $\mathbf{x}_{t-1}$ to $\mathbf{x}_t$.
- $\mathbf{z}_t$: A vector of observations taken by the robot at time t where $\mathbf{z}_t^i$ denotes the i-th observation.
- $\mathbf{c}_t$: A correspondence vector that contains indices of all features observed at time t where $\mathbf{c}_t^i$ denotes the i-th correspondence of an observation and a map feature.
- $\mathcal{M}$: A set of features $\mathcal{M} = \{\mathbf{m}_i\}$ representing the environment around the robot.
- The sets $\mathcal{X}_{1:t}, \mathcal{U}_{1:t}, \mathcal{Z}_{1:t}, \mathcal{C}_{1:t}$ are ensembles of all referred quantities for time instances 1 through t.

Two basic Bayesian approaches to SLAM are frequently used. One is known as the *online SLAM* problem with known correspondences. It involves estimating the posterior over the momentary pose $\mathbf{x}_t$ along with the map $\mathcal{M}$:

$$p\left(\mathbf{x}_t, \mathcal{M} | \mathcal{U}_{1:t}, \mathcal{Z}_{1:t}, \mathcal{C}_{1:t}\right) . \tag{3.47}$$

This approach is called online since it only involves estimating quantities at the time t. The set of correspondences $\mathcal{C}_{1:t}$ is assumed to be known and are not considered in the Bayesian formulation. In contrary, the *full SLAM* or *offline SLAM* problem seeks to calculate a posterior over all quantities:

$$p\left(\mathcal{X}_{1:t}, \mathcal{M} | \mathcal{U}_{1:t}, \mathcal{Z}_{1:t}, \mathcal{C}_{1:t}\right) . \tag{3.48}$$

Here we focus on the latter problem since we make the assumption that all data is available for the registration process. Like in Equation 3.3, probabilistic SLAM can be treated as an estimation problem. During SLAM, the most probable sequence of states of the robot has to be estimated in addition to the map. This is often solved using the Markov assumption. That is, the state transition is assumed to be a Markov process in which the next state $\mathbf{x}_t$ depends only on the immediately

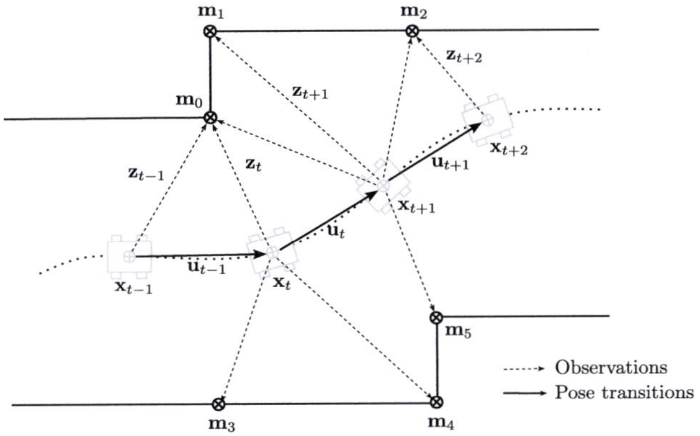

Figure 3.11: The Simultaneous Localization and Mapping (SLAM) problem. A simultaneous estimate of both robot pose $\mathbf{x}_t$ and landmark locations $\mathbf{m}_i$ is required. The true locations are never known or measured directly. Observations $\mathbf{z}_t$ are made between true robot and landmark locations and the robot controls $\mathbf{u}_t$ are issued to drive the robot to various locations.

Figure 3.12: The left figure shows the structure of traditional landmark based SLAM algorithms. The state transition is assumed to be a Markov process in which the next state $\mathbf{x}_t$ depends only on the immediately proceeding state $\mathbf{x}_{t-1}$ and the applied control $\mathbf{u}_t$, and is independent of both the observations and the map. Each observation $\mathbf{z}_t^i$ is associated with a map feature $\mathbf{m}_i$. The right figure shows our approach which incorporates correlations between features into a probabilistic estimate. Such correlations are modeled as locally supported *map priors*.

proceeding state $\mathbf{x}_{t-1}$, and the applied control $\mathbf{u}_t$, and is independent of both the observations and the map. The structure of this problem is depicted on the left side of Figure 3.12.

Bayes rule enables us to factorize the posterior in Equation 3.48:

$$\begin{aligned} &p\left(\mathcal{X}_{1:t}, \mathcal{M} | \mathcal{U}_{1:t}, \mathcal{Z}_{1:t}, \mathcal{C}_{1:t}\right) \\ &= \frac{p\left(\mathbf{z}_t | \mathcal{X}_{1:t}, \mathcal{M}, \mathcal{U}_{1:t}, \mathcal{Z}_{1:t-1}, \mathcal{C}_{1:t}\right) p\left(\mathcal{X}_{1:t}, \mathcal{M} | \mathcal{U}_{1:t}, \mathcal{Z}_{1:t-1}, \mathcal{C}_{1:t}\right)}{\underbrace{p\left(\mathbf{z}_t | \mathcal{U}_{1:t}, \mathcal{Z}_{1:t-1}, \mathcal{C}_{1:t}\right)}_{:=const.}} \\ &= \eta\, p\left(\mathbf{z}_t | \mathcal{X}_{1:t}, \mathcal{M}, \mathcal{U}_{1:t}, \mathcal{Z}_{1:t-1}, \mathcal{C}_{1:t}\right) p\left(\mathcal{X}_{1:t}, \mathcal{M} | \mathcal{U}_{1:t}, \mathcal{Z}_{1:t-1}, \mathcal{C}_{1:t}\right) , \end{aligned} \tag{3.49}$$

where $\eta = 1/p\left(\mathbf{z}_t | \mathcal{U}_{1:t}, \mathcal{Z}_{1:t-1}, \mathcal{C}_{1:t}\right)$ is a normalizer that is independent of $\mathcal{X}_{1:t}$ and $\mathcal{M}$ and thus irrelevant for the following optimization process. The first probability on the right side of Equation 3.49 is reduced by dropping the conditioning variables $\mathcal{X}_{1:t-1}$, $\mathcal{U}_{1:t}$, $\mathcal{Z}_{1:t-1}$, and $\mathcal{C}_{1:t-1}$ since an observation at time t only depends on the pose at time t and the map $\mathcal{M}$:

$$p\left(\mathbf{z}_t | \mathcal{X}_{1:t}, \mathcal{M}, \mathcal{U}_{1:t}, \mathcal{Z}_{1:t-1}, \mathcal{C}_{1:t}\right) = p\left(\mathbf{z}_t | \mathbf{x}_t, \mathcal{M}, \mathbf{c}_t\right) . \tag{3.50}$$

The second probability on the right side of Equation 3.49 can also be factored by partitioning $\mathcal{X}_{1:t}$ into $\mathbf{x}_t$ and $\mathcal{X}_{1:t-1}$

$$\begin{aligned} &p\left(\mathcal{X}_{1:t}, \mathcal{M} | \mathcal{U}_{1:t}, \mathcal{Z}_{1:t-1}, \mathcal{C}_{1:t}\right) \\ &= p\left(\mathbf{x}_t | \mathcal{X}_{1:t-1}, \mathcal{M}, \mathcal{U}_{1:t}, \mathcal{Z}_{1:t-1}, \mathcal{C}_{1:t}\right) p\left(\mathcal{X}_{1:t-1}, \mathcal{M} | \mathcal{U}_{1:t}, \mathcal{Z}_{1:t-1}, \mathcal{C}_{1:t}\right) . \end{aligned} \tag{3.51}$$

As stated above, $\mathbf{x}_t$ depends only on the immediately proceeding state $\mathbf{x}_{t-1}$ and the applied control $\mathbf{u}_t$, and is independent of the observations allowing us to drop irrelevant condition variables

$$\begin{aligned} &p\left(\mathcal{X}_{1:t}, \mathcal{M} | \mathcal{U}_{1:t}, \mathcal{Z}_{1:t-1}, \mathcal{C}_{1:t}\right) \\ &= p\left(\mathbf{x}_t | \mathbf{x}_{t-1}, \mathbf{u}_t\right) p\left(\mathcal{X}_{1:t-1}, \mathcal{M} | \mathcal{U}_{1:t-1}, \mathcal{Z}_{1:t-1}, \mathcal{C}_{1:t-1}\right) . \end{aligned} \tag{3.52}$$

Inserting Equation 3.50 and Equation 3.52 into Equation 3.49 and recursively applying the Bayes rule leads to the final definition of the *full SLAM posterior*:

$$\begin{aligned}
& p\left(\mathcal{X}_{1:t}, \mathcal{M} | \mathcal{U}_{1:t}, \mathcal{Z}_{1:t}, \mathcal{C}_{1:t}\right) \\
& = \eta\, p\left(\mathbf{x}_t | \mathbf{x}_{t-1}, \mathbf{u}_t\right) p\left(\mathbf{z}_t | \mathbf{x}_t, \mathcal{M}, \mathbf{c}_t\right) p\left(\mathcal{X}_{1:t-1}, \mathcal{M} | \mathcal{U}_{1:t-1}, \mathcal{Z}_{1:t-1}, \mathcal{C}_{1:t-1}\right) \\
& = \eta\, p\left(\mathbf{x}_1, \mathcal{M}\right) \prod_t p\left(\mathbf{x}_t | \mathbf{x}_{t-1}, \mathbf{u}_t\right) p\left(\mathbf{z}_t | \mathbf{x}_t, \mathcal{M}, \mathbf{c}_t\right) \\
& = \eta\, p\left(\mathbf{x}_1\right) p\left(\mathcal{M}\right) \prod_t p\left(\mathbf{x}_i | \mathbf{x}_{t-1}, \mathbf{u}_t\right) p\left(\mathbf{z}_t | \mathbf{x}_t, \mathcal{M}, \mathbf{c}_t\right) \\
& = \eta\, p\left(\mathbf{x}_1\right) p\left(\mathcal{M}\right) \prod_t p\left(\mathbf{x}_t | \mathbf{x}_{t-1}, \mathbf{u}_t\right) \prod_i p\left(\mathbf{z}_t^i | \mathbf{x}_t, \mathcal{M}, \mathbf{c}_t^i\right) .
\end{aligned} \tag{3.53}$$

Here, $p\left(\mathbf{x}_t | \mathbf{x}_{t-1}, \mathbf{u}_t\right)$ is known as the *motion model* which describes state transitions of the robot in terms of a probability distribution. The term $p\left(\mathbf{z}_t^i | \mathbf{x}_t, \mathcal{M}, \mathbf{c}_t^i\right)$ on the other hand denotes an *observation model* which models an observation $\mathbf{z}_t^i$ of a known feature from a known pose and a known map as a probability distribution. Both models have been studied well for a variety of robots and sensors [Thrun et al., 2005]. The two prior terms $p\left(\mathbf{x}_1\right)$ and $p\left(\mathcal{M}\right)$ characterize prior distributions of the first robot pose and of the map respectively. Usually $p\left(\mathbf{x}_1\right)$ is used to anchor the initial pose to a fixed location. The map prior $p\left(\mathcal{M}\right)$ is typically assumed to be unknown and subsumed into the normalizer η. Finding the most probable solution to the full SLAM problem is the process of finding the set of poses $\hat{\mathcal{X}}_{1:t}$ and the map $\hat{\mathcal{M}}$ that maximizes the posterior probability of Equation 3.49:

$$\hat{\mathcal{X}}_{1:t}, \hat{\mathcal{M}} = \operatorname*{argmax}_{\mathcal{X}_{1:t}, \mathcal{M}} p\left(\mathcal{X}_{1:t}, \mathcal{M} | \mathcal{U}_{1:t}, \mathcal{Z}_{1:t}, \mathcal{C}_{1:t}\right) . \tag{3.54}$$

A significant limitation of SLAM algorithms of this form lies in the necessity to select appropriate landmarks. By reducing the sensor data to a representation by landmarks, most of the information originally retrieved is usually discarded. Another critical issue which arises from using discrete landmarks in SLAM is the problem of data association. Before fusing data into the map, new measurements are associated with existing map landmarks. This step has been proven crucial in practical SLAM implementations.

3.4.2 SLAM with Map Priors

SLAM remains a challenging problem mostly due to intrinsic limitations of sensor systems. Specifically, highly structured environments with recurring patterns or plain and featureless environments often cause great problems in the early stages of SLAM algorithms, namely the landmark extraction and data association. We believe, that incorporating simple priors about the environment enables a robot to reason better about the environment. Creating an exact probabilistic model of all potential environments is not feasible and probably not even well defined, but in most cases, assumptions are reasonable. For example, assuming the existence of smooth manifolds instead of randomly distributed surfaces is a reasonable model.

In the following, we introduce prior expectations on typical environments into SLAM by means of suitable a priori distributions $p(\mathcal{M})$. First, we want to eliminate the notion of landmarks. In the previous formulation it was assumed that the correspondences $C_{1:t}$ are known beforehand, which permits a unique assignment of an observation $\mathbf{z}_t^i$ to a landmark $\mathbf{m}_i$. However, in practical SLAM implementations, this becomes a demanding task since correspondences between measurements taken at different time instances are non-unique, and the imposture thereof is a main source of deteriorated results for many SLAM implementations. Therefore, we consider the measurements directly without extraction of any landmarks and assume no immediate correspondences between measurements: For example, a mobile robot equipped with a lidar, which takes a finite number of measurements while it is in motion, is very unlikely to measure the exact same spot twice.

Here are the key modifications to the original SLAM formulation proposed in this thesis:

1. Each observation $\mathbf{z}_t^i$ stems from a unique feature in the map; no feature is seen twice. Hence, no correspondences between observations and known features are assumed.
2. Instead, a map prior $p(\mathcal{M})$ is incorporated to guide the estimation of the robot's pose and the map.

The new posterior for this formulation is:

$$
\begin{aligned}
&p\left(\mathcal{X}_{1:t}, \mathcal{M} | \mathcal{U}_{1:t}, \mathcal{Z}_{1:t}\right) \\
&= \eta\, p\left(\mathbf{x}_1\right) p\left(\mathcal{M}\right) \prod_t \left[p\left(\mathbf{x}_t | \mathbf{x}_{t-1}, \mathbf{u}_t\right) \prod_i p\left(\mathbf{z}_t^i | \mathbf{x}_t, \mathcal{M}\right) \right] .
\end{aligned}
\tag{3.55}
$$

A graphical model of this new formulation is presented on the right side of Figure 3.12. Our modifications have some interesting implications. First, the state space of our optimization problem is significantly larger than in landmark based approaches because of the one-to-one correspondence of measurements and map features. For the optimization of Equation 3.55 a good map prior is vital. This is due to the way the observation model, the motion model, as well as the prior of the first pose in Equation 3.55 considered independently are best explained by the measurements themselves. Only the map prior introduces statistical dependencies of map features and measurements. An optimization of Equation 3.55 will move points locally to comply with the map's prior model. This is fundamentally different from ICP-style rigid alignment techniques where only the robot pose is optimized. The point motion will be constraint due to the dependence of measurement and pose. In fact, a movement of a point will create a counter potential for the point and for the corresponding pose to comply with the measurement model. In other words, maximizing the posterior probability Equation 3.55 will lead to a set of poses and map features that best explain the measurements as well as the prior model. In the following sections, we will discuss the different components of Equation 3.55 in more detail.

3.4.3 Probabilistic Motion Model

The first term of Equation 3.55 is the *motion model*. Here we assume that we have some measurements of the relative motion of the robot. Most common are odometry measurements, which are obtained by integrating wheel encoder information; most robots make such measurements available in periodic intervals. If the odometry measurements where perfect, we could simply calculate the robot's pose at any time by integrating over all measurements up to that time. Let $\mathbf{u}_t = \mathbf{x}_t \ominus \mathbf{x}_{t-1}$ be the relative pose between the robot current pose t and the robots last pose $t-1$ as measured by the odometry. Consequently, the current pose is obtained by:

$$\begin{aligned} \mathbf{x}_t &= \mathbf{x}_{t-1} \oplus \mathbf{u}_t && (3.56) \\ &= \left(\mathbf{x}_{t-2} \oplus \mathbf{u}_{t-1}\right) \oplus \mathbf{u}_t && (3.57) \\ &= \mathbf{x}_1 \oplus \mathbf{u}_2 \oplus \mathbf{u}_3 \oplus \ldots \oplus \mathbf{u}_t \;. && (3.58) \end{aligned}$$

Here, $\oplus$ and $\ominus$ are pose compounding operations; refer to Appendix 8.2 for more details. In reality the odometry measurement suffers from drift and slippage. We assume that the odometry measurements are governed by a so-called probabilistic motion model $p\left(\mathbf{x}_t|\mathbf{x}_{t-1}, \mathbf{u}_t\right)$, which specifies the likelihood that the robot has the current pose $\mathbf{x}_t$ given that it previously was at $\mathbf{x}_{t-1}$, and the motion $\mathbf{u}_t$ was measured. Few publications describe and characterize the uncertainty in motion measurement; for example [Roy and Thrun, 1998] and [Eliazar and Parr, 2004] suggest decomposing the motion into the distance traveled by the robot and the turn performed. Here, we simply model the motion measurement as a random variable with a zero-centered distribution with finite variance. Let us assume the actual measurements are given by a pose increment:

$$\tilde{\mathbf{u}}_t = \begin{pmatrix} \tilde{x}_u \\ \tilde{y}_u \\ \tilde{z}_u \\ \tilde{\phi}_u \\ \tilde{\theta}_u \\ \tilde{\psi}_u \end{pmatrix} = \begin{pmatrix} x_u \\ y_u \\ z_u \\ \phi_u \\ \theta_u \\ \psi_u \end{pmatrix} + \begin{pmatrix} \Delta x_u \\ \Delta y_u \\ \Delta z_u \\ \Delta \phi_u \\ \Delta \theta_u \\ \Delta \psi_u \end{pmatrix} = \begin{pmatrix} x_u \\ y_u \\ z_u \\ \phi_u \\ \theta_u \\ \psi_u \end{pmatrix} + N_6\left(, \breve{\boldsymbol{\Sigma}}_u\right) , \tag{3.59}$$

where $\breve{\boldsymbol{\Sigma}}_u$ is the noise covariance matrix. A better model of the actual measurement is thus

$$\tilde{\mathbf{x}}_t = \mathbf{x}_{t-1} \oplus (\mathbf{u}_t + \Delta \mathbf{u}_t) \tag{3.60}$$

$$\approx \underbrace{\mathbf{x}_{t-1} \oplus \mathbf{u}_t}_{:=g(\mathbf{x}_{t-1}, \mathbf{u}_t)} + N_6\left(, \boldsymbol{\Sigma}_u\right) . \tag{3.61}$$

Here, $\boldsymbol{\Sigma}_u$ is the covariance matrix which can be derived by calculating a transform matrix $\mathbf{V}_t$ that approximates the mapping between the motion's noise in the relative frame and the motion's noise the current pose frame

$$\boldsymbol{\Sigma}_u \approx \mathbf{V}_t \breve{\boldsymbol{\Sigma}}_u \mathbf{V}_t^{\mathsf{T}} . \tag{3.62}$$

The matrix $\mathbf{V}_t$ corresponds to the derivative of $g(\mathbf{x}_{t-1}, \mathbf{u}_t)$ with respect to $\mathbf{u}_t$:

$$\mathbf{V}_t = \frac{\partial g(\mathbf{x}_{t-1}, \mathbf{u}_t)}{\partial \mathbf{u}_t} = \mathbf{J}_{\mathbf{u}_t \oplus}\{\mathbf{x}_{t-1}, \mathbf{u}_t\} \tag{3.63}$$

with $\mathbf{J}_{\mathbf{u}_t \oplus}\{\mathbf{x}_{t-1}, \mathbf{u}_t\}$ being the Jacobian of the pose compound operation. Refer to Appendix 8.2.2 for a derivation of this Jacobian. Now, we can form a Gaussian probability distribution modeling the motion:

$$p(\mathbf{x}_t | \mathbf{x}_{t-1}, \mathbf{u}_t) \propto \exp\left\{\frac{1}{2}(\mathbf{x}_t - g(\mathbf{x}_{t-1}, \mathbf{u}_t))^{\mathsf{T}} \boldsymbol{\Sigma}_u^{-1} (\mathbf{x}_t - g(\mathbf{x}_{t-1}, \mathbf{u}_t))\right\} . \tag{3.64}$$

3.4.4 Probabilistic Observation Model

In the 3D world, range sensors measure the 3D coordinates of a surface point $\mathbf{m}_i = (m_x \; m_y \; m_z)^{\mathsf{T}}$. The beam model approximates the physical properties of a range measurement by simply stating that range finders measure a distance r_m

along a beam which originates at the origin of the sensor's local coordinate system [Thrun et al., 2005]. The angular orientations of the sensor beam are denoted as the azimuth angle θ_m (x-y plane) with $0 < \theta_m < 2\pi$ and the polar angle ϕ_m (z axis) with $0 < \phi_m < \pi$. This definition corresponds to spherical coordinates, also called spherical polar coordinates [Arfken, 1985]. We denote

$$\mathbf{z}_t^i = \begin{pmatrix} r_m \\ \theta_m \\ \phi_m \end{pmatrix} \tag{3.65}$$

to be a measurement of $\mathbf{m}_i$. The endpoint of this measurement is now mapped into the sensor coordinate system via the trigonometric transformation

$$\begin{pmatrix} r_m \\ \theta_m \\ \phi_m \end{pmatrix} = \begin{pmatrix} \sqrt{(m_x - x)^2 + (m_y - y)^2 + (m_z - z)^2} \\ \tan^{-1}\left(\frac{m_y - y}{m_x - x}\right) - \theta \\ \cos^{-1}\left(\frac{m_z - z}{r_m}\right) - \phi \end{pmatrix}, \tag{3.66}$$

where $\mathbf{x}_t = \begin{pmatrix} x & y & z & \phi & \theta & \psi \end{pmatrix}^\mathsf{T}$ denotes the pose of the sensor in global coordinates. In reality, range measurements are subject to noise. In case of a laser range finder, the range measurement is mainly disturbed by variations in the structure of the measured surface. The light exits the device in form of a cone which creates an elliptical footprint when hitting a surface. It is not well defined which surface point is actually measured within this ambiguity ellipse. This may lead to significant errors in the range measurement if the cone overlaps a surface border or a steep ridge. Also the angular measurements may be subject to noise. Even very small misalignments, such as eccentricities or axis deviations, can lead to errors in the angular orientation. Error models and specific characterizations of measurement uncertainties are, for example, given in [Deumlich and Staiger, 2002, Gordon, 2008], [Benet et al., 2002], and [Gutierrez-Osuna et al., 1998] for laser, infrared, and ultrasonic range finders, respectively. We assume, the range values and angular orientations are disturbed by independent noise. We will model this noise by a zero-centered random variable with finite variance. Let us assume the actual measurements are given by

$$\begin{pmatrix} \tilde{r}_m \\ \tilde{\theta}_m \\ \tilde{\phi}_m \end{pmatrix} = \begin{pmatrix} r_m \\ \theta_m \\ \phi_m \end{pmatrix} + \begin{pmatrix} \varepsilon_{\alpha 1} \\ \varepsilon_{\alpha 2} \\ \varepsilon_{\alpha 3} \end{pmatrix} = \begin{pmatrix} r_m \\ \theta_m \\ \phi_m \end{pmatrix} + N_3\left(, \mathbf{\Sigma}_m\right) \tag{3.67}$$

and

$$\mathbf{\Sigma}_m = \begin{pmatrix} \alpha_1^2 & 0 & 0 \\ 0 & \alpha_2^2 & 0 \\ 0 & 0 & \alpha_3^2 \end{pmatrix} \tag{3.68}$$

is the noise covariance matrix in measurement space. A better model of the actual measurement is thus

$$\tilde{\mathbf{z}}_t^i = \begin{pmatrix} \tilde{r}_m \\ \tilde{\theta}_m \\ \tilde{\phi}_m \end{pmatrix} \tag{3.69}$$

$$= \underbrace{\begin{pmatrix} \sqrt{(m_x - x)^2 + (m_y - y)^2 + (m_z - z)^2} \\ \tan^{-1}(m_y - y, m_x - x) - \theta \\ \cos^{-1}\left(\frac{m_z - z}{r_m}\right) - \phi \end{pmatrix}}_{h(\mathbf{x}_t, \mathbf{m}_i)} + N_3\left(, \mathbf{\Sigma}_m\right) . \tag{3.70}$$

Now, we can form a Gaussian probability distribution modeling the observation:

$$p\left(\mathbf{z}_t^i | \mathbf{x}_t, \mathbf{m}_i\right) \propto \exp\left\{\frac{1}{2}\left(\mathbf{z}_t^i - h\left(\mathbf{x}_t, \mathbf{m}_i\right)\right)^{\mathsf{T}} \mathbf{\Sigma}_m^{-1}\left(\mathbf{z}_t^i - h\left(\mathbf{x}_t, \mathbf{m}_i\right)\right)\right\} . \tag{3.71}$$

3.4.5 Prior of the Initial Pose

The prior distribution $p(\mathbf{x}_1)$ should anchor the intial pose, for example, to the origin of the global coordinate system. It is easily expressed by a Gaussian distribution

$$p(\mathbf{x}_1) \propto \exp\left\{\frac{1}{2}\left(\mathbf{x}_1 - \tilde{\mathbf{x}}_1\right)^T \mathbf{\Sigma}_1^{-1}\left(\mathbf{x}_1 - \tilde{\mathbf{x}}_1\right)\right\} , \tag{3.72}$$

where $\tilde{\mathbf{x}}_1$ is the initial believe in the initial pose. The covariance $\mathbf{\Sigma}_1$ is a matrix with variances close to zero on the diagonal and zero else.

3.4.6 Spatial Correlation Models

The probability distribution $p(\mathcal{M})$ in Equation 3.55 represents a *prior distribution* of all measured scenes. An exact probabilistic model of this distribution is not feasible and probably not even well defined. Hence, we focus on partial models, which represent properties of the surface structure. In our approach we use locally defined spatial correlation models representing two properties: manifoldness

$f(\mathcal{M})$ and shape $g(\mathcal{M})$. The final prior $p(\mathcal{M})$ is defined as the combination of both models:

$$p(\mathcal{M}) = \frac{1}{\eta} f(\mathcal{M})\, g(\mathcal{M}) \ , \tag{3.73}$$

where η denotes a constant factor, which corresponds to the integral over all other factors and therefore normalizes $p(\mathcal{M})$ to be a probability density function. In practice, this factor can be safely omitted as the normalization does not have an effect on the optimization.

Manifold Model

The intuition of this correlation model is that map observations belong to structured surfaces in the robot's environment. This means that for a 3D map the most probable surface must be a compact, locally connected, two-dimensional manifold, possibly with boundary, and embedded in $\mathbb{R}^3$. The first step towards defining a potential function which captures this property is to compute a tangent plane associated with each map point $\mathbf{m}_i$. A tangent plane is defined by a point $\mathbf{o}_i$ and normal $\mathbf{n}_i$. For each point, we choose a local neighborhood N_ε of varying diameter (typically $\varepsilon = 10 \ldots 50$ points). The center $\mathbf{o}_i$ is taken to be the centroid of N_ε, and the normal $\mathbf{n}_i$ is determined using principal component analysis [Hoppe et al., 1992]: the eigenvector with the smallest eigenvalue corresponds to the normal $\mathbf{n}_i$. The projected distance d_i of the point onto its tangent line is defined by the dot product:

$$d_i = (\mathbf{m}_i - \mathbf{o}_i) \cdot \mathbf{n}_i \ . \tag{3.74}$$

Now, we define a Gaussian manifold potential function of the form:

$$f(\mathcal{M}) \propto \prod_i \exp\left\{ -\frac{d_i^2}{2\sigma_M^2} \right\} \ , \tag{3.75}$$

where σ_M^2 is the variance of tangent plane distances. This parameter makes it possible to taylor the optimization to specific types of environments. For example, when creating maps of office buildings, one may find a dominant use of straight and smooth surfaces. Thus the tangent plane distance variance σ_M^2 will be set to a small value. In our application this parameter was hand tuned but [Diebel et al., 2006] demonstrated that prior parameters in a Bayesian framework such as ours can be determined through supervised learning techniques.

Figure 3.13 illustrates the properties of the manifold correlation model. The data points are drawn to their corresponding tangent planes. Hence, the most probable

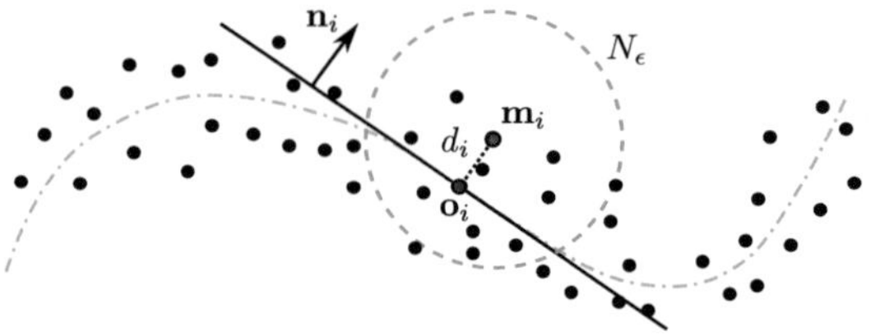

Figure 3.13: The *manifold model* uses a fixed neighborhood N_ε of points to create a tangent plane defined by a point $\mathbf{o}_i$ and the normal $\mathbf{n}_i$. The potential is then modeled as a Gaussian function over the projected distance d to the tangent plane.

arrangement of map points regarding this potential is when all points are located on a 2D plane embedded in 3D. It should be noted that the manifold potential is a set of locally supported functions. In other words, each map point is associated with a plane calculated from the points neighborhood and the size of N_ε defines the region of influence. We allow ε to adapt locally, which makes the requirement that the data is uniformly distributed over the surface less stringent. To select and adapt the neighborhood size, we use a kernel density estimator [Parzen, 1962] and set ε proportional to the computed density.

Shape Model

The shape model addresses consistency of surface orientations. If two surface regions (c.f. Figure 3.14) belong to the same physical surface, the orientation of edges representing the same portion should have a consistent orientation. In other words, we are looking for geometric relations (parallelism, orthogonality) of adjacent surface regions since we assume a predominantly rectilinear environment.

A simple approach is to examine the normals of adjacent surface regions. If the angle is close to one of 0°, 90°, 180°, or 270° the *shape potential* will draw the points towards a rectilinear case. Such a potential can be defined as follows: Let $\mathbf{m}_i$, $\mathbf{m}_j$, and $\mathbf{m}_k$ be adjacent points in the same surface region. The normal on the surface region is defined by:

$$\mathbf{n}_i = \frac{(\mathbf{m}_j - \mathbf{m}_i) \times (\mathbf{m}_k - \mathbf{m}_i)}{\|(\mathbf{m}_j - \mathbf{m}_i) \times (\mathbf{m}_k - \mathbf{m}_i)\|} \,. \tag{3.76}$$

Now, let $\mathbf{n}_i$ and $\mathbf{n}_i^*$ be the normals on two corresponding surface regions S and S^* respectively (c.f. Figure 3.14). Then the shape potential for the 0° case has the

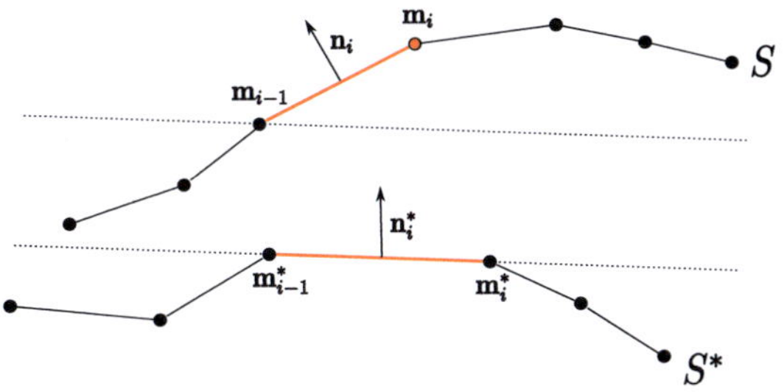

Figure 3.14: The *shape potential* uses the orientation of adjacent surface regions. The differences between two corresponding normals $\mathbf{n}_i$ and $\mathbf{n}_i^*$ are modeled as Gaussian functions over the normals differences.

following form:

$$g_0\left(\mathcal{M}\right) \propto \prod_{\{i,j\}} \exp\left\{-\frac{1}{2}\left(\mathbf{n}_i^* - \mathbf{n}_i\right)^{\mathsf{T}} \mathbf{\Sigma}_O \left(\mathbf{n}_i^* - \mathbf{n}_i\right)\right\} . \tag{3.77}$$

Here, $\mathbf{\Sigma}_O$ corresponds to a covariance matrix for the orientation of adjacent surface regions. This covariance matrix was again hand tuned to our application.

We define individual functions for the 90°, the 180°, and the 270° case, in similar ways. Ultimately, the shape model is only applied to region pairs that fall within a small margin of 10° normal angle deviation of one of the respective categories. All other cases will not contribute to the shape potential. The final shape potential is defined as a product of the individual surface potentials:

$$f_S\left(\mathcal{M}\right) = g_0\left(\mathcal{M}\right) g_{90}\left(\mathcal{M}\right) g_{180}\left(\mathcal{M}\right) g_{270}\left(\mathcal{M}\right) . \tag{3.78}$$

3.4.7 Implementation

In Equation 3.55 we defined a novel probabilistic model for the SLAM problem and in the previous sections we discussed the different components of this model. Map and pose are calculated from the Maximum A-Posteriori (MAP) solution of Equation 3.55. Now we want to focus on a practical implementation to calculate this solution. Since maxima of Equation 3.55 are unaffected by monotone transformations, we can take the negative logarithm of this expression to turn it into a sum and optimize this expression instead

$$\begin{aligned}
\hat{\mathcal{X}}_{1:t}, \hat{\mathcal{M}} &= \underset{\mathcal{X}_{1:t}, \mathcal{M}}{\operatorname{argmin}}\, p\left(\mathcal{X}_{1:t}, \mathcal{M} \mid \mathcal{U}_{1:t}, \mathcal{Z}_{1:t}\right) \\
&= \underset{\mathcal{X}_{1:t}, \mathcal{M}}{\operatorname{argmin}} - \log \eta - \log p\left(\mathbf{x}_1\right) - \log p\left(\mathcal{M}\right) \\
&\quad - \sum_t \log p\left(\mathbf{x}_t \mid \mathbf{x}_{t-1}, \mathbf{u}_t\right) \\
&\quad - \sum_t \sum_i \log p\left(\mathbf{z}_t^i \mid \mathbf{x}_t, \mathbf{m}_i\right) \\
&= \underset{\mathcal{X}_{1:t}, \mathcal{M}}{\operatorname{argmin}}\, E\left(\mathcal{X}_{1:t}, \mathcal{M}\right) . \qquad (3.79)
\end{aligned}$$

Finding the most probable solution now reduces to finding the global minimum of the function $E\left(\mathcal{X}_{1:t}, \mathcal{M}\right)$ which is a sum of log-likelihoods. The term $-\log \eta$ is constant therefore not relevant for minimizing $E\left(\mathcal{X}_{1:t}, \mathcal{M}\right)$.

Algorithm 1 Calculate

for all controls $\mathbf{u}_t$ **do**
    $\mathbf{x}_t \leftarrow$ *motion_model* $\left(\mathbf{u}_t, \mathbf{x}_{t-1}\right)$
    for all observations $\mathbf{z}_t^i$ **do**
        $\mathbf{m}_i \leftarrow$ *observation_model* $\left(\mathbf{x}_t, \mathbf{z}_t^i\right)$
    end for
end for
$\mathcal{X}_{1:t}, \mathcal{M} \leftarrow$ *global_registration* $\left(\mathcal{X}_{1:t}, \mathcal{M}\right)$ % see Section 3.3 for more details
repeat
    create prior model $p\left(\mathcal{M}\right)$
    fix state variables $\mathcal{X}_{1:t}$
    $\mathcal{M} \leftarrow$ *conjugate_gradient_iteration* $\left(\mathcal{X}_{1:t}, \mathcal{M}\right)$
    fix state variables $\mathbf{m}_{1:i}$
    $\mathcal{X}_{1:t} \leftarrow$ *conjugate_gradient_iteration* $\left(\mathcal{X}_{1:t}, \mathcal{M}\right)$
until convergence

Our Algorithm consists of three main steps: first we use the *motion model* and the *observation model* from Equation 3.58 and Equation 3.66 respectively to calculate an initial estimate for $\mathcal{X}_{1:t}$ and $\mathcal{M}$. Next, an initialization is performed to improve this estimate. Finally, we use a non-linear conjugate gradient variant to find the parameters which minimize $E\left(\mathcal{X}_{1:t}, \mathcal{M}\right)$. An outline of this algorithm is presented in Algorithm 1.

Unfortunately, the objective function $E\left(\mathcal{X}_{1:t}, \mathcal{M}\right)$ is non-linear and thus finding the global minimum is known to be difficult. For this reason, we use a scan alignment algorithm prior to the optimization. In particular, we use the global registration methods which we presented earlier in Section 3.3 in order to create an initial alignment and a better starting point for our optimization. Our experiments show that this starting point is usually sufficiently close to the global minimum of E that the following optimization procedure will converge into the correct solution.

The most probable path and the most probable map are estimated by finding the global minimum of the function $E(\mathcal{X}_{1:t}, \mathcal{M})$. The minimization itself is a high dimensional and sparse optimization problem. Therefore, the method of non-linear Conjugate Gradient (CG) is used to find a good solution. A detailed description of this a method can be found in [Shewchuk, 1994]. In our implementation we use a modified version of CG which addresses the structure of the state space. Each CG iteration consists of two sub-optimization steps. First, we fix all pose state variables and optimize the map feature positions. Next, the map features are fixed and the positions are optimized. By splitting the optimization in two steps, we loose the optimality of our solution; however, in practice, this scheme leads to a better convergence than optimizing all state variables simultaneously. Each sub-optimization step employs a standard Newton-Raphson line search and the Fletcher-Reeves formulation to linearly combine the negative gradient of the function $E(\mathcal{X}_{1:t}, \mathcal{M})$ with previous such gradients.

3.4.8 Experimental Results

2D Registration

We start with an application of our non-rigid registration method to 2D mapping. By setting insignificant state variables to 0, we can modify our approach for the 2D case. For example, the pose of a robot in 2D is defined as:

$$\mathbf{x}_{2D} = \begin{pmatrix} x \\ y \\ 0 \\ 0 \\ 0 \\ \psi \end{pmatrix} . \tag{3.80}$$

First, we use synthetic data created in a simulated 2D environment [Gerkey et al., 2003]. The dataset consists of 16 simulated 360° scans with 720 measurements in each scan. The ground truth of the entire dataset and of two details are depicted in Figure 3.15. This ground truth was then distorted by adding

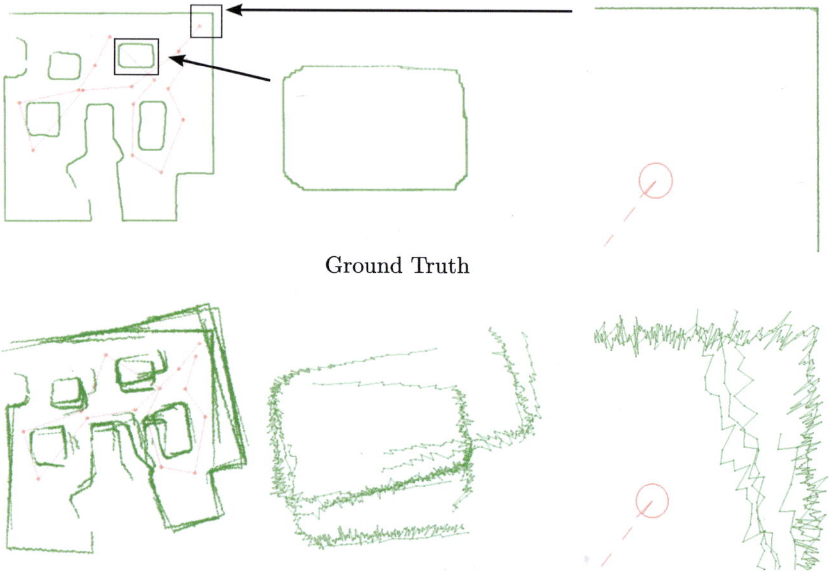

Figure 3.15: For the evaluation of our algorithms a synthetic 2D dataset is used. The first column shows the full dataset, whereas the second and third column depict magnified details. The ground truth (top) was then distorted by adding Gaussian noise (bottom) in order to create a realistic input for all algorithms.

Gaussian noise to the measurements (range and bearing) and to the odometry in order to create a realistic input for all algorithms. For a comparison, we use a the variant of the ICP algorithm described in Section 3.2, which incrementally registers all scans and the global registration described in Section 3.3. The thickness of walls is a general indication of the error distribution—a divergence of the robot pose typically results in map distortions, such as bend/double walls, while noise of the range sensor has a fixed mean and makes walls appear fuzzy and blurred (see Figure 3.16).

We also assess the algorithm performance by comparing the reconstructed trajectory and the reconstructed map with the available ground truth (see Figure 3.17). On one hand, ICP is able to align groups of scans correctly, but it fails to create a globally consistent map. This behavior is expected since ICP is a pairwise alignment algorithm. On the other hand, the global registration produces a consistent

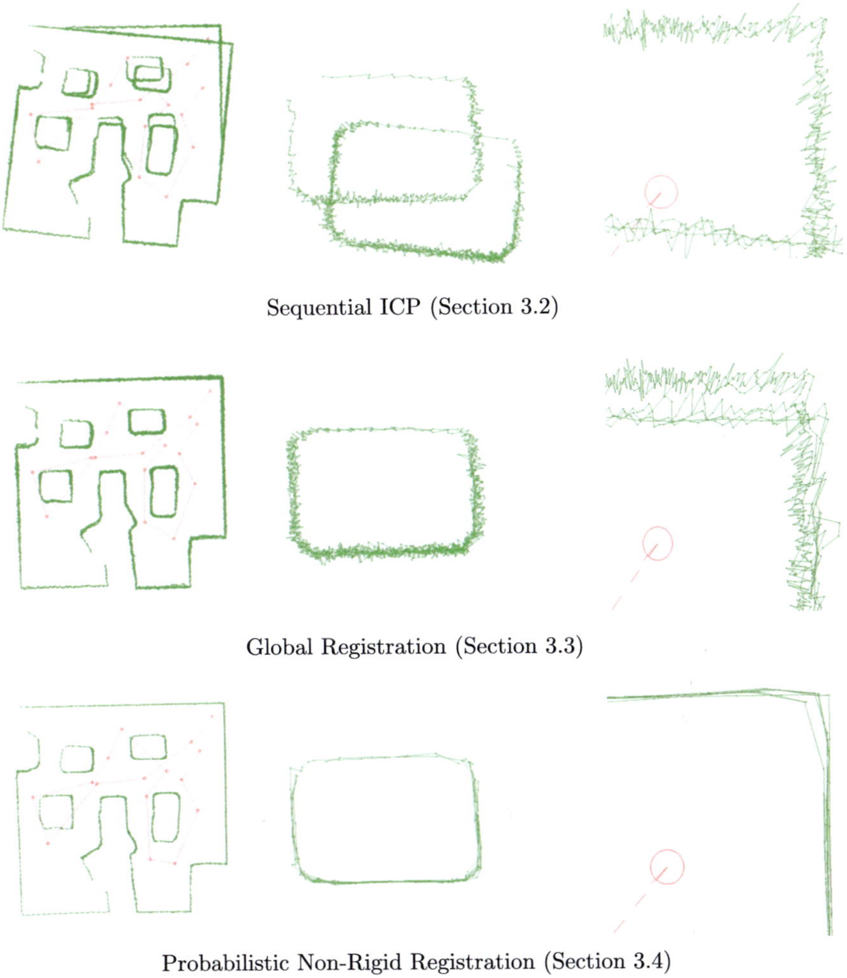

Figure 3.16: Evaluation of our algorithms on a synthetic 2D dataset. The ICP algorithm yields a good pairwise alignment but results in an inconsistent map (top). The global registration method (middle) produces a consistent map on the first glance, but the details reveal fuzzy surfaces (first detail) and small pose error residuals (second detail). The probabilistic non-rigid algorithm creates a globally consistent map and is able to eliminate measurement errors almost entirely (bottom).

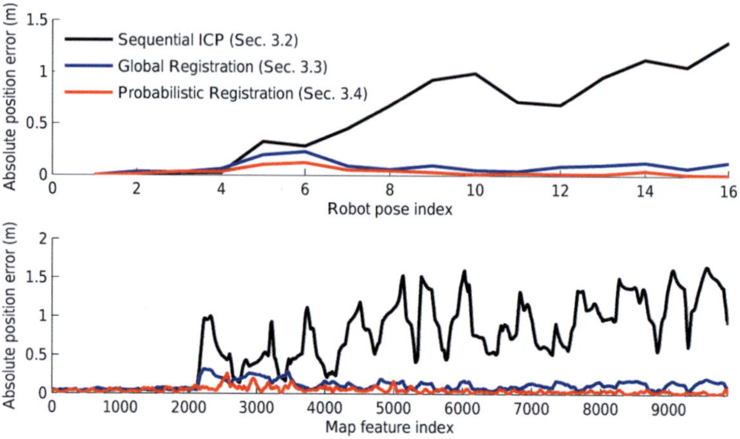

Figure 3.17: Absolute pose and map feature errors for the synthetic dataset.

map, although some residual pose errors remain. Both ICP and global registration adjust robot poses only and therefore feature measurement errors are not corrected. In contrast, the probabilistic non-rigid registration algorithm creates a globally consistent map and is able to minimize measurement errors. Figure 3.17 shows the absolute robot pose and map feature errors and the following table presents the corresponding first and second moments:

	Pose error (m)		Map error (m)	
Algorithm	mean	std-dev	mean	std-dev
ICP	0.597	0.199	0.702	0.238
Global Registration	0.088	0.115	0.115	0.005
Probabilistic Registration	0.035	0.048	0.047	0.002

In the second experiment we use data gathered by a real robot. Here, we use the fr079 dataset which is publicly available at the Robotics Dataset Repository (Radish) [Howard and Roy, 2003]. It consists of 4791 scans from a Sick LMS lidar with odometry pose estimate for each scan. For a comparison we again use the global registration described in Section 3.3. The reconstruction of the full map is presented on the right side of Figure 3.18. Both global registration and our algorithm result in a similar map. One may notice that the walls appear thinner in the map reconstructed by our algorithm, which quantitatively shows our algorithm provides a sensible estimation of the robot path. The details on the left side of Figure 3.18 reveal a significantly better registration of the data. Our algorithm

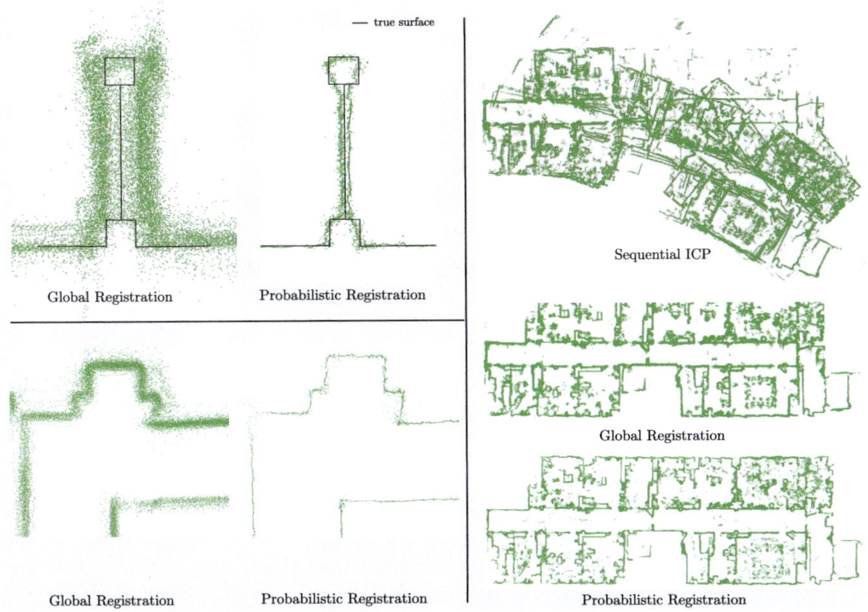

Figure 3.18: A comparison of our algorithm to sequential registration with the ICP algorithm and the global registration on the fr079 dataset. The right side shows the full dataset, and on the left side, we present magnifications of two details.

performs very well on straight walls since those features are represented best by our correlation models. Some outliers and smoothed corners are produced on sharp features since our models are not well defined at corners.

3D Registration

The second experiment shows the full functionality of the non-rigid registration algorithm in all 6 degrees of freedom. We used data from the data acquisition system presented in the previous chapter, acquired in an office of Robert Bosch LLC in Palo Alto. Figure 3.19 depicts two details from this office dataset. The left side shows the datasets aligned with the global registration method presented in Section 3.3, the right side presents the results for the probabilistic non-rigid registration method. The color coding corresponds to the surface distance d_S at the corresponding points. We define the surface distance as

$$d_S := \Big[(\mathbf{p}_i - \mathbf{q}_i) \cdot \mathbf{n}_i\Big]^2 \tag{3.81}$$

with the point $\mathbf{p}_i$ of point cloud $\mathcal{P}$ being the closest point to $\mathbf{q}_i$ of point cloud $\mathcal{Q}$ and $\mathbf{n}_i$ being the normal vector at point $\mathbf{q}_i$. This essentially is the point-to-plane metric proposed by [Besl and McKay, 1992]. The color coding reveals a signficant residual registration error of up to 50 mm in both examples. This error is effectively reduced using the probabilistic non-rigid registration.

3.4.9 Conclusion

In this section, we presented an novel approach for aligning scans in a probabilistic and non-rigid fashion. We used a map representation which stores all observations as unique features in this map. Instead of assuming correspondences between observations like it is done in traditional SLAM approaches, we incorporated two spatial correlation models as map priors to guide the optimization. With this approach, we formulated the full SLAM problem as a maximum a-posteriori estimation problem which we optimized using a nonlinear conjugate gradient method. Scans are aligned by optimizing the robot's pose as well as by optimizing the measurements. This non-rigid alignment is fundamentally different from ICP-style rigid alignment techniques where only the robot pose is optimized. The measurement point motion will be constrained due to the dependence of measurement and pose. In fact, a movement of a measurement point will create a counter potential for the point and for the corresponding pose to comply with the measurement model. Finally, we demonstrated the performance of our algorithm on synthetic data and on large real-world datasets. Our framework efficiently handles a large number of scans comprising millions of samples. In comparison to the rigid-registration methods, we demonstrate with a number of 2D and 3D datasets that our non-rigid registration significantly improves the alignment quality.

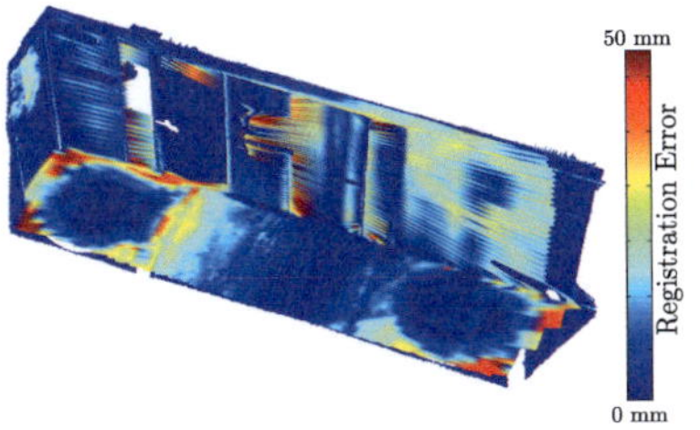

(a) Global registration.

(b) Probabilistic registration.

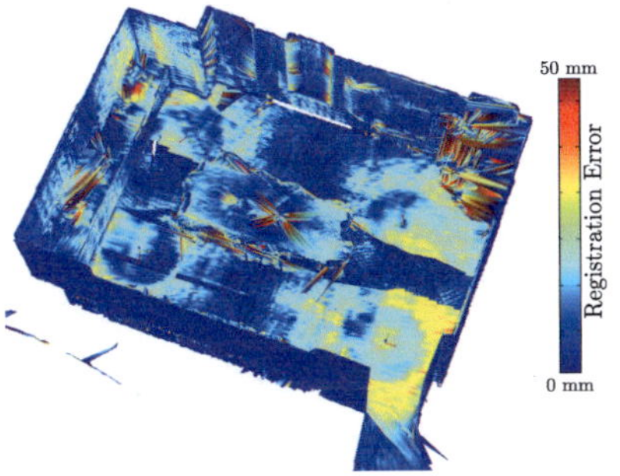

(c) Global registration.

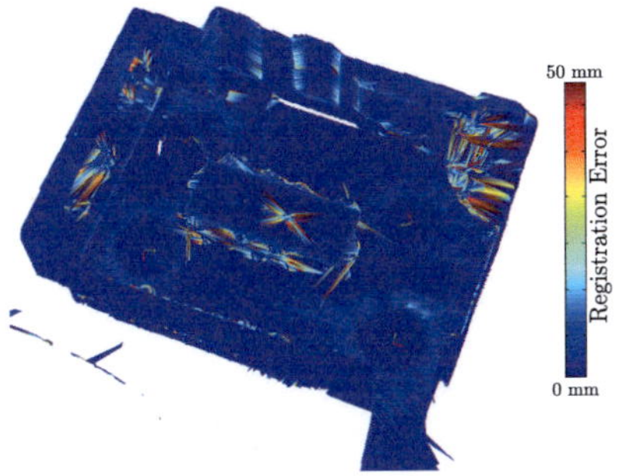

(d) Probabilistic registration.

Figure 3.19: Comparison of 3D registration algorithms: Global registration (left) and probabilistic non-rigid registration (right). The enlarged details demonstrate that using our probabilistic non-rigid method results in a more accurate registration: The registration error visualization reveals a slight miss-alignment for the ICP registered dataset, while our non-rigid technique results in a good alignment over the whole surface.

4 Surface Reconstruction

4.1 Introduction

An efficient processing of 3D maps demands – just like in any other field of computer science – the design of suitable data structures. At first glance, one might simply generate 3D maps by generalizing well known 2D map structures like grid maps to the third dimension. The resulting growth of the computational cost for accessing, modifying, and storing the map will be immense. If we store the occupancy evidence as single bytes, then an evidence grid with 1024 cells along each dimension requires a megabyte of memory in 2D and a gigabyte in 3D. Since most cells will remain empty, data structures that represent surfaces only are more suitable. In the past, various approaches for modeling environments in 3D more efficiently have been proposed. Point clouds, elevation maps [Hebert et al., 1989], multi-level surface maps [Triebel et al., 2006], and octree structures [Wurm et al., 2010] are some examples.

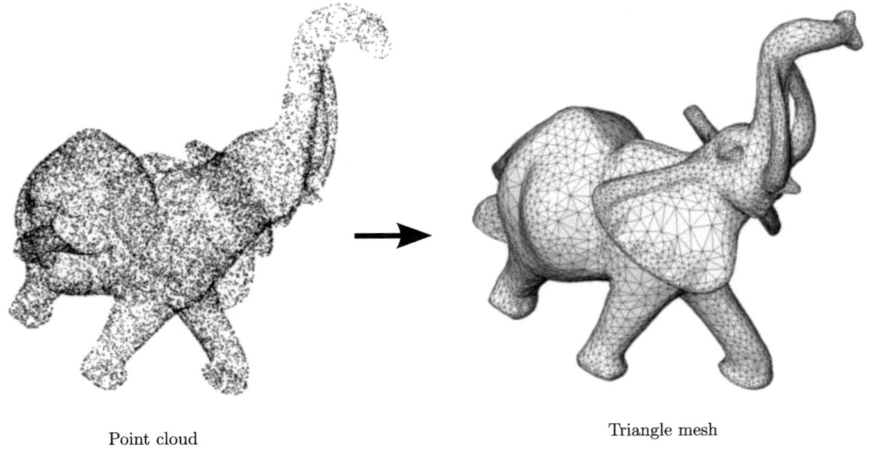

Figure 4.1: Given a set of registered scans, a surface reconstruction algorithm reconstructs a parametric surface that closely approximates the original surface. The left image shows a point cloud of 17K points sampled on a statue of an elephant and the right image presents the reconstructed surface mesh.

Typically, 3D maps are further processed (e.g., denoising, segmentation, classification) to obtain a more appropriate parametric representation. The most common parametric description of surfaces are piecewise linear surface models with polygons (e.g., triangles, quadrilaterals). Such a description allows the definition of surface attributes (normals, gradients) and they are well suited for fast rendering, efficient data reduction, and collision testing. For these reasons we have selected a triangle mesh as our basic world representation.

The input data for the surface reconstruction process is given as a point cloud $\mathcal{P} = \{\mathbf{p}_i\}$ which is a set of 3D points $\mathbf{p}_i \in \mathbb{R}^3$ stemming from a sampling process such as a 3D scanner. The goal of the surface reconstruction is then to reconstruct a parametric 2D manifold embedded in 3D space which closely approximates the true surface. Figure 4.1 presents an example for such a surface reconstruction. We define the resulting *parametric surface* as follows:

Definition 4.1.1 (Parametric surface). *A parametric surface is defined by a vector-valued function* $f : \Omega \rightarrow \mathcal{S}$*, that maps a two-dimensional parameter domain* $\Omega \in \mathbb{R}^2$ *to the surface* $\mathcal{S} = f(\Omega) \subset \mathbb{R}^3$.

In this thesis, the parametric surface is defined as a triangle mesh:

Definition 4.1.2 (Triangle mesh). *A triangle mesh* $\mathcal{M} = \{\mathcal{V}, \mathcal{F}\}$ *is defined as a graph structure (simplicial complex) with a set of vertices:* $\mathcal{V} = \{v_1, \ldots, v_V\}$*; and a set of triangular faces connecting them:* $\mathcal{F} = \{f_1, \ldots, f_F\}$, $f_i \in \mathcal{V} \times \mathcal{V} \times \mathcal{V}$. *Equivalent is a topological representation in terms of the edges of the respective graph:* $\mathcal{E} = \{e_1, \ldots, e_E\}$, $e_i \in \mathcal{V} \times \mathcal{V}$.

In a triangle mesh, each triangle defines, via its barycentric parametrization, a linear segment of a piecewise linear surface representation. We define a mesh to be *2-manifold*, which is the case if the surface is locally homeomorphic to a disk (or a half-disk at boundaries) for each vertex. This is the case for a triangle mesh in case it neither contains non-manifold edges, nor non-manifold vertices, nor self-intersections. A non-manifold edge has more than two incident triangles and a non-manifold vertex is generated by pinching two surface sheets together at that vertex, such that the vertex is incident to two fans of triangles. See [do Carmo, 1976] for more details.

Artifacts of the data acquisition process as well as complex surface topologies pose great challenges for the design of surface reconstruction algorithms. Specifically, we need to consider the imperfection of the sensing system. The sampling of the true surface may be uneven and noisy while the surface itself may have features

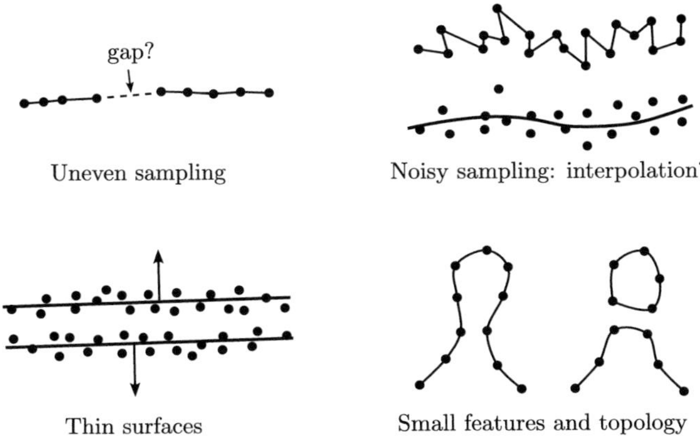

Figure 4.2: Surface reconstruction from scanned point clouds is a difficult task. The sampling of the true surface may be uneven and noisy while the surface itself may have a difficult topology such as thin surfaces or small features.

hardly more elevated than the sensor noise, features close to the sampling interval, and a complex topology. Figure 4.2 depicts some examples which often occur in real world datasets. We can summarize the following problems a surface reconstruction algorithm needs to address:

1. The size of the point cloud and so the number of input points $\mathcal{P}$ for the reconstruction can be very large, especially since many viewpoints are required to capture the entire scene. Therefore, a reconstruction algorithm to scale well with large datasets.

2. The scene may contain a variety of objects, which introduce occlusions and depth discontinuities. An algorithm needs to reliably reconstruct the correct surface topology in the presence of a considerable amount of noise and occlusions.

3. The scene may contain features at varying scales: large surfaces like walls, floors or columns, as well as small objects with a size close to the noise level. Therefore, a multi-resolutional representation of the reconstructed surface mesh is advantageous, using less triangles for smooth areas but keeping the detail of small features.

Previous approaches to surface reconstruction can be roughly put into three categories: *volumetric approaches*, *combinatorial approaches*, and *global fitting approaches*.

Pioneered by the work of [Hoppe et al., 1992], *volumetric approaches* always start with a simple scheme to estimate tangent planes and to define an implicit function as the signed distance to the tangent plane of the closest point. Signed distances can also be accumulated into a volumetric grid [Curless and Levoy, 1996]. Afterwards, a triangulation algorithm, such as marching cubes [Lorensen and Cline, 1987], is employed to reconstruct the surface at the zero level-set of the implicit function. These approaches rely on oriented points as input, which may be difficult to obtain from scanning devices. More recently, an implicit surface reconstruction method based on Fourier desciptors was developed by [Kazhdan, 2005]. The advantage to this method is that the reconstructed surface is smooth, and noise as well as gaps in the data are handled robustly. However, computing even a single Fourier coefficient requires a summation over all input samples since the basis functions are globally supported. This was later modified in [Kazhdan et al., 2006]. The modification utilizes an octree and finds the implicit function by solving a Poisson equation yielding a much more computational tractable and memory efficient algorithm [Bolitho et al., 2007]. The method of [Kazhdan et al., 2006] is one of the most promising approaches for large scale 3D reconstruction. It will serve as basis for our approach that extends the original method using bilateral filters and a subsequent data driven optimization.

The second category approaches the problem of surface reconstruction from the computational geometric point of view. Several algorithms are based on *combinatorial structures*, such as Delaunay triangulations [Boissonnat, 1984, Kolluri et al., 2004] or Voronoi diagrams [Amenta et al., 2001]. These schemes typically create a triangle mesh that interpolates all or most of the points. The computational geometric approaches typically perform poorly under the influence of noise and are, therefore, not well suited for our data. The resulting surfaces are often jagged and have to be smoothed [Kolluri et al., 2004] in subsequent processing.

Algorithms in the third category, called *surface fitting methods*, approach the reconstruction problem by deforming a base-model to optimally fit the input sample points [Terzopoulos and Vasilescu, 1991, Chen and Medioni, 1995]. These approaches represent the base-shape as a collection of points with springs between them and adapt the shape by adjusting either the spring stiffnesses or the point positions as a function of the surface information. As with the computational geometric approaches, these methods have the advantage of generating a surface whose complexity is on the order of the size of the input samples. However, these methods tend to be of limited use for our application as the topology of the reconstructed surface needs to be the same as the topology of the base shape. This limits the class of models that can be reconstructed using this method. Other global fitting methods commonly define an implicit function as the sum of Radial Basis

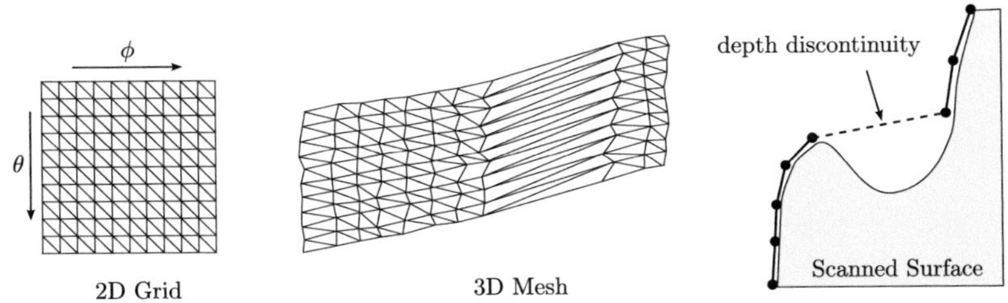

Figure 4.3: Triangulated range data in 2D grid becomes a 3D mesh. Depth discontinuities will cause wrong connections.

Functions (RBF) centered at the points [Carr et al., 2001]. However, ideal RBFs (polyharmonics) are globally supported and nondecaying, leading to a complexity that is quadratic in the number of basis functions. For our datasets, which have a large number of data points and a complex topology, surface fitting methods are not well suited.

4.2 Direct Polygonal Meshing of Range Images

The scanning process already lays out the 3D input points in a grid like structure referred to as *range image*. Each data point in this range image is represented by a depth value associated with the laser beam's two polar angles (ϕ,θ). An intuitive approach for reconstructing a surface is a triangulation of the grid points. Similar procedures have been proposed by [Turk and Levoy, 1994, Curless, 1997, Levoy et al., 2000]. A 3D mesh is created by connecting a point in the range image with two of its neighbors in each angular direction which yields a triangulation in the 2D range image space (see Figure 4.3). Since we know the corresponding 3D position in space for each range image point, the 2D triangulation can be easily transfered into a 3D mesh. If the scanned surface is perpendicular to the scanning direction, the triangles in 3D space will be isosceles. As the angle to the surface decreases, the triangles become more elongated and depth discontinuities produce very long and thin triangles. Since triangle edges may span over depth discontinuities, a plausibility check has to be performed. By thresholding the edge length and the dihedral angles, potentially bad triangles can be detected and removed.

The triangulation procedure is performed for each scan individually leading to a set of meshes with overlapping areas. We integrate the overlapping areas to reduce the size of the resulting model and to obtain a single consistent mesh representation. This is a difficult task even for noise free meshes. There is an exponential

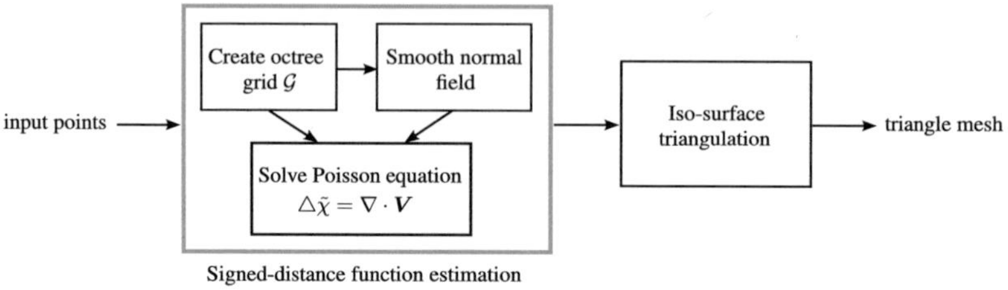

Figure 4.4: Overview of our Volumetric Surface Reconstruction approach. The input data points are used to define a signed distance function. A mesh is reconstructed by triangulating the zero-set of this function.

number of ways to connect two triangulated surfaces; however, only a few are acceptable. The *Polygon Zippering* [Turk and Levoy, 1994] algorithm removes overlapping portions of meshes, clips one mesh against another, and finally removes small triangles introduced during clipping. This approach is rather inefficient if there is a significant overlap between individual views since meshes are stitched over and over again. Another shortcoming in algorithms of this type is that overlapping measurements of a surface area are considered redundant and are therefore discarded in the process. Ideally, we would like to use all available data to reconstruct the surface.

4.3 Volumetric Surface Reconstruction

The algorithm described in the following does not make any prior assumptions about connectivity of points. Our algorithms is a *volumetric* approach for surface reconstruction that is more efficient than a direct polygonal meshing in situations where multiple scans are taken of the same surface; see [Curless and Levoy, 1996, Davis et al., 2002] for examples of volumetric surface reconstruction algorithms. Figure 4.4 depicts an overview of our algorithm. The basic idea of our volumetric surface reconstruction is using the input data points to define an *signed distance function* and compute its zero-set. The surface is therefore regarded as a level surface of an implicit function defined over the entire embedding space. The first step is concerned with estimating the signed distance function. This is done by discretizing the input points into an octree grid that is used to efficiently represent a smoothed normal field. The distance function is then estimated by solving a Poisson equation using the smoothed normal field. Finally, a mesh is reconstructed by triangulating the zero-set of this function at the octree grid cells.

(a) Oriented points $\mathcal{V}$.

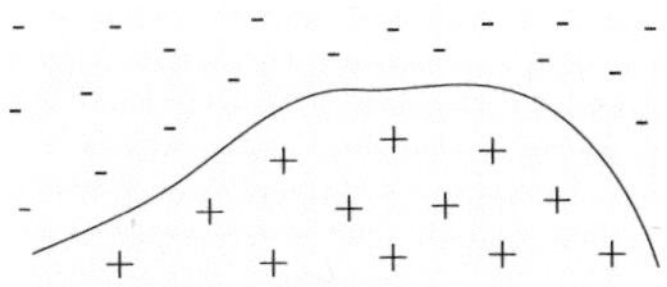

(b) Signed distance function ζ.

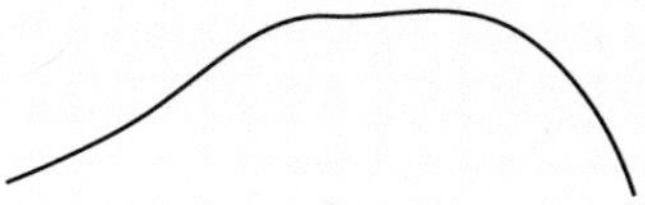

(c) Implicit surface $\mathcal{S}$.

Figure 4.5: A set of oriented points (top left) is transformed into a signed distance function (top right). The zero-set of the signed distance function (bottom) is a good estimate of the true surface.

4.3.1 Signed Distance Function Estimation

Consider the function $\zeta : \mathbb{R}^3 \to \mathbb{R}$ of a set $\mathcal{V}$ in a metric space which determines how close a given point $\mathbf{x} \in \mathbb{R}^3$ is to the boundary of $\mathcal{V}$. The function has positive values at points inside $\mathcal{V}$, it decreases in value as $\mathbf{x}$ approaches the boundary of $\mathcal{V}$ where the signed distance function is zero, and it takes negative values outside of $\mathcal{V}$. The *implicit surface* $\mathcal{S}$ is then defined as a zero-set of this (scalar) function $\mathcal{S} : \zeta(\mathbf{x}) = 0$. An implicit surface that represents the measurement data well is found if the volumetric field function $\zeta(\mathbf{x})$ is smooth and the zero-set approximates the real surface as closely as possible. Figure 4.5 presents an example for surface reconstruction using a signed distance function.

Instead of a signed distance function we seek to calculate a 3D indicator function χ with χ being defined as 1 for points inside the model, and 0 for points outside the model. [Kazhdan et al., 2006] have shown that there exists an integral relationship between points sampled from a real surface and this indicator function. Specifically, they found that the problem of finding the indicator function can be reduced to finding the scalar function χ whose gradient best approximates the vector field $\mathbf{V}$ defined by oriented points from the scans (see Figure 4.6).

The gradient vectors of χ would be unbounded at the surface, which may lead to numerical instabilities. Therefore, the indicator is convolved with a smoothing filter F and instead the gradients of the smoothed function are considered. One can

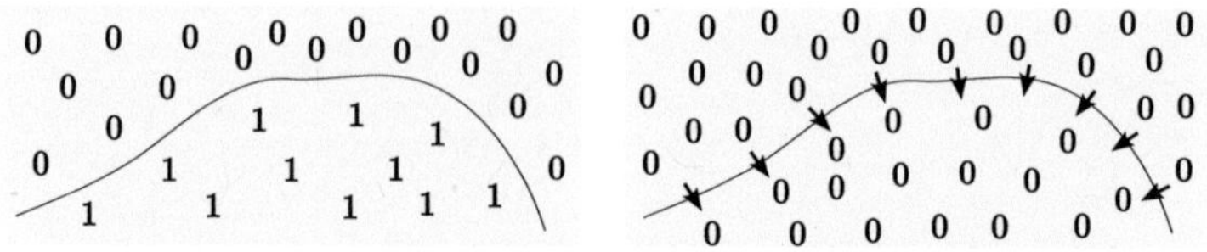

(a) Indicator function χ. (b) Indicator gradient $\nabla\chi$.

Figure 4.6: The 3D indicator function and its gradient vector field.

show [Kazhdan et al., 2006] that the gradient of the smoothed indicator function is equal to the smoothed surface normal field:

$$\nabla(\chi \star F)(\mathbf{q}) = \int_{\mathcal{S}} F(\mathbf{q})\, N_{\mathcal{S}}(\mathbf{p})\, d\mathbf{p} \tag{4.1}$$

Here $N_{\mathcal{S}}(\mathbf{p})$ corresponds to the surface normal at $\mathbf{p} \in \mathcal{S}$. If we now partition $\mathcal{S}$ into distinct patches $\mathcal{P}_{\mathbf{p}_i}$,each corresponding to a point sample $\mathbf{p}_i$, we can approximate the integral over the patch by the value at the point sample:

$$\nabla(\chi \star F)(\mathbf{q}) = \int_{\mathcal{S}} F(\mathbf{q})\, N_{\mathcal{S}}(\mathbf{p})\, d\mathbf{p} \tag{4.2}$$

$$= \sum_{\mathbf{p}_i \in \mathcal{P}} \int_{\mathcal{P}_{\mathbf{p}_i}} F(\mathbf{q})\, N_{\mathcal{S}}(\mathbf{p})\, d\mathbf{p} \tag{4.3}$$

$$\approx \sum_{\mathbf{p}_i \in \mathcal{P}} |\mathcal{P}_{\mathbf{p}_i}|\, F_{\mathbf{p}_i}(\mathbf{q})\, N_{\mathbf{p}_i}(\mathbf{p})\, d\mathbf{p} \equiv \mathbf{V}(\mathbf{q})\ . \tag{4.4}$$

Now we want to find the function $\tilde{\chi}$ which is an approximation of the smoothed indicator function such that $\nabla\tilde{\chi} = \mathbf{V}$. Since $\mathbf{V}$ is generally not integrable, we apply the divergence operator which yields a standard Poisson problem:

$$\triangle\tilde{\chi} = \nabla \cdot \nabla\tilde{\chi} = \nabla \cdot \mathbf{V}\ . \tag{4.5}$$

Equation 4.5 can be solved by discretizing the 3D space into a regular $n \times n \times n$ grid $\mathcal{G}$ and using this grid as a space of functions. This results in memory requirements growing cubically with the resolution which becomes impractical very quickly. Fortunately, the indicator function is piecewise constant (1 inside and 0 outside) and changes only around the boundary. Therefore, an octree can be used to get an accurate representation of the indicator function near the boundary. In this case, the required memory grows only approximately quadratic.

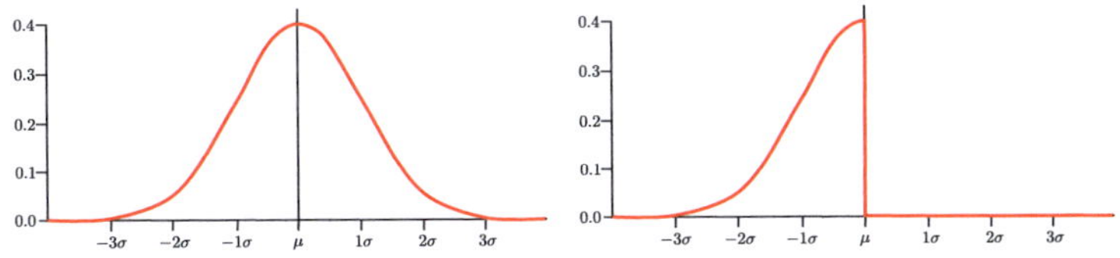

(a) Gaussian filter kernel. (b) Bilateral filter kernel at p.

(c) Noisy input data. (d) Result of Gaussian filter. (e) Result of bilateral filter.

Figure 4.7: The bilateral filter smoothes the input data (here 1D) while preserving its edges. Each point is replaced by a weighted average of its neighbors. The filter weighs each neighbor by a spatial component, which penalizes its Euclidean distance, and a normal component, which penalizes the difference in normal vectors. The combination of both components ensures that only nearby similar points contribute to the final result.

For each grid cell $c \in \mathcal{G}$, we set $F_c : \mathbb{R}^3 \to \mathbb{R}$ to be the smoothing function for a local patch. We choose F_c to be a *bilateral filter* [Aurich and Weule, 1995, Tomasi and Manduchi, 1998, Jones et al., 2003] centered at the cell's centroid:

$$F_c(\mathbf{q}) = \frac{1}{w_\mathbf{q}} \sum_{i \in \mathcal{N}_c} G_{\sigma_s}\left(\|\mathbf{o}_c - \mathbf{q}\|\right) G_{\sigma_r}\left(|\mathbf{n}_c \cdot \mathbf{n}_i|\right) \mathbf{n}_i \ , \tag{4.6}$$

where $G_\sigma(\cdot)$ denotes a Gaussian kernel, $\mathbf{n}_c$ is the cell's normal vector, $\mathbf{o}_c$ is the cell's centroid, and $\mathcal{N}_c$ is a set of the neighboring cells of c. The normalization factor $w_\mathbf{q}$ is defined as:

$$w_\mathbf{q} = \sum_{i \in \mathcal{N}_c} G_{\sigma_s}\left(\|\mathbf{o}_c - \mathbf{q}\|\right) G_{\sigma_r}\left(|\mathbf{n}_c \cdot \mathbf{n}_i|\right) \ . \tag{4.7}$$

The parameters σ_s and σ_r are parameters controlling the fall-off of weights in spatial and normal domains, respectively. Similarly to the Gaussian convolution, the bilateral filter of Equation 4.6 is a normalized weighted average where G_{σ_s} is a spatial Gaussian that decreases the influence of distant cells. G_{σ_r} corresponds to a range Gaussian that decreases the influence of cells i with a normal vector different

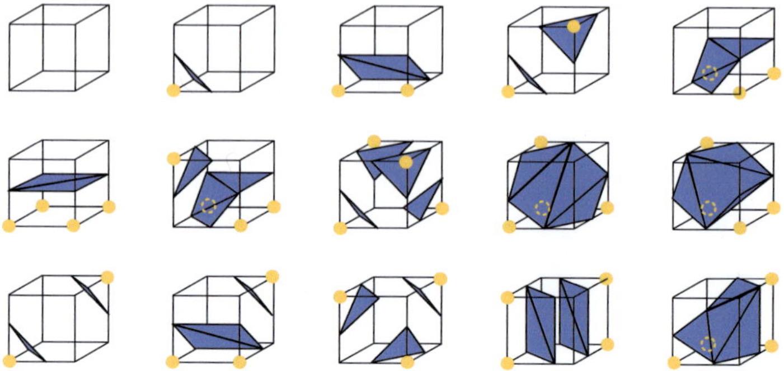

Figure 4.8: The 15 unique configurations of corner classifications in the marching cubes algorithm. Triangle vertices are formed on edges of a cube where one corner of the edge is classified as being inside the surface (marked yellow) while the other corner of the edge is classified as being outside.

from $\mathbf{n}_c$. See Figure 4.7(b) and Figure 4.7(a) for exemplary filter responses. The main difference between this and a Gaussian filter is that the bilateral filter takes the variation of normals into account in order to preserve edges. Figure 4.7 shows a sample output of the bilateral filter compared to a Gaussian filter.

To make the computation tractable, two Gaussians G_{σ_s} and G_{σ_s} are approximated by the n-th convolution of a box filter with itself scaled by the variance:

$$G_\sigma(x) \approx B(x)^{\star n} \text{ with } B(t) = \begin{cases} 1 & |t| < 0\ 5 \\ 0 & \text{otherwise} \end{cases} . \tag{4.8}$$

This limits the support for G to the domain $[-1\ 5, 1\ 5]$ for $n = 3$ and therefore the number of cells whose function overlap. An advantage of this approximation is that the basis functions are defined only locally. This leads to a sparse system when optimizing Equation 4.5 which can be solved very efficiently.

Once the smoothed vector field is defined for each grid cell, the gradient field of the indicator function defined in Equation 4.5 can be efficiently represented as linear sum of all grid cell functions. Finally, the indicator function χ is solved such that the gradient of χ is closest to $\mathbf{V}$. Refer to [Kazhdan et al., 2006] for more details.

4.3.2 Iso-Surface Triangulation

Once we have computed the indicator function χ, we can obtain the reconstructed surface $\tilde{S}$ by extracting the zero-set (iso-surface) of χ. We use a variation of the *marching cubes* algorithm [Lorensen and Cline, 1987]. This method creates vertices at zero-crossings of χ along edges of the octree leafs. The vertices are connected to triangles such that a continues manifold along S is formed.

The basic principle behind the marching cubes algorithm is to subdivide space into a series of small cubes. The algorithm then *marches* through each of the cubes evaluating the indicator function at the corner points and replacing the cube with an appropriate set of polygons.

If the corners of all grid cells in $\mathcal{G}$ are classified as either being below or above the zero-set (by evaluating χ), there are $2^8 = 256$ possible configurations of corner classifications. Two of the configurations are trivial: grid cells where all points are above or below the zero-set. In those cases the cube will not contribute to the surface. For all other configurations it is determined where along each cube edge the iso-surface crosses, and use these edge intersection points to create one or more triangular patches for the iso-surface. Accounting for symmetries, there are only 15 unique configurations of triangles which are presented in Figure 4.8.

Now, surface patches for all cubes can be created for the entire volume. For neighboring cubes edge intersections are propagated between cubes which share the edges. This results in a compact triangle mesh $\mathcal{M}$.

Figure 4.9 shows the result of iso-surface extraction with the marching cubes algorithm for different grid resolutions. The selection of an appropriate grid resolution is important for a good reconstruction. A coarse grid will lead to a low-pass filtered geometry Figure 4.9(a) while a cell size in the order of the sensor resolution (here 10mm) will reveal quantization noise as circular patterns on flat surfaces Figure 4.9(c).

4.4 Surface Optimization

In the previous section, we presented an algorithm to reconstruct a parametric surface from a set of unorganized points. As a result, we obtained a mesh which approximates the true surface and its topological type. With the knowledge of the surface topology and given the original point cloud $\mathcal{P}$, the mesh $\tilde{\mathcal{M}}$ will now be optimized to improve reconstruction accuracy. The optimization is guided by the following three constraints:

1. The mesh should perfectly fit the set of data points.
2. The topology of the mesh should remain the same.
3. The optimized surface should be a faithful approximation of the real surface.

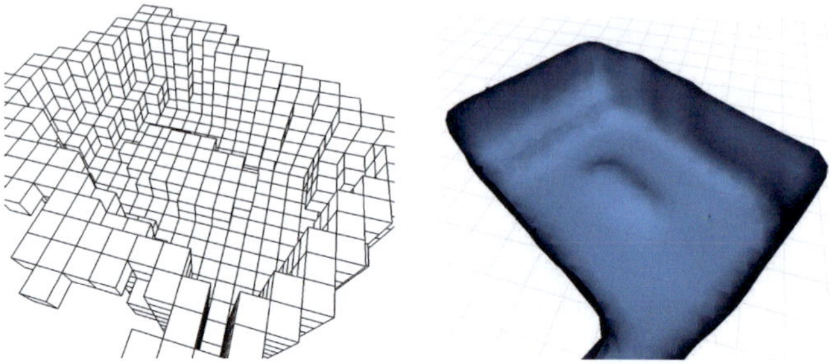

(a) Grid size 200mm.

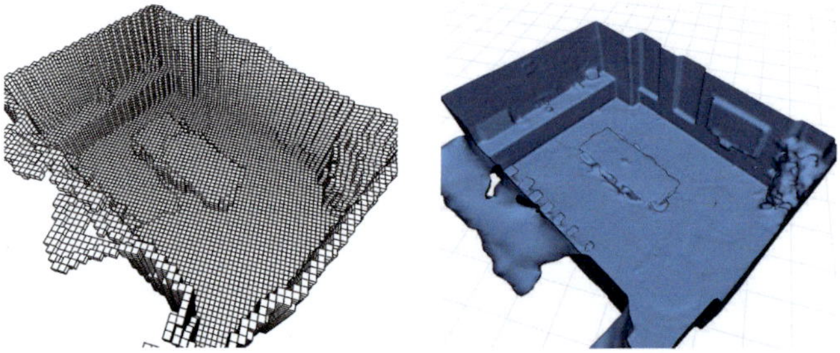

(b) Grid size 50mm.

(c) Grid size 10mm.

Figure 4.9: Iso-surface reconstruction using the *marching cubes* algorithm [Lorensen and Cline, 1987]. Each row corresponds to a reconstruction with a certain grid size. The left column shows the visited cells during the iso-surface extraction, and the right column shows the rendered triangle mesh.

To combine the three constraints, we formulate the surface optimization as an energy minimization problem and define the following energy function:

$$E\left(\tilde{\mathcal{M}},\mathcal{P}\right) = \kappa_1 E_{\text{fit}}\left(\tilde{\mathcal{M}},\mathcal{P}\right) + \kappa_2 E_{\text{topology}}\left(\tilde{\mathcal{M}}\right) + \kappa_3 E_{\text{smooth}}\left(\tilde{\mathcal{M}}\right) , \tag{4.9}$$

which we seek to minimize in order to find an optimized surface representation:

$$\mathcal{M} = \min_{\tilde{\mathcal{M}},\mathcal{P}} E\left(\tilde{\mathcal{M}},\mathcal{P}\right) . \tag{4.10}$$

The three potential functions forming this continuous optimization problem can be thought of as springs applying forces to the vertex locations. The *fitting potential* E_{fit} wants to move the vertices in a direction that minimizes the distance of the data point to their closest triangle which improves the accuracy of the surface reconstruction. The topology potential E_{topology} penalizes large deformations of triangles and therefore preserves the originally reconstructed topology. The last potential E_{smooth} is a smoothing term which prevents over-fitting and yields a smooth surface. Figure 4.10 illustrates the potential functions.

4.4.1 Fitting Potential

The first potential E_{fit} evaluates the distance of each point input point $\mathbf{p}_i$ to the reconstructed mesh (see Figure 4.10(a)). If the reconstructed surface would perfectly fit the input data, all points would be part of this surface. This potential wants to move the vertices in a direction that minimizes the distance of the data points to their closest triangle, which improves the accuracy of the surface reconstruction. The same potential function was previously suggested in [Hoppe et al., 1993]. As pointed out in their work, we are only considering piecewise linear surfaces (meshes) and the data points themselves are noisy, there is a limit to the accuracy that we can achieve.

We define the fitting potential E_{fit} as:

$$E_{\text{fit}}\left(\tilde{\mathcal{M}},\mathcal{P}\right) = \sum_{\mathbf{p}_i \in \tilde{\mathcal{M}}} d_i\left(\mathbf{p}_i,\tilde{\mathcal{M}}\right) , \tag{4.11}$$

where $d_i(\mathbf{p}_i,\tilde{\mathcal{M}})$ is the distance of a point $\mathbf{p}_i$ to a mesh $\tilde{\mathcal{M}} = \{\mathcal{V},\mathcal{F}\}$. This distance is the minimal distance of $\mathbf{p}_i$ to all faces $f_j \in \mathcal{F}$:

$$d_i\left(\mathbf{p}_i,\tilde{\mathcal{M}}\right) = \min_{f_j \in \mathcal{F}} \|\mathbf{p}_i - \xi\left(f_j,\mathbf{p}_i\right)\|^2 , \tag{4.12}$$

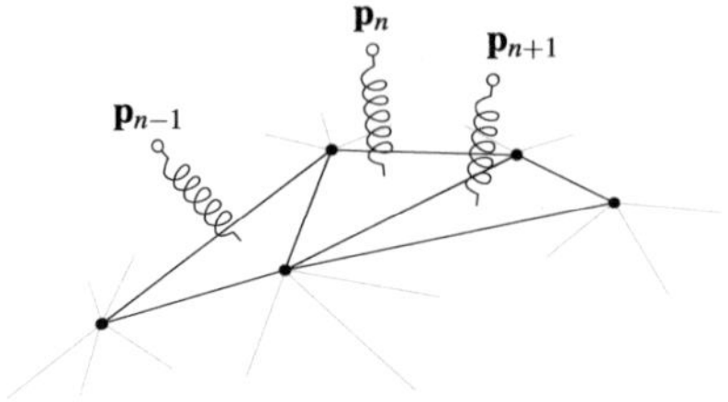

(a) Fitting potential.

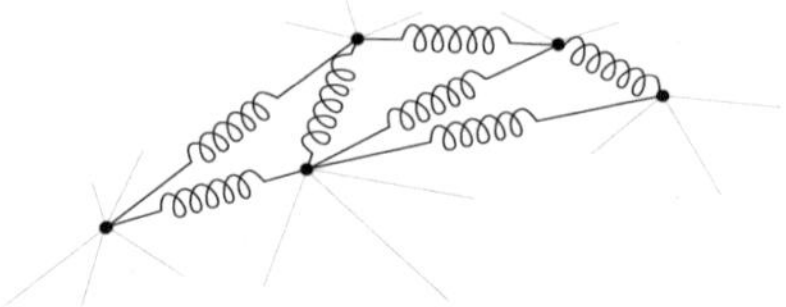

(b) Topology potential.

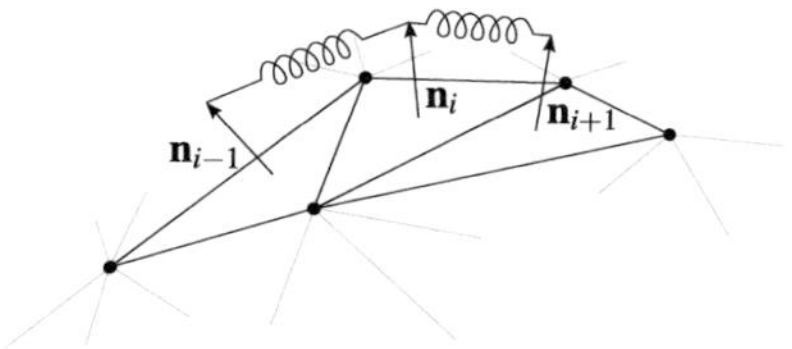

(c) Smoothness potential.

Figure 4.10: Potential functions used for the surface optimization. The fitting potential (right) brings the surface close to the data points it was sampled from the topology potential (middle) penalizes large deformations in the surface geometry. The smoothness potential smoothes the reconstruction by preferring locally consistent surface normals.

where $\xi(f_j, \mathbf{p}_i)$ is a function which returns the closest point to $\mathbf{p}_i$ on the triangle f_j. This function is more difficult than it appears at the first glance since the point $\mathbf{p}_i$ could be closest to the plane of the triangle, closest to an edge or closest to a vertex. As a first step, the projection of $\mathbf{p}_i$ into the triangle plane is calculated. Let $\mathbf{p}_1$, $\mathbf{p}_2$, and $\mathbf{p}_3$ be the vertices and $\mathbf{n}$ the normal vector of a triangle face f_j:

$$\mathbf{n} = \frac{(\mathbf{p}_2 - \mathbf{p}_1) \times (\mathbf{p}_3 - \mathbf{p}_1)}{|(\mathbf{p}_2 - \mathbf{p}_1) \times (\mathbf{p}_3 - \mathbf{p}_1)|} \,. \tag{4.13}$$

The projection $\mathbf{p}_i'$ is defined as:

$$\mathbf{p}_i' = \mathbf{p}_i + d\mathbf{n} \tag{4.14}$$

where d is the scalar distance of $\mathbf{p}_i$ to the triangle plane:

$$d = \|\mathbf{p}_1 - \mathbf{p}_i\| \cos\alpha \tag{4.15}$$

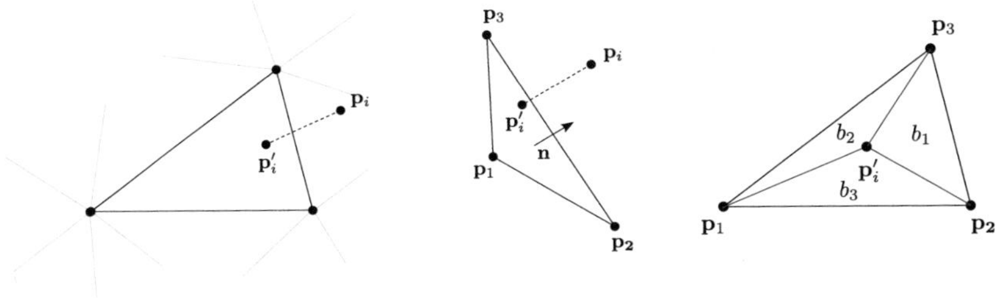

(a) Point to triangle distance. (b) Barycentric coordinates.

Figure 4.11: The distance of a point $\mathbf{p}_i$ to a triangle face is defined as the length of the vector that connects $\mathbf{p}_i$ to the closest point on the triangle. Barycentric coordinates are used to determine the position of this point.

with α being the angle of the normal $\mathbf{n}$ and the vector $\mathbf{p}_1 - \mathbf{p}_i$:

$$\cos\alpha = \frac{(\mathbf{p}_1 - \mathbf{p}_i)\cdot\mathbf{n}}{\|\mathbf{p}_1 - \mathbf{p}_i\|} . \tag{4.16}$$

In the trivial case that $\mathbf{p}'_i$ falls inside the triangle f_j, the closest point is $\mathbf{p}'_i$. If instead $\mathbf{p}'_i$ falls outside the triangle, the distance to the triangle is the distance to the closest edge or to the closest vertex. In order to determine if $\mathbf{p}'_i$ is inside/outside the triangle, and if it is outside, which edge/vertex $\mathbf{p}'_i$ is closest to, we calculate the barycentric coordinates [Coxeter, 1969]. The barycentric coordinates of the point $\mathbf{p}'_i$ with respect to the vertices $\mathbf{p}_1$, $\mathbf{p}_2$, and $\mathbf{p}_3$ of the triangle f_j are a triplet of values, $\{b_1, b_2, b_3\}$, such that $\mathbf{p}'_i = b_1\mathbf{p}_1 + b_2\mathbf{p}_2 + b_3\mathbf{p}_3$, with $b_1 + b_2 + b_3 = 1$. One can show that b_1, b_2, and b_3 are proportional to ratios of specific (signed) triangle areas. If $|\mathbf{p}_1\mathbf{p}_2\mathbf{p}_3|$ denotes the *signed* area of the triangle (given counter-clockwise in that specific order), we can use Cramer's rule which states that determinants correspond to signed areas:

$$|\mathbf{p}_1\mathbf{p}_2\mathbf{p}_3| = \det\begin{pmatrix}\mathbf{p}_1 & \mathbf{p}_2 & \mathbf{p}_3\\ 1 & 1 & 1\end{pmatrix} . \tag{4.17}$$

Then, the barycentric coordinates are simply calculated by the ratios of the triangle areas:

$$b_1 = \frac{|\mathbf{p}'_i\mathbf{p}_2\mathbf{p}_3|}{|\mathbf{p}_1\mathbf{p}_2\mathbf{p}_3|}, \; b_2 = \frac{|\mathbf{p}'_i\mathbf{p}_3\mathbf{p}_1|}{|\mathbf{p}_1\mathbf{p}_2\mathbf{p}_3|}, \; b_3 = \frac{|\mathbf{p}'_i\mathbf{p}_1\mathbf{p}_2|}{|\mathbf{p}_1\mathbf{p}_2\mathbf{p}_3|} . \tag{4.18}$$

Now, we can distinguish the following cases:

1. $\mathbf{p}'_i$ lies inside the triangle if b_1, b_2, and b_3 are positive.
2. $\mathbf{p}'_i$ lies on a triangle edge if one coordinate is zero while the other coordinates are positive. E.g., $b_1 = 0$ means the point lies on the edge $\{\mathbf{p}_2, \mathbf{p}_3\}$.
3. $\mathbf{p}'_i$ falls together with a triangle vertex if two coordinates are zero leaving the third coordinate to 1. E.g., the coordinates $\{1, 0, 0\}$ correspond to the point $\mathbf{p}_1$.
4. $\mathbf{p}'_i$ lies outside the triangle and the closest point is one of the triangle's vertices in case two coordinates are negative while the the other coordinates is positive. E.g., $b_2 < 0$ and $b_3 < 0$ means the closest vertex is $\mathbf{p}_1$.
5. $\mathbf{p}'_i$ lies outside the triangle and the closest point lies on an edge in case one coordinate is negative while the the other coordinates are positive. E.g., $b_1 < 0$ means the closest edge is $\{\mathbf{p}_2, \mathbf{p}_3\}$.

In the last case (5), we need to project $\mathbf{p}_i$ orthogonally onto the corresponding edge. Let's assume the edge is between $\mathbf{p}_1$ and $\mathbf{p}_2$, then the closest point is defined by:

$$\mathbf{p}'_i = \underline{\mathbf{p}_1\mathbf{p}_i} - \left(\underline{\mathbf{p}_1\mathbf{p}_i} \cdot \underline{\mathbf{p}_2\mathbf{p}_1}\right) \underline{\mathbf{p}_2\mathbf{p}_1} \tag{4.19}$$

with

$$\underline{\mathbf{p}_1\mathbf{p}_i} = \mathbf{p}_1 - \mathbf{p}_i \text{ and} \tag{4.20}$$

$$\underline{\mathbf{p}_2\mathbf{p}_1} = \frac{\mathbf{p}_2 - \mathbf{p}_1}{\|\mathbf{p}_2 - \mathbf{p}_1\|} . \tag{4.21}$$

Finally, we can define the function $\xi(f_j, \mathbf{p}_i)$ which returns the closest point to $\mathbf{p}_i$ on the triangle f_j based on the cases stated above.

4.4.2 Topology Potential

The second potential E_{topology} preserves the originally reconstructed topology. The goal is to prevent the triangle edges from diverging arbitrarily from the original reconstruction by penalizing changes in triangle edges. We define the topology potential E_{topology} as:

$$E_{\text{topology}}\left(\tilde{\mathcal{M}}\right) = \sum_{\mathbf{v}_i \in \mathcal{V}} \sum_{\mathbf{v}_j \in \mathcal{N}_1(\mathbf{v}_i, \mathcal{V})} \|\mathbf{v}_i - \mathbf{v}_j - \mathbf{e}_{i,j}\|^2 , \tag{4.22}$$

where $\mathbf{e}_{i,j}$ corresponds to the edge vector $\tilde{\mathbf{v}}_i - \tilde{\mathbf{v}}_j$ before the optimization. $\mathcal{N}_1(\mathbf{v}_i, \mathcal{V})$ is the one-ring vertex neighborhood of $\mathbf{v}_i$.

4.4.3 Smoothness Potential

The third potential E_{smooth} is a 'weak' smoothness prior. The desired effect is to create an optimized mesh that has a smooth curvature and enhanced sharp features at the same time. With this potential, we seek to adjust the vertices in such a way that the face normals of adjacent triangles match. In prior work [Levin et al., 2003, Diebel et al., 2006], sub-quadratic potentials of the form $\|\mathbf{n}_i - \mathbf{n}_j\|^p$ with $p < 2$ were suggested to smooth the mesh while enhancing features such as edges. In comparison, the quadratic function $p = 2$ tends to over-smooth the edges and remove fine features from the mesh. Here, we adapt the square-root potential proposed by [Diebel et al., 2006]:

$$E_{\text{smooth}}\left(\tilde{\mathcal{M}}\right) = \sum_{f_i \in \mathcal{F}} \sum_{f_j \in \mathcal{N}_1(f_i, \mathcal{F})} \sqrt{(\mathbf{n}_i - \mathbf{n}_j)^{\mathsf{T}} (\mathbf{n}_i - \mathbf{n}_j)}\,, \tag{4.23}$$

where $\mathbf{n}_i$ and $\mathbf{n}_j$ are face normals as previously defined in Equation 4.13. In this case $\mathcal{N}_1(f_i, \mathcal{F})$ is the one-ring face neighborhood of f_i.

4.4.4 Optimization

Finding an optimal surface mesh M according to Equation 4.10 results in a *sparse non-linear energy minimization* problem for which a rich family of efficient algorithms exists. The problem is sparse since only local neighborhoods (one-rings) are used, and non-linear since both E_{smooth} and E_{fit} require non-linear optimization of the vertex positions. The term E_{fit} requires a discrete optimization for finding the data point closest to a face. Those correspondences are updated after each iteration of the energy optimization. Only E_{topology} is a true quadratic-potential, and we noted that alongside its main purpose of topology preservation, it also acts as a regularizing term that helps to guide the optimization into a desirable local energy. As the optimization converges to the solution, the weight κ_2 of this potential is gradually reduced. This helps to locally adjust the mesh vertices for a tighter fit. In order to optimize Equation 4.10 we can leverage existing optimization algorithms to perform the minimization. Here we use the non-linear variant of conjugate gradient (CG) algorithm which can be found in contemporary textbooks [Shewchuk, 1994].

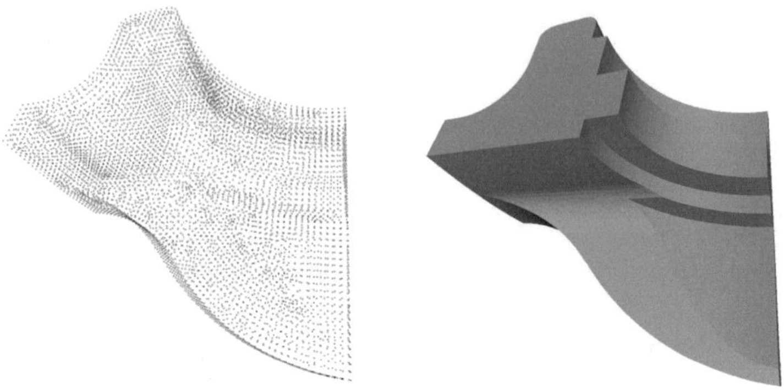

Figure 4.12: The fandisk test dataset [Hoppe, 1993]. The 3D point cloud (left) serves as input for our surface reconstruction approach and the manually created surface model (right) is used as ground-truth for quantitative evaluations.

4.5 Experimental Results

Synthetic Data

To study the properties of our surface reconstruction approach, we use a synthetic dataset. The so called *fandisk* [Hoppe, 1993] dataset was a manually created model of a mechanical part and it consists of 6,475 vertices and 12,946 triangles. The dataset is depicted in Figure 4.12. For our purposes, we ignore the triangles and use the vertices as input for our surface reconstruction algorithm. The volumetric surface reconstruction algorithm described in Section 4.3 results in a "water-tight" mesh, i.e., no hole should be allowed in the surface. In fact, the marching cubes iso-surface extraction guarantees to produce a water-tight mesh for arbitrary indicator functions. The grid discretization in conjunction with the smoothing filter that is applied to the indicator function causes smoothing artifacts in the resulting surface model. The sharp edges of the original model appear rounded in the reconstruction. In the next step, we optimize the reconstructed surface model with the method described in Section 4.4. The optimization algorithm adjusts the vertex positions in order to minimize the energy function in Equation 4.10. The resulting mesh fits the input data points considerably better than the initial reconstruction (see Figure 4.13(b)). Triangle edges are aligned in directions of sharp edges to achieve a better approximation of the true surface. The effect is surprising, since the true surface is unknown to the algorithm and can only be estimated from the input sample points. Also, no explicit heuristics are used in the optimization to prefer sharp edges.

(a) Mesh reconstruction using volumetric surface reconstruction (Section 4.3).

(b) Mesh optimization using energy minimization (Section 4.4).

Figure 4.13: Volumetric surface reconstruction and surface optimization on the *fandisk* dataset. Left column shows the normal mapped mesh where the color of a triangle corresponds to its normal direction; the middle column depicts the rendered surface using Gouraud shading [Gouraud, 1971]; and the right columns shows the reconstruction error approximated by the distance of a reconstructed vertex to the true surface. Note that the color for the reconstruction error is taken from a red-green-blue map, where red means zero error and blue means large error.

In order to quantify the reconstruction error, we use the Hausdorff distance between the reconstructed mesh and the original mesh [Cignoni et al., 1996]. The one-sided Hausdorff distances between two meshes $\mathcal{M}$ and $\mathcal{M}'$ is defined as the maximum of all vertex to mesh distances:

$$d\left(\mathcal{M}, \mathcal{M}'\right) = \max_{\mathbf{v} \in \mathcal{V}_{\mathcal{M}}} d\left(\mathbf{v}, \mathcal{M}'\right) \ , \tag{4.24}$$

where the distance $d\left(\mathbf{v}, \mathcal{M}'\right)$ between a vertex $\mathbf{v}$ belonging to the mesh $\mathcal{M}$ and a

Figure 4.14: The *conference room* dataset serves as input point cloud for our reconstruction approach.

mesh $\mathcal{M}'$ is defined as the minimal Euclidean distance:

$$d(\mathbf{v}, \mathcal{M}') = \min_{\mathbf{v}' \in \mathcal{V}_{\mathcal{M}'}} \|\mathbf{v} - \mathbf{v}'\| . \tag{4.25}$$

Since the one-sided Hausdorff distance is in general not symmetrical, i.e., $d(\mathcal{M}, \mathcal{M}') \neq d(\mathcal{M}', \mathcal{M})$, it is more convenient to introduce the symmetrical Hausdorff distance $d_s(\mathcal{M}, \mathcal{M}')$ defined as the maximum between the two one-sided Hausdorff distances:

$$d_s(\mathcal{M}, \mathcal{M}') = \max\left[d(\mathcal{M}, \mathcal{M}'), d(\mathcal{M}', \mathcal{M})\right] . \tag{4.26}$$

The symmetrical distance provides a more accurate measurement of the error between two surfaces since the computation of a one-sided error can lead to significantly underestimated distance values [Cignoni et al., 1996]. The following table presents the results for the distance computation for the *fandisk* dataset. Here the *max* presents the symmetrical Hausdorff distance as discussed before. The *mean* and *RMS* columns are similar approaches for evaluating the reconstruction error replacing the max operation in the Hausdorff equations Equation 4.26 and Equation 4.24 with the corresponding operations:

	absolute distance (mm)			w.r.t. b-box diag (%)		
Algorithm	max	mean	RMS	max	mean	RMS
Surface Reconst.	0.1966	0.0253	0.0358	2.582	0.3327	0.4705
Surface Optim.	0.1051	0.0113	0.0172	1.380	0.1488	0.2263

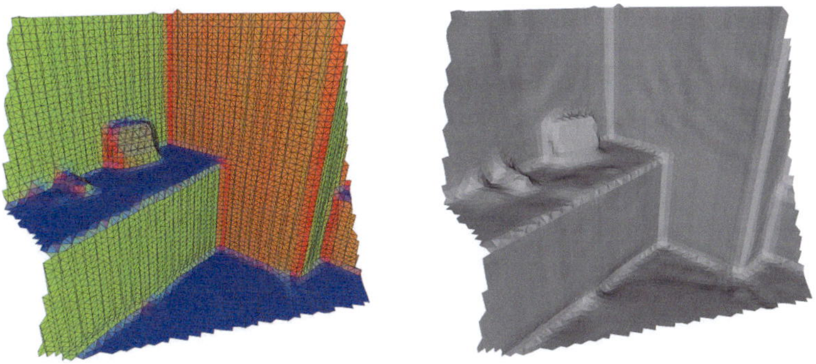

(a) Mesh reconstructed with volumetric surface reconstruction (Section 4.3).

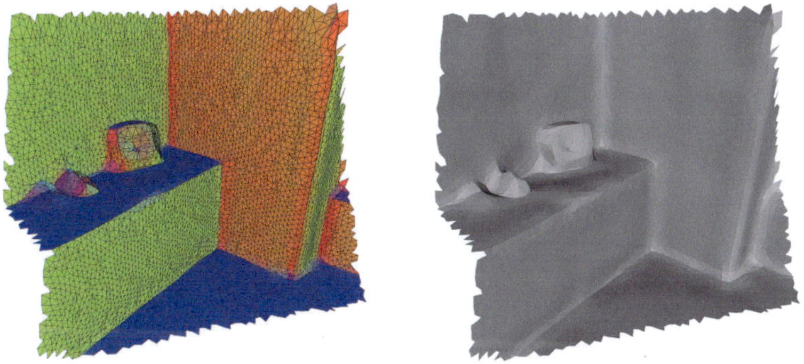

(b) Optimized with energy function (Section 4.4).

Figure 4.15: Volumetric surface reconstruction and surface optimization on the *conference room* dataset. Left column shows the normal mapped mesh where the color of a triangle corresponds to its normal direction and the right column depicts the rendered surface using Gouraud shading [Gouraud, 1971].

Real Data

In the second experiment we use scan-data. The input for the surface reconstruction is a point cloud which consists of 56,509 points from multiple overlapping scans. The scans were automatically aligned with the algorithm described in Section 3.4. The input data and a picture of the scene are depicted in Figure 4.14. Compared to the synthetic data, the reconstruction has to deal with the imperfectness of the sensing system and the complexity of the scanned scene. The point cloud sampling varies from areas of very low density with less than 1 sample per square centimeter to areas with very high density with more than 50 points per square centimeter. This makes it difficult for our algorithm to reconstruct an accurate model since the indicator function is calculated on a voxel grid and the sampling rate determines the grid cell size. For this experiment, the grid cell size was set to 2 cm in order to ensure at least one point falls into each cell. The volumetric surface reconstruction algorithm finds a good approximation of the real surface and results in a water-tight mesh with 5,993 vertices and 11,701 triangles (see Figure 4.15(a)). Again, the sharp edges (e.g., table top, wall corner) are too smoothly reconstructed. The subsequent optimization moves the triangle vertices and aligns triangle edges along sharp edges to achieve a better approximation of those features.

4.6 Conclusion

In this chapter, we presented an approach for volumetric surface reconstruction. We have shown that the surface description can be derived from a set of unorganized input points by finding a zero iso-surface of an indicator function over the 3D space. This indicator function can be efficiently expressed as a sum of functions generated by an octree discretization of the function space computed from the input data points. This octree forms a very compact representation of the environment which allows us to scale the reconstruction to large 3D models. To find the indicator function, we adopted the method of [Kazhdan et al., 2006] which uses a Poisson system defined on the grid cells. This approach was extended to use locally supported bilateral filters to smooth the normal vector field. A mesh is reconstructed by triangulating the zero iso-surface using the Marching Cubes algorithm. This mesh only approximates the true surface and its topological type. Errors may be introduced due to discretization and the necessity for smoothing the normal vector field. Therefore, we presented a novel method for optimizing the reconstructed mesh to improve reconstruction accuracy. This method moves the mesh vertices to achieve a better fit with the input data points while keeping the topology as suggested by the Poisson reconstruction. Using synthetic and real scan data we demonstrated that this method significantly reduces reconstruction errors.

We can summarize that the proposed volumetric surface reconstruction approach with subsequent surface optimization is a very suitable framework for the reconstruction of indoor environments. The presented algorithms can handle very large input point clouds that occur when scanning indoor environments with many viewpoints. Our approach handles occlusions and depth discontinuities well since the data of all viewpoints is integrated into a single representation before reconstruction. It is also robust to noise since the normal vector field is smoothed as part of the reconstruction.

5 Photo-Realistic Texture Reconstruction

5.1 Introduction

In the previous chapters we described methods to acquire 3D scans, register and integrate this data into a single representation, and reconstruct surface models. In this chapter, we present methods to reconstruct the *surface appearance*. In general, objects are made out of a variety of different materials which mainly influence their appearance. In essence, we think of the appearance of a material as being a function of how that material interacts with light. The material may simply reflect light, or it may exhibit more complex phenomena such as sub-surface scattering. Specifically, for visualization applications a realistic reconstruction and reproduction of the surface appearance greatly enhances the visual impression by adding more realism. Figure 5.1 demonstrates that reconstructing and adding a texture to a surface model results in a drastically more realistic 3D model. One will note that the textured model also suggests a higher level of geometry details (plant leaves, power cord). This illusion is due to the human perception system's lack of spatial resolution. For a human observer, however, the simulation of fine 3D structures is completely sufficient to convey realism. In computer graphics, this trick is often used for simulating bumps and wrinkles on the surface of an object and is therefore called *bump mapping* [Blinn, 1978b].

In this chapter, we describe a system to reconstruct visually realistic 3D models. We will not attempt to study the optical and semantic implications of texturing 3D models, a careful review of which is available in [Carey and Greenberg, 1985]. Rather, we present methods for the reconstruction of surface materials – namely surface textures – from sensor data.

5.1.1 Appearance Models

To further study the appearance of objects, we will introduce two fundamental radiometric quantities. The *radiance* is the amount of light that passes through a particular area and falls within a given solid angle in a specified direction. In

(a) Rendered geometry of an indoor scene. (b) Texture mapped onto the geometry.

Figure 5.1: Texture mapping is one of the most successful techniques to create high quality and visually realistic 3D models. Although the geometric model (a) gives us a good idea about the scene, we can get a much more realistic picture by reconstructing and mapping a texture onto the mesh surface (b).

contrast, the *irradiance* represents the amount of light falling onto a surface. For example, if an ideal point light source radiates uniformly in all directions and there is no absorption, then the irradiance is reduced in proportion to the inverse square of the distance to the source.

The surface appearance can be thought of as a combination of the both concepts. Whenever a light sources illuminates a surface we can measure the irradiance at a particular point. Based on its material, the surface emits all or only a portion of the irradiance, and we can measure the emitted light at a view point. The emitted light can vary with direction (directional distribution), and we are interested in the amount of light emitted per unit surface area. Hence, we arrive at the definition of radiance: namely, the power emitted per unit area (perpendicular to the viewing direction) per unit solid angle. This is perhaps the most fundamental unit in computer vision and graphics. It is easy to show that the irradiance on the observer's retina or a camera sensor is proportional to the radiance of the observed surfaces.

One way to model the surface appearance is by describing reflectance properties. Unfortunately, reflectance itself is a complex phenomenon. In general, a surface may reflect a different amount of light at each position, and for each possible direction of incident and reflected light (see Figure 5.2(a)). A common way to model the reflection is the Bidirectional Reflectance Distribution Function (BRDF)

[Nicodemus, 1965], which defines the reflection at an opaque surface. This 4-dimensional function

$$f_r(\boldsymbol{\omega}_i, \boldsymbol{\omega}_o) = \frac{L_o(\boldsymbol{\omega}_o)}{L_i(\boldsymbol{\omega}_i)} \tag{5.1}$$

returns the ratio of reflected radiance L_o exiting along the outgoing direction $\boldsymbol{\omega}_o$, to the irradiance incident L_i on the surface from the incoming light direction $\boldsymbol{\omega}_i$. Each direction $\boldsymbol{\omega}$ is itself parameterized by the two polar angles ϕ and θ with respect to the surface normal $\mathbf{n}$. Following this definition, the reflected radiance at a surface point $\mathbf{p}$ is calculated with:

$$L_o(\boldsymbol{\omega}_o) = \int_{\Omega_\mathbf{p}} L_i(\boldsymbol{\omega}_i) f_r(\boldsymbol{\omega}_i, \boldsymbol{\omega}_o) \cos\theta_i d\boldsymbol{\omega}_i \ , \tag{5.2}$$

where the integral is defined over the 3D upper hemisphere $\Omega_\mathbf{p}$ at the point $\mathbf{p}$. Here θ_i denotes the angle made between $\boldsymbol{\omega}_i$ and the surface normal $\mathbf{n}$. There exists a large variety of lower dimensional approximations for the BRDF exploiting common material properties such as homogeneity and isotropy (radiance is unchanged if the incoming and outgoing vectors are rotated by the same amount around the surface normal). Two common examples are the Lambertian BRDF [Wolff et al., 1992] which assumes $f_r := const.$ resulting in a matte or diffuse appearance, and the Blinn-Phong BRDF [Blinn, 1977], which models the reflections as a lobe centered around the direction of an ideal mirror reflection for each incident angle that contains significantly more energy than the rest. This model is designed to represent glossy materials. As we can see, the reflection functions embody a significant amount of information. They can tell us whether a surface is shiny or matte, metallic or dielectric, smooth or rough. Knowing the reflectance function of a surface allows us to make complete predictions of how that surface appears under any possible lighting. For real surfaces the BRDF is spatially varying since the surface material itself is varying. This spatial variation adds two more dimensions to the BRDF and is then called the Spatial Varying Bidirectional Reflectance Distribution Function (SVBRDF).

Even the SVBRDF is not enough to characterize all materials. Many surfaces exhibit translucency: a phenomenon in which light enters the object, is reflected inside the material, and eventually re-emerges from a different point on the surface. Such sub-surface scattering can have a dramatic effect on appearance. The Bidirectional Scattering-Surface Reflection Distribution Function (BSSRDF) models the phenomenon of light leaving the surface at a different point than the one at which it entered. This is done by adding two more dimensions to the SVBRDF:

$$BSSRDF(\mathbf{p}_i, \boldsymbol{\omega}_i, \mathbf{p}_o, \boldsymbol{\omega}_o) \tag{5.3}$$

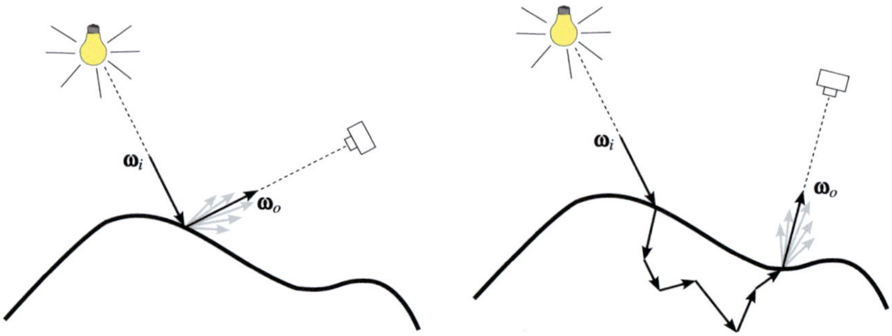

(a) Reflection. (b) Sub-surface scattering.

Figure 5.2: The reflection at an opaque surface can be thought of as a function of the incoming light direction $\boldsymbol{\omega}_i$ and the outgoing $\boldsymbol{\omega}_o$ light direction (left). Sub-surface scattering is a phenomenon in which light enters the object, is reflected inside the material, and eventually re-emerges from a different point on the surface (right).

Unfortunately, even the BSSRDF is not enough. Moreover, some surfaces are fluorescent: they emit light at different wavelengths than those present in the incident light. Some other surfaces may have appearance that changes over time because of chemical changes or physical processes such as drying or weathering. Other surfaces might capture light and re-emit it later leading to phosphorescence and other such phenomena. Thus, a complete description of light scattering at a surface needs to add at least two wavelength (λ_i, λ_o) and two time dimensions (t_i, t_o) to the BSSRDF. Thus, the full description of the material appearance is the 12-dimensional *scattering function*. A taxonomy of different reflection and appearance models is presented in Figure 5.3.

5.2 Appearance Reconstruction

So far, there has been little effort put into capturing the full scattering function since its high dimensionality leads to immense difficulties in capturing and working with it directly. However, many efforts exist to capture one or more of its low-dimensional subsets.

While a first approach for efficiently measuring the BSSRDF reflectance fields has recently been proposed by [Garg et al., 2006], an exhaustive coverage of incident light situations still has not been achieved due to the huge amount of capture effort

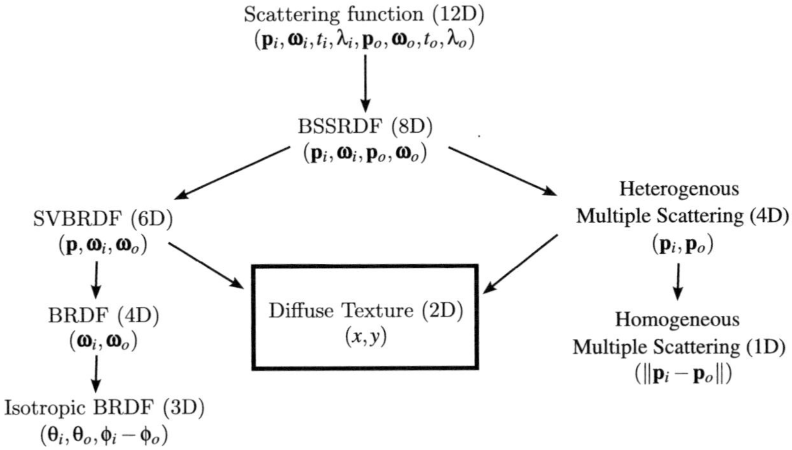

Figure 5.3: Taxonomy of different surface reflection and surface scattering functions. Our focus lies in reconstructing a diffuse texture, which is a 2D function modeling the surface appearance as a spatially varying color.

and required data storage. Therefore, usually simplifying assumptions are made to reduce the dimensionality of the problem. The methods of [Debevec et al., 2000], [Marschner et al., 2000], [Sato et al., 1997], and others have produced high quality measurements leading to the creation of very realistic visualizations. However, most of the previous work has been conducted under highly controlled lighting conditions, usually by careful active positioning of a single point light source. Even methods that work outdoors, such as those of [Yu and Malik, 1998], [Sato and Ikeuchi, 1994], are designed specifically for natural illumination, and assume a simple parametric model for skylight. [Bernardini et al., 2001] proposed a system that uses an inexpensive, electronic camera-based setup and do not assume a highly controlled lighting. They reconstruct texture and normal maps based on low-resolution range images and high-resolution intensity images. [Johnson and Kang, 1997b] proposed a similar method as they also combine information from multiple overlapping scans to avoid jumps in color appearance and to reduce noise. Both methods require multiple images to achieve a very coarse approximation of the Lambertian BRDF.

We do a simple calculation to get a sense of how much data is required to densely sample the SVBRDF of a regular surface: if the shape of the object is known and the light source and view directions are given, each pixel in a photo taken of the surface provides one sample of the SVBRDF (or the BRDF at a particular surface point). Sampling the BRDF in 1° angular increments therefore requires

1,049,760,000 samples to cover the 3D upper hemisphere a single surface point. This means, we required to capture hundreds-of millions of images to sample multiple surface points. Clearly, capturing millions of images per object is highly impractical.

5.2.1 Reconstruction of Diffuse Texture Maps

Possible solutions for capturing the surface appearance are improved acquisition systems or low dimensional approximations of the surface scattering function. Here, we choose to approximate the surface scattering function since data acquisition systems such as the ones used in [Debevec et al., 2000] or [Garg et al., 2006] are impractical to employ on a mobile platform. We assume the material to be spatially varying Lambertian, which means the appearance of a surface can be described by a two dimensional *diffuse texture* storing the constant BRDF for each surface point. This means the appearance model can be measured from as little as one image as we will see later. Here, we define a *texture map* rather loosely as a function $\tau\ :\ \mathcal{T} \subset \mathbb{R}^2$ defined on the domain $\mathcal{T}$ which is mapped onto the 2-dimensional space of a surface representation. In our case τ, is a function of the surface color [Catmull, 1974] while in computer graphics systems, a variety of other functions have been used such as normal vector perturbation (bump mapping) [Blinn, 1978b], specularity (the glossiness coefficient) [Blinn, 1978a], and transparency [Gardner, 1985].

5.2.2 Texture Mapping

The surface color is stored in 2D texture maps which are mapped onto the reconstructed 3D surface for visualization. Mathematically, *texture mapping* means the mapping of a texture $\mathcal{T}$ onto a surface $\mathcal{S} \subseteq \mathcal{M}$. The surface $\mathcal{S}$ is a continuous part of a parametric manifold $\mathcal{M}$ –a triangle mesh in our case– representing the object's surface. The texture is mapped onto the surface by a function: $f\ :\ \mathcal{S} \rightarrow \mathcal{T}$. Figure 5.4 depicts an example for such a mapping. The choice of a good mapping f is critical for visually pleasing results. *Homeomorphic* (topology-preserving) mappings that produce little geometric distortions are preferred since these mappings conserve the sampling rate across the surface. We also want the mapping to be bijective, which means that each surface point maps to a single texture point. Discontinuities at edges of texture maps are also undesirable since they cause discontinuities of texture on the surface. Mappings that fulfill those criteria are called *isometric isomorphisms*, and they map an arbitrary two-dimensional manifold embedded in $\mathbb{R}^3$ to a subset of $\mathbb{R}^2$ without geometric distortions. Unfortunately, for

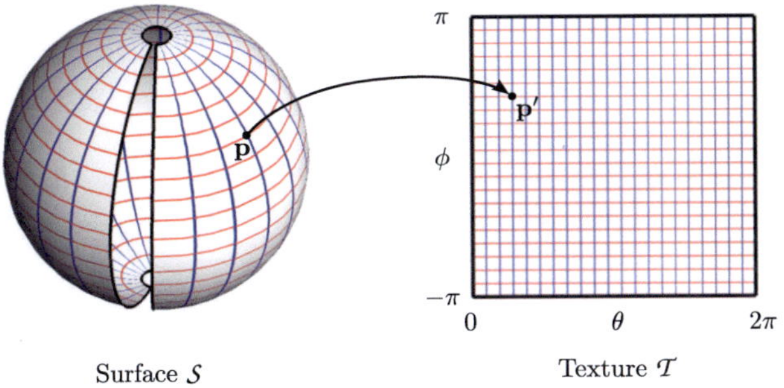

Figure 5.4: A sphere can be cut on a meridian and unfolded to create a texture map. This process will cause geometric distortions near the poles of the sphere.

reconstructed mesh models, those generally do not exist. In fact, they only exists for *developable* surfaces: those are surfaces with zero Gaussian curvature. However, we can show that a good partitioning of $\mathcal{M}$ leads to good approximations of such mappings.

An example for a texture mapping is shown in Figure 5.4. Each point $\mathbf{p} = (x, y, z)$ on the surface of the sphere is mapped to the texture coordinates $\mathbf{p}' = (\phi, \theta)$. The iso-$\phi$ and iso-θ lines form a regular grid in the texture, but a a significant distortion is noticeable near the poles when mapped back onto the sphere. In fact, the mapping results in singularities right at the poles where a single point on the surface is mapped to an infinite number of points in the texture domain.

This kind of surface mapping, also called *surface parameterization*, is a well-studied problem in computer graphics. In general, surface parameterization refers to segmenting a 3D surface into one or more patches and unfolding them onto a plane without any overlap. Borrowing terminology from mathematics, this is often referred to as creating an *atlas* of *charts* for a given surface. See [Floater and Hormann, 2005] and [Sheffer et al., 2006] for some recent surveys.

5.3 Multi-view Texture Reconstruction

In our system, we capture color images from a digital camera together with the geometry. We use the captured images to reconstruct diffuse texture maps which are mapped onto the 3D model to generate a greater realism. Our texture reconstruction approach consists of the following steps which will be explained in the following sections: *surface partitioning*, *surface unfolding*, *color reconstruction*, and *color blending*.

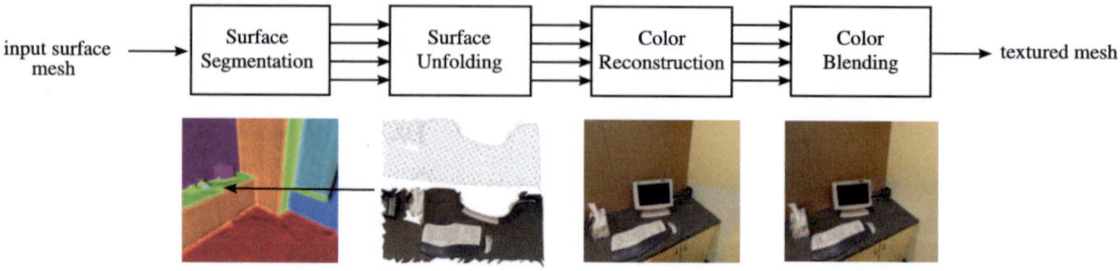

Figure 5.5: For the texture reconstruction the mesh is *segmented* into nearly planar regions and each region is unfolded onto a 2D plane. The texture of each region is reconstructed from all camera images observing this part of the surface, and the resulting color composite is blended afterwards to avoid discontinuity artifacts.

5.3.1 Surface Partitioning

The first subproblem we have to address is the *surface partitioning*. In other words: which partitions $\mathcal{S} \subseteq \mathcal{M}$ are suitable for a good mapping? There are two common approaches to this problem. The first is to find a single cut for the surface that makes the modified surface homeomorphic to a disk [Sheffer and Hart, 2002, Ni et al., 2004]. This method is unsuitable for meshes with complex topology and creases. The other approach is to divide the surface into a collection of patches that can be unfolded with little stretch [Alliez et al., 2002, Lévy et al., 2002]. Though stretch is minimized, this approach creates seams between the patches. This may lead to noticeable discontinuities if color variation across the seams is not treated with care.

We seek to break the surface into several segments such that the distortion when unfolding each segment onto a plane is sufficiently small while the number of segments remains small at the same time. Since planes are developable (zero curvature) by definition, one possible approach is to segment the surface into nearly planar segments [Cohen-Steiner et al., 2004, Diebel et al., 2006, Jenke et al., 2006]. We employ an incremental clustering approach with a subsequent merging strategy which is explained in this section.

The segmentation starts by randomly selecting an initial mesh face as a seed. The initial segment is now the exact location of this seed. The segment is then grown from this seed face to adjacent faces if the orientation matches with the seed face. The segment is finished when no more faces can be added and the algorithm starts over by selecting a new seed face. The procedure stops when all the faces are classified as belonging to a segment. The outline of this seeded region growing algorithm is as follows:

Algorithm 2 Cluster mesh faces into nearly planar partitions.

while not all faces $\mathcal{F} \in \mathcal{M}$ are assigned to a segment **do**
  randomly choose a seed face f_{seed} which is not assigned to a partition yet
  create a new segment $\mathcal{S}$ and add f_{seed} to $\mathcal{S}$
  let $\mathbf{n}_{\text{seed}}$ be the normal vector on f_{seed}
  add all one-ring neighbors of f_{seed} to open list $\mathcal{L}$
  while $\mathcal{L}$ is not empty **do**
    pop face f from open list
    if f is not assigned to a partition **then**
      let $\mathbf{n}$ be the normal vector on f
      if $\|\mathbf{n}_{\text{seed}} - \mathbf{n}\| < \epsilon$ **then**
        add f to $\mathcal{S}$
        add all one-ring neighbors of f to open list $\mathcal{L}$
      end if
    end if
  end while
end while

Often, this segmentation procedure results in a highly segmented surface (compare Figure 5.6(a)). In order to reduce this over-segmentation, we append an optimization procedure to merge neighboring segments by incorporating information about their similarity. The basic concept of such a procedure was developed by [Haris et al., 1998] for Region Adjacency Graphs (RAG) in image segmentation and can be applied to the mesh segmentation as well, if the scalar dissimilarity measures are adequately modified to evaluate normal features.

We define an objective function $F(\mathcal{P})$ that evaluates the error of a partition $\mathcal{P}$. The optimal partition $\mathcal{P}_o$ can then be found by minimizing $F(\mathcal{P})$ for a certain partition size. This is a combinatorial optimization problem which can be efficiently approximated in an incremental manner: at each iteration all pairs of adjacent regions are selected and tested, however, only the pair which introduces the least error is merged.

The square error of the piecewise planar approximation of the input mesh is chosen here as objective function $F(\mathcal{P})$. For a segment $\mathcal{S}_i$ the square error is given by:

$$E(\mathcal{S}_i) = \sum_{\mathbf{n}_i \in \mathcal{S}_i} \left(\mathbf{n}_i - \boldsymbol{\mu}_{\mathcal{S}_i}\right)^{\mathsf{T}} \left(\mathbf{n}_i - \boldsymbol{\mu}_{\mathcal{S}_i}\right) , \tag{5.4}$$

where the value $\boldsymbol{\mu}_{\mathcal{S}_i}$ that minimizes $E(\mathcal{S}_i)$ is equal to the mean normal value of the segment

$$\boldsymbol{\mu}_{\mathcal{S}_i} = \frac{1}{|\mathcal{S}_i|} \sum_{\mathbf{n}_i \in \mathcal{S}_i} \mathbf{n}_i \ . \tag{5.5}$$

Now, the objective function is simply defined as

$$F(\mathcal{P}) = \sum_{\mathcal{S}_i \in \mathcal{P}} E(\mathcal{S}_i) \ , \tag{5.6}$$

(a) 1385 segments. (b) 53 segments. (c) 11 segments.

Figure 5.6: Mesh partitioning into nearly-planar segments.

Given a surface partition $\mathcal{P}_n$ with n segments, and assuming it to be optimal for its size, a new partition $\mathcal{P}_{n-1}$ of cardinality $n-1$ is sought such that $F(\mathcal{P}_{n-1})$ has the smallest value among all possible merges of just one segment pair in $\mathcal{P}_n$. It can be shown [Alvarado, 2004] that the best $n-1$ segments are obtained by merging the segment pair that minimizes the function

$$\gamma\left(\mathcal{S}_i, \mathcal{S}_j\right) = \begin{cases} \frac{|\mathcal{S}_i| \cdot |\mathcal{S}_j|}{|\mathcal{S}_i| + |\mathcal{S}_j|} \left(\boldsymbol{\mu}_{\mathcal{S}_i} - \boldsymbol{\mu}_{\mathcal{S}_j}\right)^{\mathsf{T}} \left(\boldsymbol{\mu}_{\mathcal{S}_i} - \boldsymbol{\mu}_{\mathcal{S}_j}\right) & \text{for } \mathcal{S}_i \text{ adjacent to } \mathcal{S}_j \ , \\ +\infty & \text{otherwise} \ . \end{cases} \tag{5.7}$$

We can now derive an iterative optimization as follows:

Algorithm 3 Iterative merging of mesh segments.

1: **while** $\min \gamma\left(\mathcal{S}_i, \mathcal{S}_j\right) < \epsilon_\gamma$ **do**
2: find $\left\{\mathcal{S}_i^*, \mathcal{S}_j^*\right\} = \min \gamma\left(\mathcal{S}_i, \mathcal{S}_j\right)$
3: merge segments $\mathcal{S}_i^*$ and $\mathcal{S}_j^*$ into new segment $\mathcal{S}_k$
4: **end while**

Here, ϵ_γ is a dissimilarity threshold which regulates the resulting number of segments. Figure 5.6 depicts the results of the previously described seeded region growing algorithm with subsequent merging.

In our experiment, the initial partition found by the surface segmentation in Algorithm 2 consists of 1385 segments (see Figure 5.6(a)). The merging procedure with a stop criterion $\epsilon_\gamma = 0\ 02$ and $\epsilon_\gamma = 0\ 05$ results in 53 and 11 segments respectively (see Figure 5.6(b) and Figure 5.6(c)). Once we have determined a good partition, we can break the mesh into several pieces, one for each segment, and reconstruct a texture for each piece individually. The cuts will introduce discontinuities in the texture. In practice, the cuts naturally fall together with edges and corners in the geometry where we also expect to see abrupt changes in texture and shading.

5.3.2 Surface Unfolding

The second step considers the surface-to-texture mapping which is often called *unfolding*. This means, once a set of disjoint surface regions is obtained, a mapping is computed that maps each point on the surface of a region onto the corresponding texture domain. The classical approach treats the unfolding problem as finding the minimum of some functional that measures the stretch introduced by the parameterization [Eck et al., 1995, Floater and Hormann, 2005]. In this approach the boundary vertices of the surface patch $\mathcal{S}$ are assigned to initial positions (e.g., a circle or a square). Then, the parameterization for the interior vertices is determined by solving a large linear system or through a nonlinear optimization process. This works well if the shape of $\mathcal{S}$ resembles the initial position. To allow the boundary vertices of a patch to be free from the arbitrary initial assignment, [Lévy et al., 2002] use a least-squares conformal mapping. These methods are typically based on differential geometry which cannot be directly applied in the presence of creases since the differential quantities they estimate are undefined on the creases. Also, ill-shaped triangles, which are common in scanned meshes, may cause numerical instabilities.

A rather simple idea for constructing an unfolding of a triangle mesh draws form the previously described segmentation procedure, which results in almost planar surface segments. Suppose a surface segment $\mathcal{S}_\mathcal{T}$ is contained in a plane so that its vertices have coordinates $\mathbf{p}_i = (x_i, y_i, 0)$ with respect to some appropriately chosen coordinate frame. A mapping can then be defined by just using the local coordinates itself by setting $\mathbf{u}_i = (x_i, y_i)$. As we can easily see, this parameterization is *globally isometric* and thus optimal in our sense. As discussed above, only isometric mappings are topology-preserving and without geometric distortions.

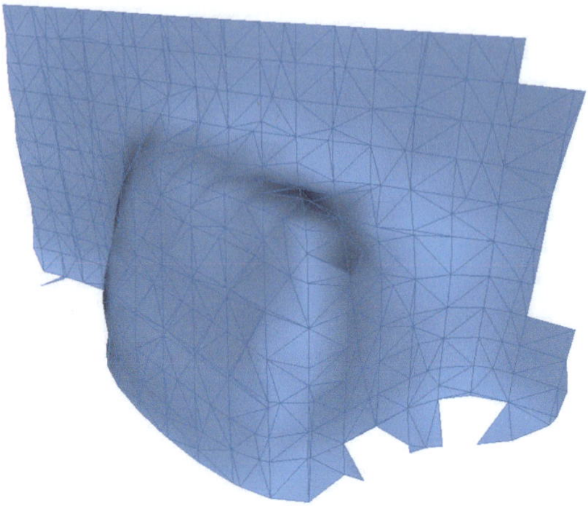

Figure 5.7: Example mesh for a typical mesh segment that should be unfolded onto a plane for texture reconstruction.

Typically, the vertices of $\mathcal{S}_\mathcal{T}$ are not perfectly contained in a plane since the segmentation procedure balances the planarity of each segment and the number of resulting segments. An example for a typical mesh segment is depicted in Figure 5.7. In this case, we can find the best fitting plane in a least squares sense by using *principal component analysis* (PCA). The result is an orthogonal linear transformation W that transforms the data point $\mathbf{p}_i = (x_i, y_i, z_i)$ to a new coordinate system $\tilde{\mathbf{p}}_i = (\tilde{x}_i, \tilde{y}_i, \tilde{z}_i)$ such that the greatest variance of the data is along the first coordinate and the smallest variance along the third coordinate respectively. Then a mapping can be defined by projecting the transformed coordinates onto the plane spanned by the first and the second coordinate axis:

$$\mathbf{u}_i = \begin{pmatrix} \tilde{x}_i \\ \tilde{y}_i \end{pmatrix} = \begin{pmatrix} 1 & 0 & 0 \\ 0 & 1 & 0 \end{pmatrix} \tilde{\mathbf{p}}_i \,. \tag{5.8}$$

Figure 5.9(a) presents such an *orthogonal parameterization.* One will note in Figure 5.9(c) that a texture is mapped to the surface with little distortions (white) in flat areas, but with significant distortions (red) in areas where surface triangles have an oblique angle in respect to the x-y plane. In fact, the distortion even causes some of the mapped triangles to intersect and flip. This violates our requirement for the mapping to be bijective. This resulting distortion becomes apparent once we map a homogeneous checkerboard pattern onto the surface (Figure 5.9(e)).

From a theoretical point of view, as pointed out by [Floater and Hormann, 2005], there are two independent qualities that quantify the distortion: angular distor-

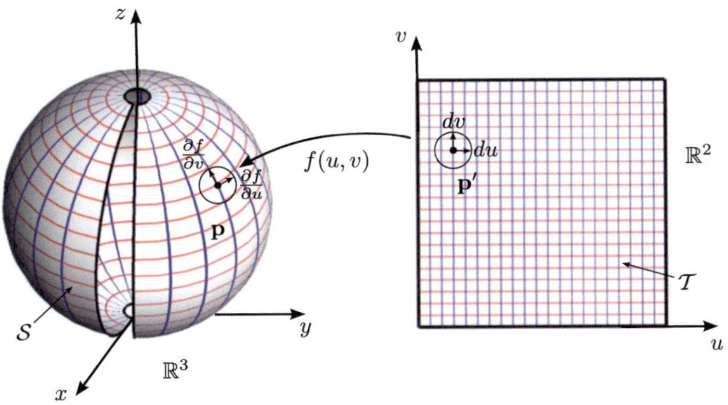

Figure 5.8: A conformal parameterization $f(u, v)$ transforms an elementary circle in the texture domain into an elementary circle in the surface domain.

tion and area distortion. For texture mapping, finding a *conformal mapping* which preserves the angular distortion is typically more beneficial than finding an *authalic mapping* which preserves the area. One reason is that for continuous surfaces conformal mappings are nearly unique, whereas authalic mappings are not [Floater and Hormann, 2005]. Often there exists a number of area-preserving mappings which introduce a large amount of angular distortion.

Here, we focus on minimizing the angular distortion, or shear, of the parameterization. In mathematics, a *conformal map* is a function between domains which preserves angles. In other words, a conformal parameterization transforms an elementary circle in the texture domain into an elementary circle on the surface (see Figure 5.8). If we now consider a triangle $\{\mathbf{p}_i, \mathbf{p}_j, \mathbf{p}_k\}$ of the surface, we can define a local orthonormal basis $B = \{\mathbf{x}, \mathbf{y}\}$ in the supporting plane by setting:

$$\begin{aligned} \mathbf{x} &= \frac{\mathbf{p}_j - \mathbf{p}_i}{\|\mathbf{p}_j - \mathbf{p}_i\|}, \\ \mathbf{n} &= \frac{\mathbf{x} \times (\mathbf{p}_k - \mathbf{p}_i)}{\|\mathbf{x} \times (\mathbf{p}_k - \mathbf{p}_i)\|}, \\ \mathbf{y} &= \mathbf{n} \times \mathbf{x}. \end{aligned} \tag{5.9}$$

In this basis, we can define the parameterization f, the function that maps a point $\mathbf{p}'_i = (u_i, v_i)$ in the texture space $\mathcal{T}$ to a point $\mathbf{p}_i = (x_i, y_i, 0)$ defined in B. The gradients of this function are given by:

$$\begin{aligned}
\nabla u &= \begin{pmatrix} \frac{\partial u}{\partial x} \\ \frac{\partial u}{\partial y} \end{pmatrix} , \\
&= \frac{1}{2|T|} \begin{pmatrix} y_j - y_k & y_k - y_i & y_i - y_j \\ x_k - x_j & x_i - x_k & x_j - x_i \end{pmatrix} \begin{pmatrix} u_i \\ u_j \\ u_k \end{pmatrix} , \\
&= \mathbf{M}_T \begin{pmatrix} u_i \\ u_j \\ u_k \end{pmatrix} , && (5.10) \\
\nabla v &= \mathbf{M}_T \begin{pmatrix} v_i \\ v_j \\ v_k \end{pmatrix} . && (5.11)
\end{aligned}$$

where the matrix $\mathbf{M}_T$ is constant over the triangle T and $|T|$ denotes the area of T. Next, we want the mapping to be conformal and more precisely to preserve angles. With the previously derived gradients this property can be expressed as:

$$\nabla v = \mathrm{rot}_{90}(\nabla u) = \begin{pmatrix} 0 & -1 \\ 1 & 0 \end{pmatrix} \nabla u . \tag{5.12}$$

Here rot_{90} denotes the anti-clockwise rotation by 90 degrees. Only mappings that fulfill this property for all points are called *conformal maps*. In the continuous setting, Riemann proved that any surface admits a conformal parameterization [Petersen, 2006]. However, in our case of piecewise linear functions on a triangle mesh, only developable surface parts admit a conformal parameterization. Therefore, we seek to minimize the *discrete conformal energy* that corresponds to the "non-conformality" in a least-square sense:

$$\min \sum_{\{i,j,k\} \in \mathcal{F}} \left\| \mathbf{M}_T \begin{pmatrix} v_i \\ v_j \\ v_k \end{pmatrix} - \begin{pmatrix} 0 & -1 \\ 1 & 0 \end{pmatrix} \mathbf{M}_T \begin{pmatrix} u_i \\ u_j \\ u_k \end{pmatrix} \right\|^2 . \tag{5.13}$$

This formulation is equivalent to the *complex conformal energy* proposed by [Lévy et al., 2002]. The quadratic form in Equation 5.13 can be minimized by setting its gradient to zero and solving the resulting sparse linear system of the form $\mathbf{Ax} = 0$. The matrix $\mathbf{A}$ has the form:

$$\mathbf{A}_{i,j} = \begin{cases} w_{ij} & (i,j) \in \mathcal{N}_1 , \\ 0 & \text{otherwise} , \end{cases} \tag{5.14}$$

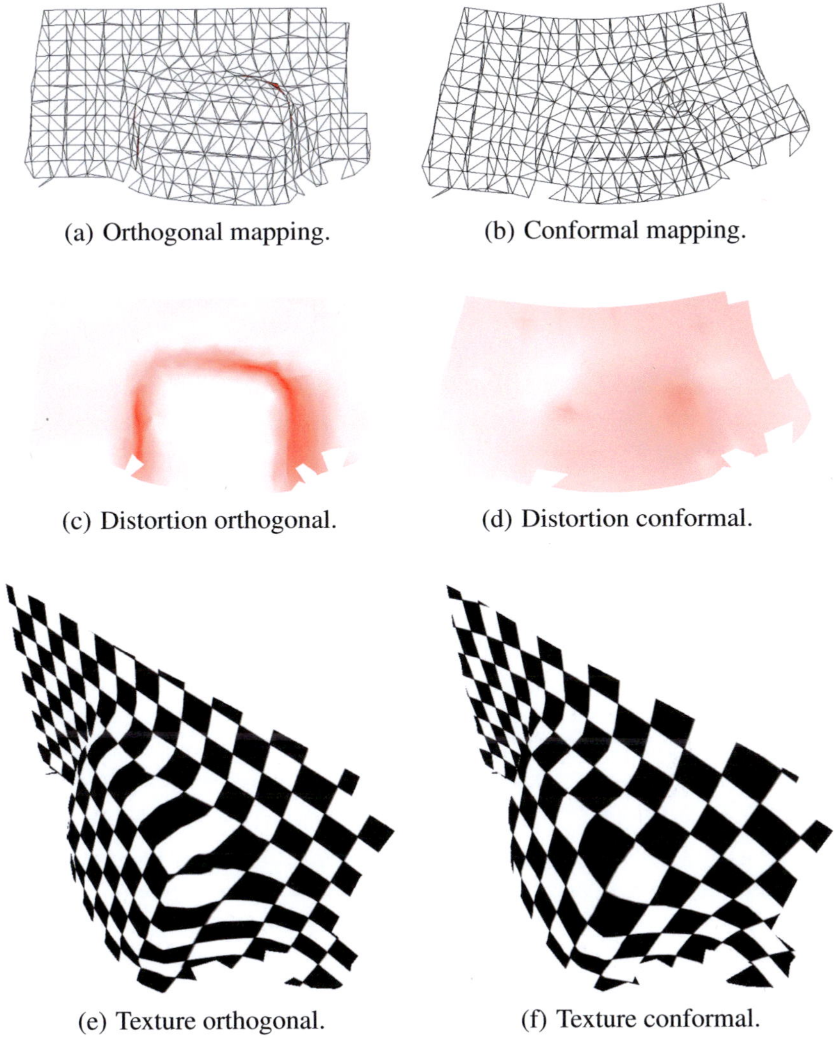

(a) Orthogonal mapping. (b) Conformal mapping.

(c) Distortion orthogonal. (d) Distortion conformal.

(e) Texture orthogonal. (f) Texture conformal.

Figure 5.9: Unfolding of triangular meshes onto the two-dimensional texture domain. The *orthogonal mapping* creates a significant angular distortion in areas where triangles are not parallel to the plane of projection while the conformal mapping minimizes the overall angular distortion by globally optimizing the vertex positions.

where $\mathcal{N}_1$ denotes the one-ring neighborhood and w_{ij} are edge weights as a result of Equation 5.13. The matrix $\mathbf{A}$ is singular, since conformality is invariant through similarities, namely affine transformations in Euclidean space. By fixing the *u,v*-coordinates of two vertices, we obtain 4 degrees of freedom what yields a positive definite system. The coordinates for these two vertices as well as initial coordinates for all other points $\mathbf{p}'_i$ can be determined by an orthogonal mapping as described earlier.

Figure 5.9(b) presents a least-square *conformal parameterization*. The distortion introduced by this parameterization, visualized in Figure 5.9(d), is lower than introduced using the orthogonal projection (see Figure 5.9(c)). Specifically, areas where surface triangles have an oblique angle in respect to the x-y plane experience significantly less distortion compared to the orthogonal parameterization method. We observe that the distortion is more evenly spread over the entire texture domain. This is expected since the described procedure globally minimizes distortion over all triangles.

5.3.3 Color Reconstruction

After having determined a mapping for each segment, we now want to reconstruct a diffuse texture for each segment. Knowing the pose and the intrinsic calibration of our scanner allows us to project any 3D surface point into any of the original camera images to retrieve the color from this particular view. However, each view carries only information for one part of the reconstructed surface. The color reconstruction process first finds the camera images that have information about a particular 3D point and then determines the best color for this location.

To find out if a given 3D point is visible in a certain view, we first transform the point into the camera coordinate system using the known view pose. Next, we use the intrinsic camera calibration to project the point to pixel coordinates. If the resulting coordinates are valid (i.e., in the range of the image dimensions) we can conclude that the 3D point is in the camera's view. However, the geometry of the environment may create complex occlusions. This makes it difficult to recognize if a 3D point was truly observable by the camera. The most accurate way to test if the 3D point is occluded in this view would be to trace the rays originating at the point to the center of the camera and determine if it intersects with any surface. However, this is a very inefficient method since the amount of points and surfaces is large.

We propose a method to estimate the correct camera image for each point by considering the original point-cloud. First, for each point we want to colorize, we

(a) Reconstruction of vertex colors.

(b) Reconstruction of high-resolution texture.

Figure 5.10: Visualization of a mesh using colored vertices only leads to poor texture resolution. Our texture mapping algorithm automatically generates stitched textures for parts of the mesh by composing parts from images captured by different scans.

find the n nearest neighbor points in the original point-cloud. This can be efficiently done by using *k*D-Trees. For each point in the scanned point-cloud we can uniquely identify the corresponding camera image as discussed earlier. We then calculate a histogram of images and project the 3D point into the image used most often among the n neighbors and use the color resulting from this projection. The rational for this procedure is that it identifies the most likely camera image based on a local neighborhood.

We perform this procedure for all vertices in the triangle mesh and change the color in the corresponding point on the texture map. The result for this color reconstruction is presented on the left side of Figure 5.10. The colors at positions that were previously occluded by the robot were successfully reconstructed from other scans. However, one will notice that the texture resolution is very poor, and it varies over the model. The reason for this behavior is that the described process does not actually create textures, it merely retrieves a color for each vertex of the reconstructed mesh. The color between vertices is interpolated from the surrounding vertex colors by the rendering system. This effect is even more drastic once simplification algorithms are applied to the geometry. In order to obtain a high-resolution texture we first re-parameterize the mesh to obtain a densely sampled surface, then reconstruct a texture for the dense mesh, and finally apply the texture to the original mesh.

For the re-parameterization we use an equidistant point grid in texture space (c.f. Figure 5.11(a)) where each grid point corresponds to a texture pixel. The space spanned by this grid will become our texture space $\mathcal{T}$. The resolution of the pixel grid is kept constant for all segments in order to achieve a constant texture resolution over the whole 3D model. Now, we assume that our surface to texture mapping f is bijective[1]. In other words, the surface area $\mathcal{S}_T$ of a triangle T uniquely maps to a part of the texture space $\mathcal{T}_T \subset \mathcal{T}$. The mapping $f : \mathcal{S} \rightarrow \mathcal{T}_S \subset \mathcal{T}$ does not guarantee that the texture space will be used completely. We can conclude that any point $\tilde{\mathbf{p}} \in \mathcal{T}$ either uniquely falls inside one mapped triangle or is not part of the mapped surface at all.

In order to determine if $\tilde{\mathbf{p}}_i = (u_i, v_i)$ is inside or outside of a mapped triangle, we calculate the barycentric coordinates [Coxeter, 1969]. See Section 4.4.1 for more details on the calculation of barycentric coordinates. In this way, we find the corresponding triangles for all points of the grid and use the barycentric coordinates to interpolate the mapping f at the point's coordinates. Grid points that are not part of the mapped surface are discarded. Figure 5.11(b) shows the resulting equally sampled surface points compared with the original mesh.

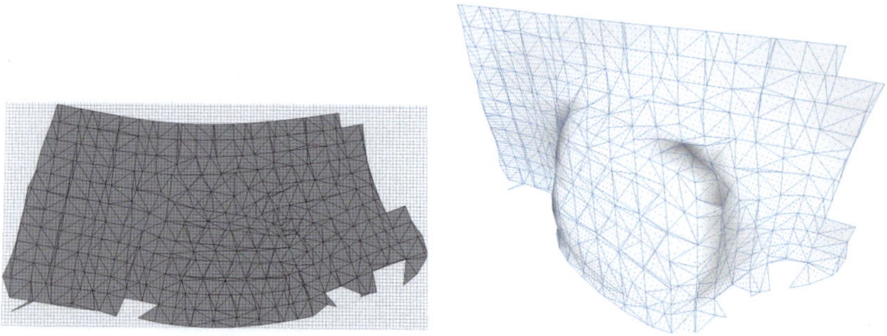

(a) Mapped surface with point grid. (b) Re-parameterization grid points.

Figure 5.11: Mesh re-parameterization is used to create an equally sampled surface grid in which each point uniquely corresponds to a texture pixel.

[1]Even though the methods described in the previous section are not guaranteed to be bijective, we can easily check this criterion for each mapping. In a bijective map, the order of the triangle vertices (anti-clockwise) will be preserved. In practice, the conformal mapping is bijective in our case since the surfaces are almost developable and the fixed vertices are well chosen.

5.3.4 Color Interpolation

Since the reconstructed texture maps are composites from multiple camera images, discontinuity artifacts usually become visible. The reason for those artifacts is that the true surface appearance varies by distance and incidence angle while our simple model assumes a Lambertian BRDF. For a consistent texturing we want to minimize the visibility of these discontinuity artifacts. We approach this problem by using a blending technique, which globally adjusts the color of all pixels.

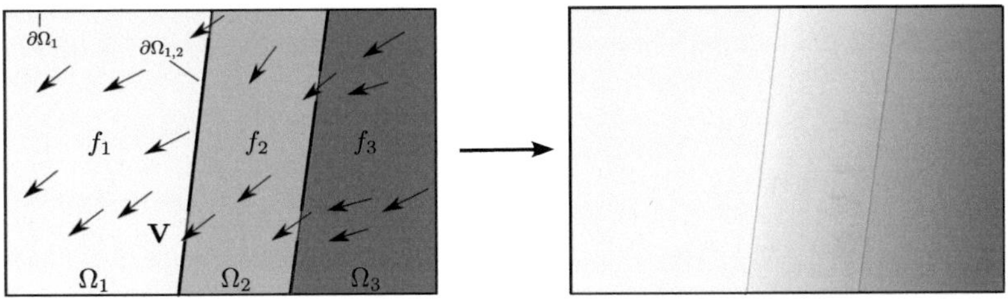

Figure 5.12: Our poisson blending approach uses a guidance vector field **V** composed from color gradients and boundary constraints to guarantee smooth boundaries between texture regions reconstructed from different photos $(\Omega_1 \ldots \Omega_3)$. The result is a blended composite with no visible discontinuities at region boundaries.

Our algorithm extends the ideas of [Pérez et al., 2003] to use a Poisson formulation for the multi-view blending problem. The procedure is as follows: for a texture with regions reconstructed from n camera images, we can treat the regions as separate functions: $f_{1:n}$. Now, let $\Omega_{1:n}$ be the definition space of $f_{1:n}$, $\partial\Omega_{i,j}$ be the boundary between Ω_i and Ω_j, and $\partial\Omega_i$ the texture boundary of the ith texture. Finally, we define **V** to be a guidance vector field defined over $\Omega_{1:n}$. See Figure 5.12 (left) for an illustration of this notation.

Our goal is to find a new set of functions $f'_{1:n}$ which have the same definition space as $f_{1:n}$ and no visible discontinuities at their boundaries. We cast this problem as a membrane interpolant that satisfies:

$$f'_{1:n} = \min_{f_{1:n}} \sum_i \iint_{\Omega_i} |\nabla f_i - \mathbf{V}|^2 \ , \tag{5.15}$$

with the Dirichlet boundary conditions $f_i \mid_{\partial\Omega_{i,j}} = f_j \mid_{\partial\Omega_{i,j}}$ and $f_i \mid_{\partial\Omega_i} = f_i \mid_{\partial\Omega_i}$. We set the guidance vector field **V** to equal the derivatives of $f_{1:n}$, which means we constrain the derivatives of $f_{1:n}$ to be the same as the derivatives of $f_{1:n}$. The first boundary constraint guarantees a smooth boundary between texture regions, while the second constraint is necessary because the gradient operator is invariant through multiplicative factors. The solution of Equation 5.15 is the unique solution of the following Poisson equation:

$$\nabla \cdot \nabla f_{1:n} = \triangle f_{1:n} = \nabla \mathbf{V} \text{ over } \Omega_{1:n} , \tag{5.16}$$

with the same boundary conditions as Equation 5.15. In the discrete texture domain, this can be efficiently solved as a sparse linear system. For each pixel $\mathbf{p} \in \mathcal{T}$, let $\mathcal{N}_\mathbf{p}$ be the set of its 4-connected neighbors and let $\{\mathbf{p}, \mathbf{q}\}$ be a pixel pair such that $\mathbf{q} \in \mathcal{N}_\mathbf{p}$. The boundary between the two regions i and j is now defined as:

$$\partial\Omega_{i,j} = \{\mathbf{p} \in \Omega_i : \mathcal{N}_\mathbf{p} \cap \Omega_j \neq \emptyset\} \tag{5.17}$$

and the texture boundary of region i is:

$$\partial\Omega_i = \{\mathbf{p} \in \Omega_i : |\mathcal{N}_\mathbf{p} \cap \mathcal{T}| < 4\} . \tag{5.18}$$

The finite difference discretization of Equation 5.15 yield the following quadratic optimization problem:

$$f'_{1:n} = \min_{f_{1:n}} \sum_{i \in 1:n} \sum_{\{\mathbf{p},\mathbf{q}\} \cap \Omega_i} \left(f_i(\mathbf{p}) - f_i(\mathbf{q}) - v_{\mathbf{pq}} \right)^2 \tag{5.19}$$

with

$$f_i(\mathbf{p}) = f_j(\mathbf{p}) \text{ for all } \mathbf{p} \in \partial\Omega_{i,j} \tag{5.20}$$

and

$$f_i(\mathbf{p}) = f_i(\mathbf{p}) \text{ for all } \mathbf{p} \in \partial\Omega_i \tag{5.21}$$

where $v_{\mathbf{pq}}$ equals the projection of the guidance vector field $\mathbf{V}$ onto the oriented edge $\overrightarrow{\mathbf{pq}} = \mathbf{q} - \mathbf{p}$:

$$v_{\mathbf{pq}} = \mathbf{V}\left(\frac{\mathbf{p}+\mathbf{q}}{2}\right) \cdot \overrightarrow{\mathbf{pq}} \tag{5.22}$$

The solution for this optimization problem satisfies the following simultaneous linear equations for all $i \in 1 : n$ and $\mathbf{p} \in \Omega_i$:

$$|\mathcal{N}_\mathbf{p}| f_i(\mathbf{p}) - \sum_{\mathbf{q} \in \mathcal{N}_\mathbf{p} \cap \Omega_i} f_i(\mathbf{q}) = \sum_{\mathbf{q} \in \mathcal{N}_\mathbf{p} \cap \partial\Omega_{i,j}} f_j(\mathbf{q}) + \sum_{\mathbf{q} \in \mathcal{N}_\mathbf{p}} v_{\mathbf{pq}} \tag{5.23}$$

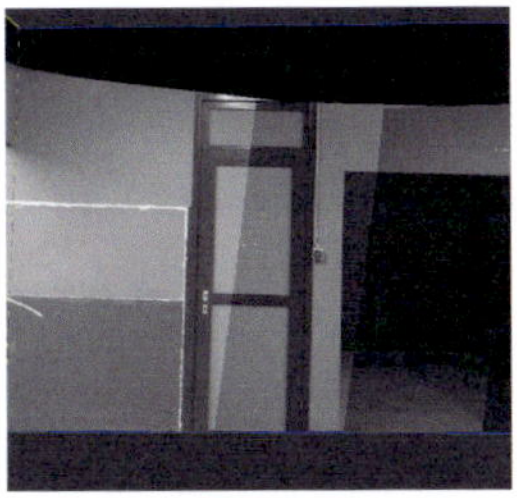

(a) Stitched textures.

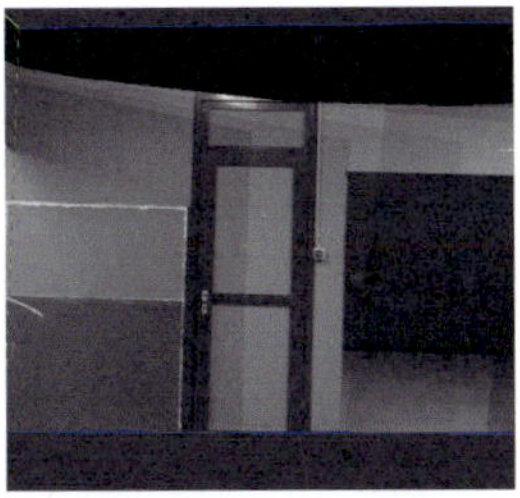

(b) Naïve blending.

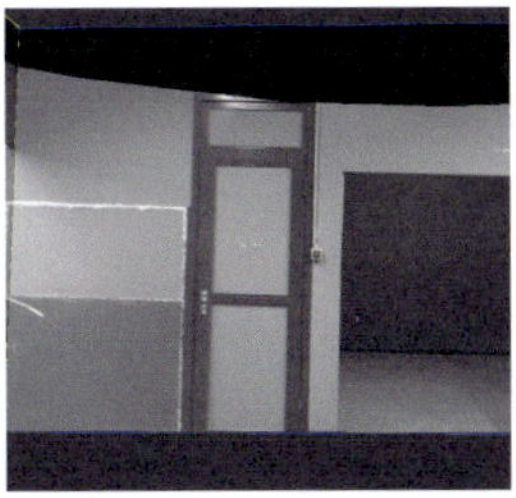

(c) Poisson blending.

(d) Texture panorama without blending.

(e) Texture panorama blended with poisson blending.

Figure 5.13: The texture blending globally optimizes the texture color and removes discontinuities at boundaries between texture regions reconstructed from different camera images. Compared to a naïve blending method, such as averaging, the proposed algorithm results in consistent texture maps without visible discontinuities.

This sparse, symmetric, positive-definite system can be solved using a sparse linear solver. We directly solve the system through LU decomposition with partial pivoting and forward/back substitution. For large $\mathcal{T}$, the size of the resulting system can easily reach an order of 10^6 and LU decomposition becomes intractable. In this case, a well-known iterative solver (e.g., Gauss-Seidel or Conjugate Gradient) can be used to achieve an approximate solution within a few iterations. Results of this blending approach are presented in Figure 5.13.

5.4 Conclusion

In this chapter, we described algorithms for the reconstruction of the surface appearance and, in particular, the reconstruction of a two-dimensional *diffuse texture*. The texture stores a constant BRDF for each surface point and is mapped onto the reconstructed 3D surface for visualization. This technique results in a very realistic reconstruction and reproduction of the surface appearance and greatly enhances the visual impression by adding more realism.

Our reconstruction approach consists of the following steps: surface partitioning (segmentation and slicing), surface unfolding, color reconstruction, and color blending. The surface partitioning is a pre-processing step used to slice a complex surface mesh in pieces with less complexity. This is necessary to permit an unfolding of each piece onto a plane. We presented an efficient split-and-merge approach which first segments the mesh into almost regions based on surface normal similarity followed by an iterative merging of mesh segments to avoid over segmentation. Empirically, we found that this procedure results in segments with low complexity. The unfolding step computes a mappping which maps the surface of each segment onto a corresponding texture. We presented an approach using a least-squares conformal mapping computed from the surface triangles. This mapping minimizes geometric distortions, which is very important as to avoid artifacts in the texture reconstruction. We demonstrated that this approach globally minimizes distortion over all surface triangles and clearly outperforms naïve orthogonal mappings. The texture domain is then discretized and the color reconstruction step retrieves a color for each texture pixel. This is done by finding the best camera images that carry information about the surface area corresponding to the texture pixel. This procedure results in one texture map per mesh segment composed of multiple camera images. This compositing may lead to visible discontinuity artifacts. Hence, we proposed a novel variational blending technique which globally adjusts the color of all pixels within one texture and eliminates compositing artifacts. This blending method enforces smooth transitions between texture regions reconstructed from different camera images and employs a vector guidance field constructed from the texture gradients to propagate those constraints throughout the texture.

In the quest for more realistic imagery, we can conclude that reconstruction of the surface appearance is a key component of the 3D modeling system. Reconstructing diffuse textures and mapping those onto the reconstructed surface mesh is a relatively efficient mean to create a realistic surface appearance. We presented a pipeline for a way of automatically reconstructing such texture maps from multiple camera images. For a visualization system it is typically true that realism demands complexity, or at least the appearance of complexity. We demonstrated that with diffuse texture maps, the appearance of complex 3D models can be achieved without actually modeling and rendering every 3D detail of a surface.

6 Results and Applications

6.1 Photo-Realistic Reconstruction of Indoor Environments

The 3D reconstruction and visualization of architectural scenes is an increasingly important research problem, with large scale efforts underway to recover models of cities at a global scale (e.g., Street View, Google Earth, Virtual Earth). The process of creating a realistic virtual model of an environment begins with modeling the geometry and surface attributes of objects in an environment along with any lights. An image of the environment is subsequently rendered from the vantage point of a virtual camera. Great effort has been expended to develop CAD systems that allow the specification of complex geometry and material attributes. Similarly, a great deal of work has been undertaken to produce systems that simulate the propagation of light through virtual environments to create realistic images. Unfortunately, current methods of modeling existing architecture, in which a modeling program is used to manually position the elements of the scene, have several drawbacks. First, the process is extremely labor-intensive, typically involving surveying the site, locating and digitizing architectural plans (if available), or converting existing CAD data (again, if available). Second, it is difficult to verify whether the resulting model is accurate. Most disappointing, though, is that the renderings of the resulting models are noticeably computer-generated; even those that employ liberal texture-mapping generally fail to resemble real photographs.

The system presented in this thesis can be used to effectively create photo-realisic reconstructions of large indoor environments. A number of experiments have been conducted using the described approach. In particular, we have created a 3D model of Bosch's office in Palo Alto. Snapshots of this model are depicted in Figure 6.1. The largest fraction of the time required for the complete 3D reconstruction process was spent on the data acquisition; 6 hours were necessary to scan one office floor by taking 127 scans (approx. 3 min per scan). Registration, surface and texture reconstruction took around 100 minutes for the Bosch dataset on a standard desktop computer (3.4 GHz, 4GB RAM). About 70% of this time was spend on IO operations on the 8GB of compressed raw data. The registration was performed on a sub-sampled dataset and took 20 minutes to converge. Projecting the registration results onto the high-resolution data yielded good results. Our volumetric

(a) Reconstructed 3D Model of Bosch's RTC.

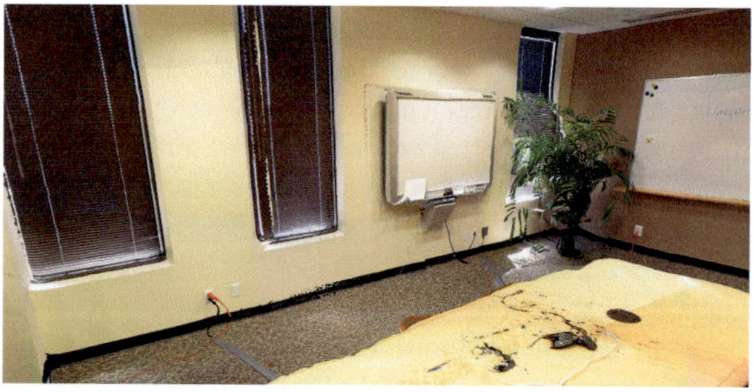

(b) A conference room rendered from a virtual camera.

(c) Kitchen.

Figure 6.1: Reconstruction of photo-realistic models from real indoor environments. The reconstructed office model presented here consists of 28,167,234 vertices and 54,745,336 triangles covering an area of 50 m by 140 m.

surface reconstruction approach found a highly detailed approximation of the real surface in approximately 65 minutes. Again, we employed a multi-grid scheme to speed up the reconstruction. Structures such as legs of chairs, as well as plants, due to fine leaf and branch structures turned out to be problematic. The reconstruction typically fused multiples of such structures into a single blob or merged them with a nearby wall. Improvements are certainly possible by scanning using a higher resolution, with the obvious drawback of increased memory requirements and extended acquisition and processing times. For the final step of model reconstruction, we found that the automatic texture reconstruction procedure resulted in high-quality texture maps in only 15 minutes for the Bosch dataset.

6.2 Rapid Inspection

Reconstructed 3D models are also directly applicable usable in inspection tasks. In many industrial applications, it is important to detect changes made in a given installation or track the progression of work in a new construction site. Typically, it is necessary to verify that the actual installation or construction complies with the design and that it continues to be correct over time. The size of installations, such as power plants and laboratories, as well as the complexity of their design and process, poses an enormous challenge when considering 100% verification before the facility comes into operation. Nowadays, inspectors prioritize equipment or randomize the inspection since an in-depth verification of everything is not feasible. In settings like nuclear power plants, the inspections continue over the lifetime of the facility. Being able to maintain a consistent knowledge of previously inspected areas and changes made over time is a critical issue for the safe operation of the facility.

Using technologies such as described in this thesis allow a rapid generation of accurate 3D models of large environments. This will help to make the inspection task easier and more accurate. Our system allows the creation of realistic "as built"[1] 3D models and and it can be used to detect and verify deviations from a reference model, such as a CAD design or a previously reconstructed and inspected model. In the first step, the reconstructed model is aligned to a reference model using the same techniques as described in Chapter 3. Subsequently, we can use geometric metrics (see Section 4.5) or visual metrics (see [Lindstrom and Turk, 2000]) to quantify the difference in both models. These differences can be displayed as color

[1]The phrase "as-built" in construction is equivalent to "as-is". 3D models deemed "as-built" are thus models that show the *existing* conditions as they are, or "as-is" – these are the actual existing conditions as opposed to designs or proposed conditions.

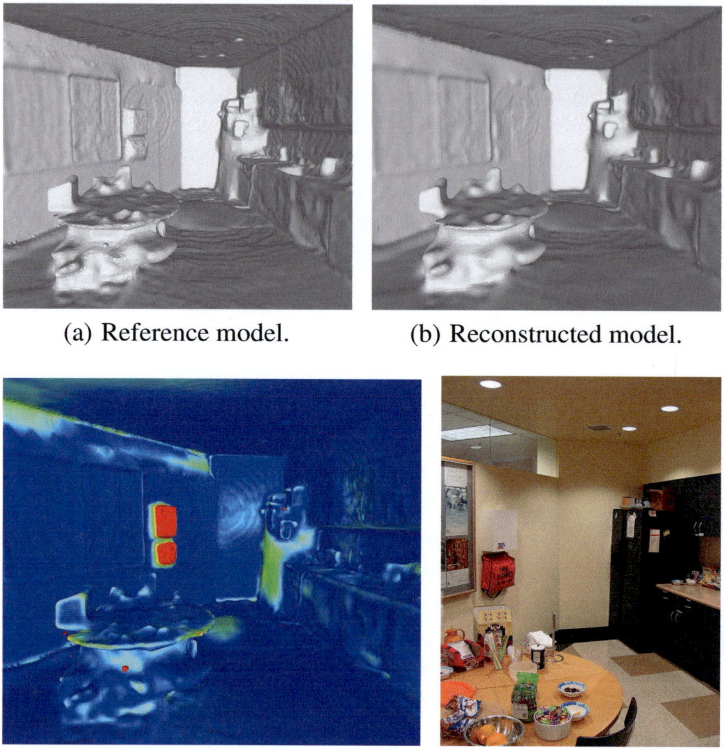

(a) Reference model. (b) Reconstructed model.

(c) Automatically detected deviations. (d) Picture of the scene.

Figure 6.2: Automatic model reconstruction can be used for inspection tasks. In this experiment, a reconstructed model is compared to a reference model by calculating Hausdorff distances [Cignoni et al., 1996] for each surface element. Pseudo coloring based gives an intuitive way of showing deviations between the models and highlights the removed first aid kit and fire blanket.

maps that give a visual indicator of the deviation between the reconstructed model and the reference model.

6.3 Model Reconstruction for Augmented Reality

Augmented Reality (AR) is the synthesis of real imagery and computer generated models. It can be used to give the user senses, which are not ordinarily available. Data from arbitrary sensors can be presented visually in a meaningful way, for example, in an industrial plant, the sensed temperature or flow rate in coolant pipes could be visually represented by color or motion, directly superimposed on a user's view of the plant. Besides visualizing real data, which is otherwise invisible, AR can be used to preview objects which do not exist, for example in architecture or design: Virtual furniture or fittings could be rearranged in a walk-through of a real building. The primary technical hurdle for AR is a robust and accurate registration between the real images and the virtual objects. Without accurate alignment, a convincing AR is impossible. The most promising approaches for accurate and robust registration use visual tracking [Klein and Murray, 2007, Davison et al., 2007]. Visual Tracking attempts to track the head pose by analyzing features detected in a video stream. Typically, a camera is mounted to the head-mounted display, and a computer calculates this camera's pose in relation to known features seen in the world. Unfortunately, real-time visual tracking is a very difficult problem. Extracting a pose from a video frame requires software to make correspondences between elements in the image and known 3D locations in the world, and establishing these correspondences in live video streams is challenging. The majority of current AR systems operate with prior knowledge of the user's environment. This could be CAD model or a sparse map of fiducials known to be present in the scene.

The 3D models generated by our system provide a comprehensive description of an environment since they contain detailed geometric and material information. A registration of an AR system could be performed directly from those models which allows for a camera-based AR tracking.

7 Summary and Conclusion

7.1 Summary

Data Acquisition In chapter 2 we presented solutions to the first step of every 3D reconstruction system: data acquisition. For 3D reconstruction of indoor environments, the data acquisition problem can be divided into three subproblems: *exploration, navigation, scanning*. We described, a 3D scanning robot that enables autonomous exploration and scanning of large environments. This hardware configuration was specifically designed to match our requirements for scanning indoor environments. It represents, however, a much larger group of scanning devices that combine distance sensors, such as laser range finders, stereo-cameras, etc., with imaging sensors, such as cameras. Further, we presented a novel calibration procedure to calculate the external calibratrion between camera and laser range finder using a planar calibration target. Lastly, we addressed the subproblem of exploration and presented an algorithm using active exploration which allows the robot to select optimal viewpoints for 3D scans. Regarding economic aspects, the data acquisition is probably the most important part of a 3D reconstruction system to automate. Labor cost is currently the dominating factor in current reconstruction approaches. The proposed robotic system and the method for exploration provide a framework for efficient data acquisition.

Multi-View Registration Chapter 3 was dedicated to solutions for the alignment of multiple scans into a common coordinate system. We presented a novel method for *multi-view registration* that directly uses information obtained from pairwise registration, yet distributes the registration error evenly over all views. Our approach resembles the concept of GraphSLAM by using the poses of the scanner as graph nodes and observations as graph edges. We optimize the graph by linearizing the compound operator and minimizing the resulting least squares energy function. We demonstrated that this method is capable of optimizing large datasets with hundreds of scans. Essentially, this method distributes the errors introduced by uncertain pose measurements over the entire graph. Systematic data acquisition errors and non-linear point cloud deformations are inherent in data acquired by real 3D scanners. Those errors are impossible to model in a rigid registration framework; however, they lead to artifacts that may drastically decrease the result of subsequent processing steps, such as surface reconstruction. To address this issue, we presented a novel approach for aligning scans in a probabilistic and non-rigid fashion. This approach incorporates spatial correlation models as map priors to guide the optimization towards a consistent registration. The key difference of this approach to traditional GraphSLAM approaches is that scans are aligned by adjusting robot poses as well as scan points. This non-rigid alignment is fundamentally different from ICP-style rigid alignment techniques where only robot poses are optimized. We demonstrated a practical algorithm that has been evaluated on synthetic data and on large real world datasets. A good alignment is very important for a 3D reconstruction application. Even small misalignments will cause the subsequent surface reconstruction to fail. So far, most effort in scan-based SLAM was spent on large scale environments while only little attention was put on the true accuracy of the resulting map. With our non-rigid alignment we showed that compared to other state-of-the-art techniques, we can improve the alignment for a variety of 2D and 3D datasets.

Surface Reconstruction In chapter 4 we were concerned with the problem of reconstructing a consistent 3D surface representation from aligned point clouds. We proposed a *volumetric surface reconstruction* method based on a Poisson framework with subsequent surface optimization. Our method estimates the surface description from a set of unorganized 3D input points by finding a zero iso-surface of an indicator function over 3D space. To find the indicator function, we adopted the method of [Kazhdan et al., 2006] which uses a Poisson system defined on the grid cells of an octree discretiztion generated from the input data points. There exists an integral relationship between the input points and this indicator function which allows using a Poisson system to efficiently solve for the indicator function on the octree grid. Our approach extended the Poisson framework to use locally supported bilateral filters to define the normal vector field. Finally, a triangle mesh is reconstructed by triangulating the indicator function's zero-set. We found that the resulting mesh approximates the true surface and its topological type well but results in an overly smooth surface representation due to discretization and the necessity for filtering the normal vector field. Therefore, we presented a novel method for optimizing the reconstructed mesh to improve reconstruction accuracy. This method moves the mesh vertices to achieve a better fit with the input data points while keeping the topology as suggested by the initial reconstruction. Using synthetic and real scan data, we demonstrated that this method significantly reduces reconstruction errors. The proposed surface reconstruction approach can handle very large input point clouds which occur when scanning large environments with many viewpoints. Our approach handles occlusions and depth discontinuities well since the the data of all viewpoints is integrated into a single representation before reconstruction. It is also robust to noise since the normal vector field is smoothed as part of the reconstruction.

Photo-Realistic Texture Reconstruction Chapter 5 was dedicated to the reconstruction of photo-realistic textures from multiple scans. We demonstrated that reconstructing and adding a texture to the surface model results in a drastically more realistic 3D model. We presented an algorithm for reconstructing a high-quality spatially varying diffuse texture using only a small number of images. Our reconstruction approach consists of the following steps: surface partitioning (segmentation and slicing), surface unfolding, color reconstruction, and color blending. This composition of multiple images into one texture is the most critical part in our texture reconstruction approach to generate realistic texture maps. Hence, we proposed a novel variational blending technique which globally adjusts the color of all pixels within one texture and eliminates compositing artifacts. Our blending method enforces smooth transitions between texture regions reconstructed from different camera images and employs a vector guidance field constructed from the texture gradients to propagate those constraints throughout the texture. By mapping the reconstructed textures onto the surface mesh our system is able to reconstruct visually realistic 3D models. When visualized, the textured models often suggest very fine geometric detail which is not represented in the acquired mesh. We showed that surface appearance reconstruction is a key component of the 3D modeling system to create photo-realistic 3D models.

7.2 Conclusion

The goal of this thesis was to address two fundamental problems preventing a broader adoption of 3D modeling techniques: 1) A lack of affordable 3D scanning devices that enable an easy acquisition of range data, and 2) algorithms capable of automatically processing range data into 3D models, in particular, algorithms for data registration, surface reconstruction, and texture reconstruction. The main contributions of this dissertation are: a systematic analysis of the 3D reconstruction problem; a complete system for an automatic creation of large scale 3D models, including a robotic data acquisition system that enables scanning large indoor environments in a short amount of time; a novel probabilistic algorithm for non-rigid registration of scans that incorporates surface prior distributions to optimize the alignment; an algorithm for the reconstruction and optimization of a consistent 3D surface representation from registered point clouds; and a novel method that blends multiple images into a photo-realistic texture composite. While the presented techniques extend the current state-of-the-art, a significant contribution of this research is a functional system that covers all steps required to automatically reconstruct textured 3D models of large indoor environments.

A common restriction made in 3D reconstruction systems is the assumption of a static environment. Our system obliges the same restriction. Although the registration is fairly robust to artifacts created by a limited amount of dynamic objects during the scan process, the methods presented for geometry and texture reconstruction will fail. More research is required to distinguish dynamic and static parts in a scene and to then consider only the latter for 3D modeling. The ultimate goal remains a system being able to operate autonomous in dynamic or even crowded environments for an indefinite amount of time.

A second direction worth more investigation lies in the application of photorealistic 3D models of indoor scenes. In this work, we mostly focused on methodologies enabling to efficiently create such models. However, we believe that once those methodologies are broadly available a variety of novel applications will also emerge. Chapter 6 highlighted a selection of those potential applications.

8 Appendix

8.1 Pose Vectors and Rigid Body Transforms

This section described the fundamental representations for the position and orientation of a rigid body in 3D Cartesian space.

8.1.1 Position

The position of a rigid body in 3D Cartesian space is described by a column vector of the coordinates *x*, *y*, *z*

$$\mathbf{p} := \begin{pmatrix} x \\ y \\ z \end{pmatrix} \tag{8.1}$$

A position vector is not only used to specify a 3D point, in this case it is typically denoted as $\mathbf{p}$, but also it is used to describe a 3D location, in which case it is denoted as $\mathbf{t}$.

8.1.2 Orientation

The most common way to represent the *orientation* or *attitude* of a rigid body is a set of three Euler angles. These are popular because they are easy to understand and easy to use. Euler angles are expressed as rotations

$$\mathbf{o} := \begin{pmatrix} \phi \\ \theta \\ \psi \end{pmatrix} \tag{8.2}$$

about three orthogonal axes, as shown in Figure 8.1. It can be shown that with a sequences of three consecutive rotations about the three orthogonal axes a rigid body can be moved into any orientation. In fact, of the 27 possible sequences of three rotations, there are only 12 that satisfy the constraint that no two consecutive rotations in a valid sequence may have the same axes. Borrowing aviation terminology, we use the sequence *roll*, *pitch*, and *yaw*. This means the first rotation is

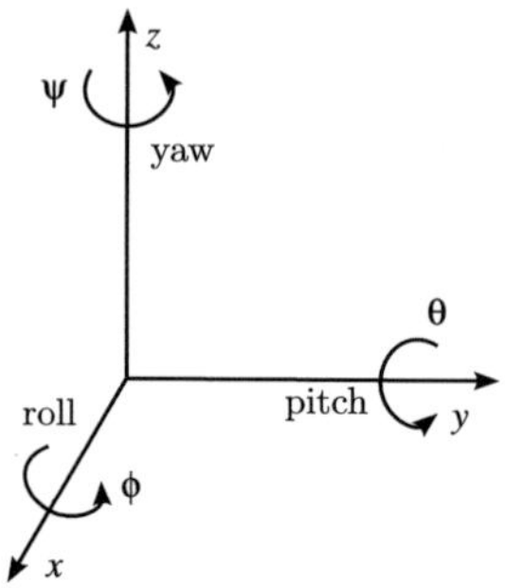

Figure 8.1: Any three-dimensional rotation can be described as a sequence of yaw, pitch, and roll rotations.

an angle ϕ about the x-axis, the second rotation is the angle θ about the y-axis, and the third rotation is the angle ψ about the z-axis.

Rotations about a single coordinate axis are called *coordinate rotations*. The coordinate rotations $\mathbf{R}_i : \mathbb{R} \rightarrow SO(3)$, for $i \in \{x, y, z\}$ are:

$$\mathbf{R}_x = \begin{pmatrix} 1 & 0 & 0 \\ 0 & \cos(\phi) & -\sin(\phi) \\ 0 & \sin(\phi) & \cos(\phi) \end{pmatrix} \tag{8.3}$$

$$\mathbf{R}_y = \begin{pmatrix} \cos(\theta) & 0 & \sin(\theta) \\ 0 & 1 & 0 \\ -\sin(\theta) & 0 & \cos(\theta) \end{pmatrix} \tag{8.4}$$

$$\mathbf{R}_z = \begin{pmatrix} \cos(\psi) & -\sin(\psi) & 0 \\ \sin(\psi) & \cos(\psi) & 0 \\ 0 & 0 & 1 \end{pmatrix} \tag{8.5}$$

Here $\mathbf{R}_i$ denotes a rotation matrix whose multiplication with a vector rotates the vector while preserving its length. The so called *special orthogonal group* of all 3×3 rotation matrices is denoted by

$$SO(3) = \{\mathbf{R} \mid \mathbf{R} \in \mathbb{R}^{3\times3},\ \mathbf{R}^\mathsf{T}\mathbf{R} = \mathbf{R}\mathbf{R}^\mathsf{T} = \mathbf{I}\} \ . \tag{8.6}$$

Thus, if $\mathbf{R} \in SO(3)$, then

$$\det(\mathbf{R}) = \pm 1 \text{ and } \mathbf{R}^{-1} = \mathbf{R}^\mathsf{T} \ . \tag{8.7}$$

A matrix representing the end result of all three rotations is formed by successive multiplication of the matrices representing the three axis rotations, as in the correct order

$$\mathbf{R} = \mathbf{R}_z \mathbf{R}_y \mathbf{R}_x = \begin{pmatrix} c_\psi c_\theta & c_\psi s_\theta s_\phi - s_\psi c_\phi & c_\psi s_\theta c_\phi + s_\psi s_\phi \\ s_\psi c_\theta & s_\psi s_\theta s_\phi + c_\psi c_\phi & s_\psi s_\theta c_\phi - c_\psi s_\phi \\ -s_\theta & c_\theta s_\phi & c_\theta c_\phi \end{pmatrix} \tag{8.8}$$

where $c_x := \cos(x)$ and $s_x := \sin(x)$. We define the rotation matrix that encodes the orientation of a rigid body to be the matrix that when pre-multiplied by a vector expressed in the body fixed coordinates yields the same vector expressed in the worked coordinates. The set of all proper rotation matrices is called the *group of rotations* in three dimensions.

8.1.3 Rigid Body Pose

The *pose* of a rigid body is the position and attitude of that body. It is defined as six dimensional vector

$$\mathbf{x}_F = \begin{pmatrix} x \\ y \\ z \\ \phi \\ \theta \\ \psi \end{pmatrix} \tag{8.9}$$

consisting of a three Cartesian coordinates and the orientation expressed as the rotations about the three coordinate axes relative to the coordinate system *F*. The order of rotations is: roll ϕ, pitch θ, yaw ψ.

8.1.4 Rigid Body Transforms

The displacement of a rigid body can be described via a *homogeneous transformation matrix*:

$$\mathbf{T} := \begin{pmatrix} t_{1,1} & t_{1,2} & t_{1,3} & t_{1,4} \\ t_{2,1} & t_{2,2} & t_{2,3} & t_{2,4} \\ t_{3,1} & t_{3,2} & t_{3,3} & t_{3,4} \\ 0 & 0 & 0 & 1 \end{pmatrix}$$

$$= \begin{pmatrix} c_\psi c_\theta & c_\psi s_\theta s_\phi - s_\psi c_\phi & c_\psi s_\theta c_\phi + s_\psi s_\phi & t_x \\ s_\psi c_\theta & s_\psi s_\theta s_\phi + c_\psi c_\phi & s_\psi s_\theta c_\phi - c_\psi s_\phi & t_y \\ -s_\theta & c_\theta s_\phi & c_\theta c_\phi & t_z \\ 0 & 0 & 0 & 1 \end{pmatrix}$$

$$= \begin{pmatrix} \mathbf{R} & \mathbf{t} \\ & 1 \end{pmatrix} \tag{8.10}$$

The 4×4 matrix $\mathbf{T}$ represents a rotation given by ϕ, θ, and ψ followed by a translation given by t_x, t_y, and t_z. The set of all displacements or the set of all such matrices with the composition rule above, is called $SE(3)$, the *special Euclidean group* of rigid body displacements in three-dimensions:

$$SE(3) = \left\{ \mathbf{T} \mid \mathbf{T} = \begin{pmatrix} \mathbf{R} & \mathbf{t} \\ & 1 \end{pmatrix}, \ \mathbf{R} \in SO(3), \ \mathbf{t} \in \mathbb{R}^3 \right\} \tag{8.11}$$

The homogeneous transformation matrix is a convenient representation of the combined transformations; therefore, it is frequently used in robotics, mechanics, computer graphics, and elsewhere.

For every rigid body pose a function which maps between coordinates defined in the rigid body frame and a global coordinate frame exists. The function

$$f_{\mathbf{x_W}}(\mathbf{p}) = \begin{pmatrix} c_\psi c_\theta & c_\psi s_\theta s_\phi - s_\psi c_\phi & c_\psi s_\theta c_\phi + s_\psi s_\phi \\ s_\psi c_\theta & s_\psi s_\theta s_\phi + c_\psi c_\phi & s_\psi s_\theta c_\phi - c_\psi s_\phi \\ -s_\theta & c_\theta s_\phi & c_\theta c_\phi \end{pmatrix} \mathbf{p} + \begin{pmatrix} x \\ y \\ z \end{pmatrix} \tag{8.12}$$

$$= \mathbf{R}\mathbf{p} + \mathbf{t} \tag{8.13}$$

maps 3D points $\mathbf{p}$ from the local coordinate frame of rigid body to global coordinates. $f_{\mathbf{x}_W}(\mathbf{p})$ is equal to applying the rigid body transform defined by the parameters of the rigid body pose to the 3D point. Thus, we can define a function which converts from a rigid body pose $\mathbf{x_W}$ to a homogenous transform matrix $\mathbf{T}$

$$T(\mathbf{x_W}) = \begin{pmatrix} c_\psi c_\theta & c_\psi s_\theta s_\phi - s_\psi c_\phi & c_\psi s_\theta c_\phi + s_\psi s_\phi & x \\ s_\psi c_\theta & s_\psi s_\theta s_\phi + c_\psi c_\phi & s_\psi s_\theta c_\phi - c_\psi s_\phi & y \\ -s_\theta & c_\theta s_\phi & c_\theta c_\phi & z \\ 0 & 0 & 0 & 1 \end{pmatrix} \tag{8.14}$$

The back conversion from a homogeneous matrix $\mathbf{T}$ to a rigid body pose $\mathbf{x}_W$ is given by:

$$x(\mathbf{T}) = \begin{pmatrix} x \\ y \\ z \\ \phi \\ \theta \\ \psi \end{pmatrix} \tag{8.15}$$

with

$$x = t_{1,4} \tag{8.16}$$
$$y = t_{2,4} \tag{8.17}$$
$$z = t_{3,4} \tag{8.18}$$
$$\phi = \operatorname{atan2}(t_{2,1}, t_{1,1}) \tag{8.19}$$
$$\theta = \operatorname{atan2}(-t_{3,1}, \cos(\phi)\, t_{1,1} + \sin(\phi)\, t_{2,1}) \tag{8.20}$$
$$\psi = \operatorname{atan2}(\sin(\phi)\, t_{1,3} - \cos(\phi)\, t_{2,3}, -\sin(\phi)\, t_{1,2} + \cos(\phi)\, t_{2,2}) \tag{8.21}$$

Here, the function atan2 is a special kind of inverse tangent that takes the quadrant into account

$$\operatorname{atan2}(y, x) = \begin{cases} \arctan(\frac{y}{x}) & x > 0 \\ \pi + \arctan(\frac{y}{x}) & y \geq 0, x < 0 \\ -\pi + \arctan(\frac{y}{x}) & y < 0, x < 0 \\ \frac{\pi}{2} & y > 0, x = 0 \\ -\frac{\pi}{2} & y < 0, x = 0 \\ \text{undefined} & y = 0, x = 0 \end{cases} . \tag{8.22}$$

For arguments x and y not both equal to zero, the value returned by atan2 is the angle in radians between the positive x-axis of a plane and the point given by the coordinates (x, y) on it.

8.2 Pose Operations in 3D

8.2.1 The Pose Compounding Operations in 3D

Mainly two operations are required to transform a rigid body in 3D space: The positive compounding operation denoted by $\oplus$ and the inversion denoted by $\ominus$. Those operations are similar to the pose compounding operation in 2D space defined in [Smith and Cheeseman, 1987] and [Brooks, 1987]. Let $\mathbf{x}_A$ and $\mathbf{x}_B$ be two rigid body pose defined in a global coordinate frame and $\mathbf{x}_{A,B}$ the relative displacement between the poses. The compounding operation is given by:

$$\mathbf{x}_B = \mathbf{x}_A \oplus \mathbf{x}_{A,B} \tag{8.23}$$
$$= x\Big(T(\mathbf{x}_A)\, T(\mathbf{x}_{A,B})\Big) . \tag{8.24}$$

The inversion of this operation is given by:

$$\mathbf{x}_{A,B} = \mathbf{x}_B \ominus \mathbf{x}_A \tag{8.25}$$
$$= x\Big(T\left(\mathbf{x}_A\right)^{-1} T\left(\mathbf{x}_B\right)\Big) \tag{8.26}$$

and one can also verify the reverse relative pose is given by:

$$\mathbf{x}_{B,A} = \begin{pmatrix}0 & 0 & 0 & 0 & 0 & 0\end{pmatrix}^{\mathsf{T}} \ominus \mathbf{x}_{A,B} \tag{8.27}$$
$$= \ominus \mathbf{x}_{A,B} \tag{8.28}$$

When for example a robot moves from pose $\mathbf{x}_t$ to the pose $\mathbf{x}_{t+1}$ and the transition is defined by an odometry reading $\mathbf{x}_{t+1,t}$, the new pose of the robot w.r.t. the world reference is given by $\mathbf{x}_{t+1} = \mathbf{x}_t \oplus \mathbf{x}_{t+1,t}$. Note, that the compounding operation is not commutative, but associative. This means, we can define the compounding of a series of poses.

8.2.2 Jacobian of the Pose Compounding Operation

The Jacobians of the positive compounding operation $\mathbf{x}_C = \mathbf{x}_A \oplus \mathbf{x}_B$ are given by

$$\mathbf{J}_{A\oplus}\left\{\mathbf{x}_A, \mathbf{x}_B\right\} = \frac{\partial\left(\mathbf{x}_A \oplus \mathbf{x}_B\right)}{\partial \mathbf{x}_A} \tag{8.29}$$
$$\mathbf{J}_{B\oplus}\left\{\mathbf{x}_A, \mathbf{x}_B\right\} = \frac{\partial\left(\mathbf{x}_A \oplus \mathbf{x}_B\right)}{\partial \mathbf{x}_B}\ . \tag{8.30}$$

Their values can be calculated by

$$\mathbf{J}_{A\oplus} = \begin{pmatrix}\mathbf{I}_3 & \mathbf{M} \\ & \mathbf{K_1}\end{pmatrix} \qquad \text{and} \qquad \mathbf{J}_{B\oplus} = \begin{pmatrix}\mathbf{R_A} & \\ & \mathbf{K_2}\end{pmatrix} \tag{8.31}$$

with

$$\mathbf{M} = \begin{pmatrix} -(y_C - y_A) & (z_C - z_A)c_{\phi_A} & t^A_{1,3}y_B - t^A_{1,2}z_B \\ x_C - x_A & (z_C - z_A)s_{\phi_A} & t^A_{2,3}y_B - t^A_{2,2}z_B \\ 0 & -x_B c_{\theta_A} - y_B s_{\theta_A} s_{\psi_A} - z_B s_{\theta_A} s_{\psi_A} & t^A_{3,3}y_B - t^A_{3,2}z_B \end{pmatrix}$$

$$\mathbf{K}_1 = \begin{pmatrix} 1 & [s_{\theta_C} s_{(\phi_C - \phi_A)}]/c_{\theta_C} & [t^B_{1,2}s_{\psi_3} + t^B_{1,3}c_{\psi_C}]/c_{\theta_C} \\ 0 & c_{(\phi_C - \phi_A)} & -c_{\theta_A} s_{(\phi_C - \phi_A)} \\ 0 & [s_{(\phi_C - \phi_A)}]/c_{\theta_C} & [c_{\theta_A} c_{(\phi_C - \phi_A)}]/c_{\theta_C} \end{pmatrix}$$

$$\mathbf{K}_2 = \begin{pmatrix} [c_{\theta_B} c_{(\psi_C - \psi_B)}]/c_{\theta_C} & s_{(\psi_C - \psi_B)} & 0 \\ -c_{\theta_B} s_{(\psi_C - \psi_B)} & c_{(\psi_C - \psi_B)} & 0 \\ [t^A_{1,3}c_{\phi_C} + t^A_{2,3}s_{\phi_C}]/c_{\theta_C} & [s_{\theta_C} s_{(\psi_C - \psi_B)}]/c_{\theta_C} & 1 \end{pmatrix}$$

$$\mathbf{R}_A = \begin{pmatrix} c_{\psi_A}c_{\theta_A} & c_{\psi_A}s_{\theta_A}s_{\phi_A} - s_{\psi_A}c_{\phi_A} & c_{\psi_A}s_{\theta_A}c_{\phi_A} + s_{\psi_A}s_{\phi_A} \\ s_{\psi_A}c_{\theta_A} & s_{\psi_A}s_{\theta_A}s_{\phi_A} + c_{\psi_A}c_{\phi_A} & s_{\psi_A}s_{\theta_A}c_{\phi_A} - c_{\psi_A}s_{\phi_A} \\ -s_{\theta_A} & c_{\theta_A}s_{\phi_A} & c_{\theta_A}c_{\phi_A} \end{pmatrix}$$

Note that x_A, y_A, etc., are elements of the rigid body pose vector $\mathbf{x}_A$ and $t^A_{i,j}$ are elements of the corresponding homogeneous transform matrix according to Equation 8.10.

8.2.3 Jacobian of the Inverse Pose Compounding Operation

The Jacobian of the inverse compound operation $\mathbf{x}_B = \ominus\mathbf{x}_A$ is given by

$$\mathbf{J}_{\ominus}\{\mathbf{x}_A\} = \frac{\partial(\ominus\mathbf{x}_A)}{\partial\mathbf{x}_A} \tag{8.32}$$

$$= \begin{pmatrix} -\mathbf{R_A}^{\mathsf{T}} & \mathbf{N} \\ & \mathbf{Q} \end{pmatrix} \tag{8.33}$$

with

$$\mathbf{N} = \begin{pmatrix} t^A_{2,1}x - t^A_{1,1}y & -t^A_{3,1}xc_\phi - t^A_{3,1}ys_\phi & 0 \\ t^A_{2,2}x - t^A_{1,2}y & -t^A_{3,2}xc_\phi - t^A_{3,2}ys_\phi + zs_\theta s_\psi & z_B \\ t^A_{2,3}x - t^A_{1,3}y & -t^A_{3,3}xc_\phi - t^A_{3,3}ys_\phi + zs_\theta c_\psi & -y_B \end{pmatrix}$$

$$\mathbf{Q} = \begin{pmatrix} -t^A_{3,3}/(1-(t^A_{1,3})^2) & -t^A_{2,3}c_\phi/(1-(t^A_{1,3})^2) & t^A_{1,1}t^A_{1,3}/(1-(t^A_{1,3})^2) \\ t^A_{2,3}/\sqrt{(1-(t^A_{1,3})^2)} & -t^A_{3,3}c_\phi/\sqrt{(1-(t^A_{1,3})^2)} & t^A_{1,2}/\sqrt{(1-(t^A_{1,3})^2)} \\ t^A_{3,3}t^A_{1,3}/(1-(t^A_{1,3})^2) & -t^A_{1,2}c_\psi/(1-(t^A_{1,3})^2) & -t^A_{1,1}/(1-(t^A_{1,3})^2) \end{pmatrix}$$

8.3 Linear Algebra

8.3.1 Solving Linear Systems

Assume we have to solve the following system of linear equations:

$$\mathbf{A}\mathbf{x} = \mathbf{b} \, , \tag{8.34}$$

where is an $\mathbf{x}$ is an unknown vector, $\mathbf{b}$ is a known vector, and $\mathbf{A}$ is a known, square matrix. There are many algorithms available for solving Equation 8.34, e.g.,

Gaussian Elimination

The standard algorithm for solving a system of linear equations is based on Gaussian Elimination. The process of Gaussian elimination has two parts. The first part (Forward Elimination) reduces a given system to either triangular form. This is accomplished through the use of elementary row operations. If this results in a degenerate equation it means the system has no solution. The second step uses back substitution to find the solution of the system.

LU Decomposition

The matrix $\mathbf{A}$ is decomposed into a lower triangular matrix and an upper triangular matrix such that

$$\mathbf{A}\mathbf{x} = \mathbf{L}\mathbf{U}\mathbf{x} = \mathbf{b} \, . \tag{8.35}$$

The solution $\mathbf{x}$ is now done in two logical steps: First, solving the equation $\mathbf{L}\mathbf{y} = \mathbf{b}$ for $\mathbf{y}$, and second, solving the equation $\mathbf{U}\mathbf{x} = \mathbf{y}$ for $\mathbf{x}$. Note that in both cases we have triangular matrices (lower and upper) which can be solved directly using forward and backward substitution without using the Gaussian elimination process. Thus the LU decomposition is computationally efficient only when we have to solve a matrix equation multiple times for different $\mathbf{b}$; it is faster in this case to do an LU decomposition of the matrix $\mathbf{A}$ once and then solve the triangular matrices for the different $\mathbf{b}$, than to use Gaussian elimination each time.

Cholesky Decomposition

If the matrix A has some special structure, this can be exploited to obtain faster or more accurate algorithms. For instance, systems with a symmetric positive definite matrix can be solved twice as fast with the Cholesky decomposition. Here, $\mathbf{A}$ is decomposed such that

$$\mathbf{A}\mathbf{x} = \mathbf{L}\mathbf{L}^{\mathsf{T}}\mathbf{x} = \mathbf{b}\ , \tag{8.36}$$

where $\mathbf{L}$ is a lower triangular matrix with strictly positive diagonal entries, then solving $\mathbf{L}\mathbf{y} = \mathbf{b}$ for $\mathbf{y}$, and second, solving the equation $\mathbf{L}^{\mathsf{T}}\mathbf{x} = \mathbf{y}$ for $\mathbf{x}$. When it is applicable, the Cholesky decomposition is roughly twice as efficient as the LU decomposition for solving systems of linear equations [Trefethen and Bau, 1997].

8.3.2 Linear Least Squares

The method of least squares is a standard approach to the approximate solution of overdetermined systems, i.e., sets of equations in which there are more equations than unknowns. "Least squares" means that the overall solution minimizes the sum of the squares of the errors made in solving every single equation. A common problem is to find the solution of the least square problem

$$\min_{\mathbf{x}} \|\mathbf{A}\mathbf{x} - \mathbf{b}\|^2\ . \tag{8.37}$$

A solution can be found by setting the partial derivatives of Equation 8.37 to zero:

$$\mathbf{A}^{\mathsf{T}}\mathbf{A}\mathbf{x} = \mathbf{A}^{\mathsf{T}}\mathbf{b}\ . \tag{8.38}$$

If $\mathbf{A}$ is square and nonsingular, the solution to Equation 8.38 is the solution to $\mathbf{A}\mathbf{x} = \mathbf{b}$ and the methods described above can be applied to solve for $\mathbf{x}$. If is not square than $\mathbf{A}\mathbf{x} = \mathbf{b}$ is overconstrained which means it has more linearly independent equations than variables. In this case there may or may not be a solution to $\mathbf{A}\mathbf{x} = \mathbf{b}$ but it is always possible to find a value of that minimizes Equation 8.37. In situation where $\mathbf{A}$ is not symmetric, not positive-definite, and even not square, the method of Conjugate Gradients [Shewchuk, 1994] can be used to find the minimum.

Bibliography

[Allen et al., 2001] Allen, P., Stamos, I., Gueorguiev, A., Gold, E., and Blaer, P. (2001). AVENUE: Automated site modeling in urban environments. In *Proceedings of 3rd Conference on Digital Imaging and Modeling*, pages 357–364, Quebec City, Canada.

[Alliez et al., 2002] Alliez, P., Meyer, M., and Desbrun, M. (2002). Interactive geometry remeshing. *ACM Trans. Graph.*, 21(3):347–354.

[Alvarado, 2004] Alvarado, J. P. (2004). *Segmentation of color images for interactive object retrieval.* PhD thesis, RWTH Aachen University.

[Amenta et al., 2001] Amenta, N., Choi, S., and Kolluri, R. K. (2001). The power crust. In *Proceedings of the sixth ACM symposium on Solid modeling and applications*, pages 249–266, New York, NY, USA. ACM.

[Arfken, 1985] Arfken, G. (1985). *Mathematical Methods for Physicists*, chapter Spherical Polar Coordinates, pages 102–111. Academic Press.

[Aurich and Weule, 1995] Aurich, V. and Weule, J. (1995). Non-linear Gaussian filters performing edge preserving diffusion. In *Mustererkennung 1995, 17. DAGM-Symposium*, pages 538–545, London, UK. Springer-Verlag.

[Bailey and Durrant-Whyte, 2006a] Bailey, T. and Durrant-Whyte, H. (2006a). Simultaneous localisation and mapping (SLAM): Part i - state of the art. *Robotics and Automation Magazine*, 13(2):99–110.

[Bailey and Durrant-Whyte, 2006b] Bailey, T. and Durrant-Whyte, H. (2006b). Simultaneous localisation and mapping (SLAM): Part ii - state of the art. *Robotics and Automation Magazine*, 13(3):108–117.

[Benet et al., 2002] Benet, G., Blanes, F., Simó, J. E., and Pérez, P. (2002). Using infrared sensors for distance measurement in mobile robots. *Robotics and Autonomous Systems*, 40(4):255–266.

[Bengtsson and Baerveldt, 2003] Bengtsson, O. and Baerveldt, A.-J. (2003). Robot localization based on scan-matching - estimating the covariance matrix for the IDC algorithm. *Robotics and Autonomous Systems*, 44(1):29–40.

[Bernardini et al., 2001] Bernardini, F., Martin, I. M., and Rushmeier, H. (2001). High-quality texture reconstruction from multiple scans. *IEEE Transactions on Visualization and Computer Graphics*, 7(4):318–332.

[Besl and McKay, 1992] Besl, P. J. and McKay, N. D. (1992). A method for registration of 3D shapes. *IEEE Transactions on Pattern Analysis and Machine Intelligence (TPAMI)*, 14(2):239–256.

[Biber et al., 2006] Biber, P., Fleck, S., and Strasser, W. (2006). The Wägele: A mobile platform for acquisition of 3D models of indoor outdoor environments. In *9th Tübingen Perception Conference (TWK 2006)*.

[Blinn, 1977] Blinn, J. F. (1977). Models of light reflection for computer synthesized pictures. In *Proceedings of the 4th Annual Conference on Computer Graphics and Interactive Techniques (SIGGRAPH)*, pages 192–198, New York, NY, USA. ACM.

[Blinn, 1978a] Blinn, J. F. (1978a). *Computer display of curved surfaces*. PhD thesis, The University of Utah.

[Blinn, 1978b] Blinn, J. F. (1978b). Simulation of wrinkled surfaces. *SIGGRAPH Computer Graphics*, 12(3):286–292.

[Böhler et al., 2003] Böhler, W., Bordas Vincent, M., and Marbs, A. (2003). Investigating laser scanner accuracy. In *Proceedings of the XIXth CIPA International Symposium*, pages 696–702, Antalya, Turkey.

[Bohren et al., 2008] Bohren, J., Foote, T., Keller, J., Kushleyev, A., Lee, D. D., Stewart, A., Vernaza, P., Derenick, J. C., Spletzer, J. R., and Satterfield, B. (2008). Little Ben: The Ben Franklin Racing Team's entry in the 2007 DARPA Urban Challenge. *Journal of Field Robotics*, 25(9):598–614.

[Boissonnat, 1984] Boissonnat, J.-D. (1984). Geometric structures for three-dimensional shape representation. *ACM Transactions on Graphics*, 3(4):266–286.

[Bolitho et al., 2007] Bolitho, M., Kazhdan, M., Burns, R., and Hoppe, H. (2007). Multilevel streaming for out-of-core surface reconstruction. In *Proceedings of the 5th Eurographics Symposium on Geometry processing (SGP)*, pages 69–78, Aire-la-Ville, Switzerland, Switzerland. Eurographics Association.

[Bonin-Font et al., 2008] Bonin-Font, F., Ortiz, A., and Oliver, G. (2008). Visual navigation for mobile robots: A survey. *J. Intell. Robotics Syst.*, 53:263–296.

[Borrmann et al., 2008] Borrmann, D., Elseberg, J., Lingemann, K., Nüchter, A., and Hertzberg, J. (2008). The efficient extension of globally consistent scan matching to 6 DoF. In *Proceedings of the 4th International Symposium on 3D Data Processing, Visualization and Transmission (3DPVT)*, pages 29–36.

[Bosse et al., 2003] Bosse, M., Newman, P. M., Leonard, J. J., Soika, M., Feiten, W., and Teller, S. J. (2003). An atlas framework for scalable mapping. In *Proceedings of the IEEE International Conference on Robotics and Automation (ICRA)*, pages 1899–1906, Taipei, Taiwan.

[Brooks, 1987] Brooks, R. A. (1987). *Visual map making for a mobile robot.* Morgan Kaufmann Publishers Inc., San Francisco, CA, USA.

[Carey and Greenberg, 1985] Carey, R. J. and Greenberg, D. P. (1985). Textures for realistic image synthesis. *Computers & Graphics*, 9(2):125 – 138.

[Carr et al., 2001] Carr, J. C., Beatson, R. K., Cherrie, J. B., Mitchell, T. J., Fright, W. R., McCallum, B. C., and Evans, T. R. (2001). Reconstruction and representation of 3D objects with radial basis functions. In *Proceedings of the 28th annual Conference on Computer Graphics and Interactive Techniques (SIGGRAPH)*, pages 67–76, New York, NY, USA. ACM.

[Catmull, 1974] Catmull, E. E. (1974). *A subdivision algorithm for computer display of curved surfaces.* PhD thesis, The University of Utah.

[Chen and Medioni, 1992] Chen, Y. and Medioni, G. (1992). Object modelling by registration of multiple range images. *Image Vision Computation*, 10(3):145–155.

[Chen and Medioni, 1995] Chen, Y. and Medioni, G. (1995). Description of complex objects from multiple range images using an inflating balloon model. *Computer Vision and Image Understanding*, 61(3):325–334.

[Cignoni et al., 1996] Cignoni, P., Rocchini, C., and Scopigno, R. (1996). Metro: measuring error on simplified surfaces. Technical report, Paris, France, France.

[Cohen-Steiner et al., 2004] Cohen-Steiner, D., Alliez, P., and Desbrun, M. (2004). Variational shape approximation. *ACM Transactions on Graphics (TOG)*, 23(3):905–914.

[Coxeter, 1969] Coxeter, H. S. M. (1969). *Introduction to Geometry*, chapter Barycentric Coordinates, pages 216–221. Wiley, New York.

[Curless, 1997] Curless, B. (1997). *New Methods for Surface Reconstruction from Range Images*. PhD thesis, Stanford University.

[Curless and Levoy, 1996] Curless, B. and Levoy, M. (1996). A volumetric method for building complex models from range images. In *Proceedings of the 23rd annual conference on Computer Graphics and Interactive Techniques (SIGGRAPH)*, pages 303–312, New York, NY, USA. ACM.

[Dang et al., 2009] Dang, T., Hoffmann, C., and Stiller, C. (2009). Continuous stereo self-calibration by camera parameter tracking. *IEEE Transactions on Image Processing*, 18(7):1536–1550.

[Davis et al., 2002] Davis, J., Marschner, S. R., Garr, M., and Levoy, M. (2002). Filling holes in complex surfaces using volumetric diffusion. *First International Symposium on 3D Data Processing Visualization and Transmission (3DPVT)*, 00:428.

[Davison et al., 2007] Davison, A. J., Reid, I. D., Molton, N. D., and Stasse, O. (2007). MonoSLAM: Real-time single camera SLAM. *IEEE Transactions on Pattern Analysis and Machine Intelligence*, 26(6):1052–1067.

[Debevec et al., 2000] Debevec, P., Hawkins, T., Tchou, C., Duiker, H.-P., Sarokin, W., and Sagar, M. (2000). Acquiring the reflectance field of a human face. In *Proceedings of the 27th annual conference on Computer graphics and interactive techniques (SIGGRAPH)*, pages 145–156, New York, NY, USA. ACM Press/Addison-Wesley Publishing Co.

[Deumlich and Staiger, 2002] Deumlich, F. and Staiger, R. (2002). *Instrumentenkunde der Vermessungstechnik*. Wichmann Herbert.

[Diebel et al., 2006] Diebel, J., Thrun, S., and Bruenig, M. (2006). A Bayesian method for probable surface reconstruction and decimation. *ACM Transactions on Graphics (TOG)*, 25(1):39–59.

[Dissanayake et al., 2001] Dissanayake, M., Newman, P., Clark, S., Durrant-Whyte, H., and Csorba, M. (2001). A solution to the simultaneous localization and map building (SLAM) problem. *IEEE Transactions on Robotics and Automation*, 17(3):229–241.

[do Carmo, 1976] do Carmo, M. P. (1976). *Differential Geometry of Curves and Surfaces*. Prentice Hall, Upper Saddle River, New Jersey 07458.

[Duckett et al., 2002] Duckett, T., Marsland, S. R., and Shapiro, J. L. (2002). Fast, on-line learning of globally consistent maps. *Autonomous Robots*, 12(3):287–300.

[Eck et al., 1995] Eck, M., DeRose, T., Duchamp, T., Hoppe, H., Lounsbery, M., and Stuetzle, W. (1995). Multiresolution analysis of arbitrary meshes. In *Proceedings of the 22nd annual conference on Computer graphics and interactive techniques*, SIGGRAPH '95, pages 173–182, New York, NY, USA. ACM.

[Eggert et al., 1997] Eggert, D. W., Lorusso, A., and Fisher, R. B. (1997). Estimating 3D rigid body transformations: a comparison of four major algorithms. *Machine Vision Applications*, 9(5-6):272–290.

[Elfes, 1989] Elfes, A. (1989). Using occupancy grids for mobile robot perception and navigation. *Computer*, 22(6):46–57.

[Eliazar and Parr, 2004] Eliazar, A. I. and Parr, R. (2004). Learning probabilistic motion models for mobile robots. In *Proceedings of the 21st International Conference on Machine Learning*, page 32, New York, NY, USA. ACM.

[Fernandez-Madrigal and Gonzalez, 2002] Fernandez-Madrigal, J.-A. and Gonzalez, J. (2002). Multihierarchical graph search. *IEEE Transactions on Pattern Analysis and Machine Intelligence*, 24(1):103–113.

[Floater and Hormann, 2005] Floater, M. S. and Hormann, K. (2005). Surface parameterization: a tutorial and survey. In Dodgson, N. A., Floater, M. S., and Sabin, M. A., editors, *Advances in Multiresolution for Geometric Modelling*, Mathematics and Visualization, pages 157–186. Springer, Berlin, Heidelberg.

[Frese and Duckett, 2003] Frese, U. and Duckett, T. (2003). A multigrid approach for accelerating relaxation-based SLAM. In *Proceedings of the IJCAI Workshop on Reasoning with Uncertainty in Robotics*, pages 39–46, Acapulco, Mexico.

[Früh and Zakhor, 2003] Früh, C. and Zakhor, A. (2003). Constructing 3D city models by merging aerial and ground views. *IEEE Computer Graphics and Applications*, 23(6):52–61.

[Furukawa et al., 2009] Furukawa, Y., Curless, B., Seitz, S. M., and Szeliski, R. (2009). Reconstructing building interiors from images. In *Proceedings of the International Conference on Computer Vision (ICCV)*.

[Gardner, 1985] Gardner, G. Y. (1985). Visual simulation of clouds. *Computer Graphics (SIGGRAPH)*, 19(3):297–304.

[Garg et al., 2006] Garg, G., Talvala, E.-V., Levoy, M., and Lensch, H. P. A. (2006). Symmetric photography: Exploiting data-sparseness in reflectance fields. In *Proceedings of Eurographics Symposium on Rendering*, pages 251–262.

[Garulli et al., 2005] Garulli, A., Giannitrapani, A., Rossi, A., and Vicino, A. (2005). Mobile robot SLAM for line-based environment representation. In *44th IEEE European Control Conference on Decision and Control*, pages 2041–2046.

[Gelfand et al., 2003] Gelfand, N., Ikemoto, L., Rusinkiewicz, S., and Levoy, M. (2003). Geometrically stable sampling for the ICP algorithm. In *Proceedings of the 4th International Conference on 3D Digital Imaging and Modeling (3DIM)*, pages 260–267.

[Gerkey et al., 2003] Gerkey, B., Vaughan, R., and Howard, A. (2003). The player/stage project: Tools for multi-robot and distributed sensor systems. In *11th International Conference on Advanced Robotics (ICAR)*, Coimbra, Portugal.

[Gindele et al., 2008] Gindele, T., Jagszent, D., Pitzer, B., and Dillmann, R. (2008). Design of the planner of team AnnieWAY's autonomous vehicle used in the DARPA Urban Challenge 2007. In *Proceedings of the IEEE Intelligent Vehicles Symposium*, Eindhoven, Netherlands.

[Gordon, 2008] Gordon, B. (2008). *Zur Bestimmung von Messunsicherheiten terrestrischer Laserscanner*. PhD thesis, TU Darmstadt.

[Gouraud, 1971] Gouraud, H. (1971). Continuous shading of curved surfaces. *IEEE Transactions on Computers*, 20(6):623–629.

[Grisetti et al., 2007a] Grisetti, G., Grzonka, S., Stachniss, C., Pfaff, P., and Burgard, W. (2007a). Efficient estimation of accurate maximum likelihood maps in 3D. *Proceedings of the IEEE/RSJ International Conference on Intelligent Robots and Systems (IROS)*, pages 3472–3478.

[Grisetti et al., 2007b] Grisetti, G., Tipaldi, G. D., Stachniss, C., Burgard, W., and Nardi, D. (2007b). Fast and accurate SLAM with Rao-Blackwellized particle filters. *Robots and Autonomous Systems*, 55(1):30–38.

[Guivant and Nebot, 2002] Guivant, J. E. and Nebot, E. M. (2002). Improving computational and memory requirements of simultaneous localization and map building algorithms. In *IEEE International Conference on Robotics and Automation (ICRA)*, pages 2731–2736.

[Gutierrez-Osuna et al., 1998] Gutierrez-Osuna, R., Janet, J. A., and Luo, R. C. (1998). Modeling of ultrasonic range sensors for localization of autonomous mobile robots. *IEEE Transactions on Industrial Electronics*, 45:654–662.

[Hähnel et al., 2003a] Hähnel, D., Burgard, W., Fox, D., and Thrun, S. (2003a). A highly efficient FastSLAM algorithm for generating cyclic maps of large-scale environments from raw laser range measurements. In *Proceedings of the IEEE/RSJ International Conference on Intelligent Robots and Systems (IROS)*.

[Hähnel et al., 2003b] Hähnel, D., Burgard, W., and Thrun, S. (2003b). Learning compact 3D models of indoor and outdoor environments with a mobile robot. *Robotics and Autonomous Systems*, 44(1):15–27.

[Harati and Siegwart, 2007] Harati, A. and Siegwart, R. (2007). Orthogonal 3D-SLAM for indoor environments using right angle corners. In *3rd European Conference on Mobile Robotics*.

[Haris et al., 1998] Haris, K., Efstratiadis, S., Maglaveras, N., and Katsaggelos, A. (1998). Hybrid image segmentation using watersheds and fast region merging. *IEEE Transactions on Image Processing*, 7(12):1684–1699.

[Hartley and Zisserman, 2004] Hartley, R. I. and Zisserman, A. (2004). *Multiple View Geometry in Computer Vision.* Cambridge University Press, ISBN: 0521540518, second edition.

[Hebert et al., 1989] Hebert, M., Caillas, C., Krotkov, E., Kweon, I. S., and Kanade, T. (1989). Terrain mapping for a roving planetary explorer. In *Proceedings of the IEEE International Conference on Robotics and Automation (ICRA)*, volume 2, pages 997–1002.

[Hecker and Bolle, 1994] Hecker, Y. and Bolle, R. (1994). On geometric hashing and the generalized hough transform. *IEEE Transactions on Systems, Man and Cybernetics*, 24(9):1328–1338.

[Heikkila and Silven, 1997] Heikkila, J. and Silven, O. (1997). A four-step camera calibration procedure with implicit image correction. In *Proceedings of the Conference on Computer Vision and Pattern Recognition (CVPR)*, page 1106, Washington, DC, USA. IEEE Computer Society.

[Hoppe, 1993] Hoppe, H. (1993). Test datasets for surface reconstruction.

[Hoppe et al., 1992] Hoppe, H., Derose, T., Duchamp, T., Mcdonald, J., and Stuetzle, W. (1992). Surface reconstruction from unorganized points. *Computer Graphics*, 26(2):71–78.

[Hoppe et al., 1993] Hoppe, H., DeRose, T., Duchamp, T., McDonald, J., and Stuetzle, W. (1993). Mesh optimization. In *Proceedings of the 20th Annual Conference on Computer Graphics and Interactive Techniques (SIGGRAPH)*, pages 19–26, New York, NY, USA. ACM Press.

[Howard and Roy, 2003] Howard, A. and Roy, N. (2003). The robotics data set repository (radish).

[Howard et al., 2004] Howard, A., Wolf, D. F., and Sukhatme, G. S. (2004). Towards autonomous 3D mapping in urban environments. In *Proceedings of the IEEE/RSJ International Conference on Intelligent Robots and Systems (IROS)*.

[Huber et al., 2000] Huber, D., Carmichael, O., and Hebert, M. (2000). 3d map reconstruction from range data. In *Proceedings of the IEEE International Conference on Robotics and Automation (ICRA)*, volume 1, pages 891–897.

[Jenke et al., 2006] Jenke, P., Wand, M., Bokeloh, M., Schilling, A., and Strasser, W. (2006). Bayesian point cloud reconstruction. In *Proceedings of Eurographics*.

[Johnson and Kang, 1997a] Johnson, A. and Kang, S. B. (1997a). Registration and integration of textured 3D data. *First International Conference on Recent Advances in 3-D Digital Imaging and Modeling (3DIM)*, 1:234.

[Johnson and Kang, 1997b] Johnson, A. E. and Kang, S. B. (1997b). Registration and integration of textured 3D data. In *Proceedings of the International Conference on Recent Advances in 3-D Digital Imaging and Modeling*, page 234, Washington, DC, USA. IEEE Computer Society.

[Jones et al., 2003] Jones, T. R., Durand, F., and Desbrun, M. (2003). Non-iterative, feature-preserving mesh smoothing. *ACM Transactions on Graphics (TOG)*, 22(3):943–949.

[Kammel and Pitzer, 2008] Kammel, S. and Pitzer, B. (2008). Lidar-based lane marker detection and mapping. In *Proceedings of the IEEE Intelligent Vehicles Symposium*, Eindhoven, Netherlands.

[Kammel et al., 2008] Kammel, S., Ziegler, J., Pitzer, B., Werling, M., Gindele, T., Jagszent, D., Schröder, J., Thuy, M., Goebl, M., von Hundelshausen, F., Pink, O., Frese, C., and Stiller, C. (2008). Team AnnieWAY's autonomous system for the 2007 DARPA Urban Challenge. *Journal Field Robotics*, 25(9):615–639.

[Kazhdan, 2005] Kazhdan, M. (2005). Reconstruction of solid models from oriented point sets. In *Proceedings of the third Eurographics Symposium on Geometry Processing (SGP)*, page 73, Aire-la-Ville, Switzerland, Switzerland. Eurographics Association.

[Kazhdan et al., 2006] Kazhdan, M., Bolitho, M., and Hoppe, H. (2006). Poisson surface reconstruction. In *Proceedings of the fourth Eurographics Symposium on Geometry Processing (SGP)*, pages 61–70, Aire-la-Ville, Switzerland, Switzerland. Eurographics Association.

[Klein and Murray, 2007] Klein, G. and Murray, D. (2007). Parallel tracking and mapping for small AR workspaces. In *Proceedings of the ACM International Symposium on Mixed and Augmented Reality (ISMAR)*, Nara, Japan.

[Kolluri et al., 2004] Kolluri, R., Shewchuk, J. R., and O'Brien, J. F. (2004). Spectral surface reconstruction from noisy point clouds. In *Proceedings of the Eurographics/ACM SIGGRAPH Symposium on Geometry Processing (SGP)*, pages 11–21, New York, NY, USA. ACM.

[Kuipers and Byun, 1993] Kuipers, B. and Byun, Y.-T. (1993). A robot exploration and mapping strategy based on a semantic hierarchy of spatial representations. pages 47–63.

[Levin et al., 2003] Levin, A., Zomet, A., and Weiss, Y. (2003). Learning to perceive transparency from the statistics of natural scenes. In S. Becker, S. T. and Obermayer, K., editors, *Advances in Neural Information Processing Systems 15*, pages 1247–1254. MIT Press, Cambridge, MA.

[Levoy et al., 2000] Levoy, M., Pulli, K., Curless, B., Rusinkiewicz, S., Koller, D., Pereira, L., Ginzton, M., Anderson, S., Davis, J., Ginsberg, J., Shade, J., and Fulk, D. (2000). The digital michelangelo project: 3D scanning of large statues. In *Proceedings of the 27th Annual Conference on Computer Graphics and Interactive Techniques (SIGGRAPH)*, pages 131–144, New York, NY, USA. ACM Press/Addison-Wesley Publishing Co.

[Lévy et al., 2002] Lévy, B., Petitjean, S., Ray, N., and Maillot, J. (2002). Least squares conformal maps for automatic texture atlas generation. *ACM Transactions on Graphics*, 21(3):362–371.

[Lindstrom and Turk, 2000] Lindstrom, P. and Turk, G. (2000). Image-driven simplification. *ACM Transactions on Graphics*, 19(3):204–241.

[Lorensen and Cline, 1987] Lorensen, W. E. and Cline, H. E. (1987). Marching cubes: A high resolution 3D surface construction algorithm. In *Proceedings of the 14th annual conference on Computer graphics and interactive techniques (SIGGRAPH)*, pages 163–169, New York, NY, USA. ACM Press.

[Lowe, 2004] Lowe, D. G. (2004). Distinctive image features from scale-invariant keypoints. *International Journal of Computer Vision*, 60:91–110.

[Lu and Milios, 1997] Lu, F. and Milios, E. (1997). Globally consistent range scan alignment for environment mapping. *Autonomous Robots*, 4(4):333–349.

[Marschner et al., 2000] Marschner, S. R., Westin, S. H., Lafortune, E. P. F., and Torrance., K. E. (2000). Image-based BRDF measurement. *Applied Optics*, 39(16).

[Miller et al., 2008] Miller, I., Campbell, M., Huttenlocher, D., Kline, F.-R., Nathan, A., Lupashin, S., Catlin, J., Schimpf, B., Moran, P., Zych, N., Garcia, E., Kurdziel, M., and Fujishima, H. (2008). Team Cornell's Skynet: Robust perception and planning in an urban environment. *Journal Field Robotics*, 25(8):493–527.

[Montemerlo et al., 2008] Montemerlo, M., Becker, J., Bhat, S., Dahlkamp, H., Dolgov, D., Ettinger, S., Hähnel, D., Hilden, T., Hoffmann, G., Huhnke, B., Johnston, D., Klumpp, S., Langer, D., Levandowski, A., Levinson, J., Marcil, J., Orenstein, D., Paefgen, J., Penny, I., Petrovskaya, A., Pflueger, M., Stanek, G., Stavens, D., Vogt, A., and Thrun, S. (2008). Junior: The stanford entry in the Urban Challenge. *Journal of Field Robotics*, 25(9):569–597.

[Montemerlo and Thrun, 2004] Montemerlo, M. and Thrun, S. (2004). A multi-resolution pyramid for outdoor robot terrain perception. In *Proceedings of the AAAI National Conference on Artificial Intelligence*, San Jose, CA. AAAI.

[Montemerlo et al., 2002] Montemerlo, M., Thrun, S., Koller, D., and Wegbreit, B. (2002). FastSLAM: a factored solution to the simultaneous localization and mapping problem. In *18th National Conference on Artificial Intelligence*, pages 593–598.

[Ni et al., 2004] Ni, X., Garland, M., and Hart, J. C. (2004). Fair morse functions for extracting the topological structure of a surface mesh. In *ACM Transactions on Graphics*, pages 613–622, New York, NY, USA. ACM.

[Nicodemus, 1965] Nicodemus, F. E. (1965). Directional reflectance and emissivity of an opaque surface. *Applied Optics*, 4(7):767–773.

[Nieto et al., 2006] Nieto, J., Bailey, T., and Nebot, E. (2006). Scan-SLAM: Combining EKF-SLAM and scan correlation. In *Field and Service Robotics : Results of the 5th International Conference (FSR)*, volume 25 of *Springer Tracts in Advanced Robotics*, pages 167–178. Springer Berlin / Heidelberg.

[Nieto et al., 2007] Nieto, J., Bailey, T., and Nebot, E. (2007). Recursive scan-matching SLAM. *Robotics and Autonomous Systems*, 55(1):39–49.

[Nüchter et al., 2003a] Nüchter, A., Surmann, H., Lingemann, K., and Hertzberg, J. (2003a). Consistent 3D model construction with autonomous mobile robots. In *Proceedings of the 26th German Conference on Artificial Intelligence (KI)*, Hamburg, Germany.

[Nüchter et al., 2003b] Nüchter, A., Surmann, H., Lingemann, K., and Hertzberg, J. (2003b). Semantic scene analysis of scanned 3D indoor environments. In Ertl, T., editor, *Proceedings of the Vision, Modeling, and Visualization Conference (VMV)*, pages 215–221, München, Germany. Aka GmbH.

[Nüchter et al., 2004] Nüchter, A., Surmann, H., Lingemann, K., Hertzberg, J., and Thrun, S. (2004). 6D SLAM with application in autonomous mine mapping. In *Proceedings of the IEEE International Conference Robotics and Automation (ICRA)*, pages 1998 – 2003, New Orleans, USA.

[Nüchter et al., 2005] Nüchter, A., Wulf, O., Lingemann, K., Hertzberg, J., Wagner, B., and Surmann, H. (2005). 3d mapping with semantic knowledge. In *Proceedings of the RoboCup International Symposium*, Osaka, Japan.

[Olson et al., 2006] Olson, E., Leonard, J., and Teller, S. (2006). Fast iterative alignment of pose graphs with poor initial estimates. In *Proceedings of the IEEE International Conference on Robotics and Automation (ICRA)*, pages 2262–2269.

[Parzen, 1962] Parzen, E. (1962). On estimation of a probability density function and mode. *The Annals of Mathematical Statistics*, 33(3):1065–1076.

[Paskin, 2003] Paskin, M. A. (2003). Thin junction tree filters for simultaneous localization and mapping. In *18th International Joint Conference on Artificial Intelligence*, pages 1157–1166.

[Pérez et al., 2003] Pérez, P., Gangnet, M., and Blake, A. (2003). Poisson image editing. *ACM Transactions on Graphics*, 22(3):313–318.

[Petersen, 2006] Petersen, P. (2006). *Riemannian geometry*.

[Pitzer et al., 2010] Pitzer, B., Kammel, S., DuHadway, C., and Becker, J. (2010). Automatic reconstruction of textured 3D models. In *IEEE International Conference on Robotics and Automation (ICRA)*, pages 3486–3493.

[Pitzer et al., 2006] Pitzer, B., Libuda, L., and Kraiss, K.-F. (2006). Knowledge-based scene analysis in indoor environments using colour and range images. In Kobbelt, L., Kuhlen, T., Aach, T., and Westermann, R., editors, *Proceedings of the Vision, Modeling, and Visualization Conference (VMV)*, pages 33–40, Aachen, Germany. Aka GmbH.

[Pitzer and Stiller, 2010] Pitzer, B. and Stiller, C. (2010). Probabilistic mapping for mobile robots using spatial correlation models. In *IEEE International Conference on Robotics and Automation (ICRA)*, pages 5402–5409, Anchorage, Alaska, USA.

[Pulli, 1999] Pulli, K. (1999). Multiview registration for large data sets. In *2nd International Conference on 3D Digital Imaging and Modeling (3DIM)*, pages 160–168, Ottawa, Canada. IEEE Computer Society.

[Quigley et al., 2009] Quigley, M., Conley, K., Gerkey, B., Faust, J., Foote, T. B., Leibs, J., Wheeler, R., and Ng, A. Y. (2009). ROS: an open-source robot operating system. In *International Conference on Robotics and Automation*, Open-Source Software workshop.

[Roy and Thrun, 1998] Roy, N. and Thrun, S. (1998). Online self-calibration for mobile robots. In *Proceeding of the IEEE International Conference on Robotics and Automation*, pages 2292–2297. IEEE Computer Society Press.

[Rusinkiewicz and Levoy, 2001] Rusinkiewicz, S. and Levoy, M. (2001). Efficient variants of the ICP algorithm. In *Third International Conference on 3D Digital Imaging and Modeling (3DIM)*.

[Sato and Ikeuchi, 1994] Sato, Y. and Ikeuchi, K. (1994). Reflectance analysis under solar illumination. Technical report, Pittsburgh, PA, USA.

[Sato et al., 1997] Sato, Y., Wheeler, M. D., and Ikeuchi, K. (1997). Object shape and reflectance modeling from observation. In *Proceedings of the 24th annual conference on Computer graphics and interactive techniques (SIGGRAPH)*, pages 379–387, New York, NY, USA. ACM Press/Addison-Wesley Publishing Co.

[Schönemann, 1966] Schönemann, P. H. (1966). A generalized solution of the orthogonal Procrustes problem. *Psychmoetrika*, 31:1–10.

[Segal et al., 2009] Segal, A., Hähnel, D., and Thrun, S. (2009). Generalized-ICP. In *Proceedings of Robotics: Science and Systems*, Seattle, USA.

[Seitz et al., 2006] Seitz, S. M., Curless, B., Diebel, J., Scharstein, D., and Szeliski, R. (2006). A comparison and evaluation of Multi-View Stereo reconstruction algorithms. In *Proceedings of the IEEE Conference on Computer Vision and Pattern Recognition (CVPR)*, pages 519–528, Washington, DC, USA. IEEE Computer Society.

[Sequeira et al., 1999] Sequeira, V., Ng, K., Wolfart, E., Gonçalves, J., and Hogg, D. (1999). Automated reconstruction of 3D models from real environments. *Journal of Photogrammetry & Remote Sensing*, 55(1):1–22.

[Sheffer and Hart, 2002] Sheffer, A. and Hart, J. C. (2002). Seamster: inconspicuous low-distortion texture seam layout. In *Proceedings of the Conference on Visualization (VIS)*, pages 291–298, Washington, DC, USA. IEEE Computer Society.

[Sheffer et al., 2006] Sheffer, A., Praun, E., and Rose, K. (2006). Mesh parameterization methods and their applications. *Foundations and Trends in Computer Graphics and Vision*, 2(2):105–171.

[Shewchuk, 1994] Shewchuk, J. R. (1994). An introduction to the conjugate gradient method without the agonizing pain.

[Smith and Cheeseman, 1987] Smith, R. C. and Cheeseman, P. (1987). On the representation and estimation of spatial uncertainly. *International Journal on Robotics Research*, 5(4):56–68.

[Stiller et al., 2008] Stiller, C., Kammel, S., Pitzer, B., Ziegler, J., Werling, M., Gindele, T., and Jagszent, D. (2008). Team AnnieWAYs autonomous system. In *Robot Vision*, volume 4931 of *Lecture Notes in Computer Science*, pages 248–259. Springer Berlin / Heidelberg.

[Stockman, 1987] Stockman, G. (1987). Object recognition and localization via pose clustering. *Computer Vision, Graphics, and Image Processing*, 40(3):361–387.

[Stoddart et al., 1998] Stoddart, A. J., Lemke, S., Hilton, A., and Renn, T. (1998). Estimating pose uncertainty for surface registration. *Image and Vision Computing*, 16(2):111–120.

[Surmann et al., 2003] Surmann, H., Nüchter, A., and Hertzberg, J. (2003). An autonomous mobile robot with a 3D laser range finder for 3D exploration and digitalization of indoor environments. *Robotics and Autonomous Systems*, 45(3–4):181–198.

[Terzopoulos and Vasilescu, 1991] Terzopoulos, D. and Vasilescu, M. (1991). Sampling and reconstruction with adaptive meshes. In *Proceedings of the Conference on Computer Vision and Pattern Recognition*, pages 70–75. IEEE.

[Thrun, 2002] Thrun, S. (2002). Robotic mapping: A survey. In Lakemeyer, G. and Nebel, B., editors, *Exploring Artificial Intelligence in the New Millenium*. Morgan Kaufmann.

[Thrun et al., 2000] Thrun, S., Burgard, W., and Fox, D. (2000). A real-time algorithm for mobile robot mapping with applications to multi-robot and 3D mapping. In *Proceedings of the IEEE International Conference on Robotics and Automation (ICRA)*, San Francisco, CA. IEEE.

[Thrun et al., 2005] Thrun, S., Burgard, W., and Fox, D. (2005). *Probabilistic Robotics*. MIT Press.

[Thrun and Montemerlo, 2005] Thrun, S. and Montemerlo, M. (2005). The GraphSLAM algorithm with applications to large-scale mapping of urban structures. *International Journal on Robotics Research*, 25(5/6):403–430.

[Thrun et al., 2004] Thrun, S., Thayer, S., Whittaker, W., Baker, C., Burgard, W., Ferguson, D., Hähnel, D., Montemerlo, M., Morris, A., Omohundro, Z., Reverte, C., and Whittaker, W. (2004). Autonomous exploration and mapping of abandoned mines. *IEEE Robotics and Automation Magazine*, 11(4):79–91. Forthcoming.

[Tomasi and Manduchi, 1998] Tomasi, C. and Manduchi, R. (1998). Bilateral filtering for gray and color images. In *Proceedings of the 6th International Conference on Computer Vision*, page 839, Washington, DC, USA. IEEE Computer Society.

[Trefethen and Bau, 1997] Trefethen, L. N. and Bau, D. (1997). *Numerical Linear Algebra*. SIAM: Society for Industrial and Applied Mathematics.

[Triebel et al., 2006] Triebel, R., Pfaff, P., and Burgard, W. (2006). Multi-level surface maps for outdoor terrain mapping and loop closing. In *IEEE/RSJ International Conference on Intelligent Robots and Systems (IROS)*, pages 2276–2282.

[Triggs et al., 2000] Triggs, B., Mclauchlan, P. F., Hartley, R. I., and Fitzgibbon, A. W. (2000). Bundle adjustment – a modern synthesis. *Lecture Notes in Computer Science*, 1883:298.

[Tsai, 1987] Tsai, R. (1987). A versatile camera calibration technique for high-accuracy 3D machine vision metrology using off-the-shelf TV cameras and lenses. *IEEE Journal on Robotics and Automation*, 3(4):323–344.

[Turk and Levoy, 1994] Turk, G. and Levoy, M. (1994). Zippered polygon meshes from range images. In *Proceedings of the 21st annual conference on Computer graphics and interactive techniques (SIGGRAPH)*, pages 311–318, New York, NY, USA. ACM Press.

[Urmson et al., 2008] Urmson, C., Anhalt, J., Bagnell, D., Baker, C. R., Bittner, R., Clark, M. N., Dolan, J. M., Duggins, D., Galatali, T., Geyer, C., Gittleman, M., Harbaugh, S., Hebert, M., Howard, T. M., Kolski, S., Kelly, A., Likhachev, M., McNaughton, M., Miller, N., Peterson, K., Pilnick, B., Rajkumar, R., Rybski, P. E., Salesky, B., Seo, Y.-W., Singh, S., Snider, J., Stentz, A., Whittaker, W., Wolkowicki, Z., Ziglar, J., Bae, H., Brown, T., Demitrish, D., Litkouhi, B., Nickolaou, J., Sadekar, V., Zhang, W., Struble, J., Taylor, M., Darms, M., and Ferguson, D. (2008). Autonomous driving in urban environments: Boss and the Urban Challenge. *Journal Field Robotics*, 25(8):425–466.

[Wolff et al., 1992] Wolff, L. B., Shafer, S. A., and Healey, G., editors (1992). *Radiometry*. Jones and Bartlett Publishers, Inc., USA.

[Wolfson and Rigoutsos, 1997] Wolfson, H. J. and Rigoutsos, I. (1997). Geometric hashing: An overview. *Computing in Science and Engineering*, 4:10–21.

[Wurm et al., 2010] Wurm, K. M., Hornung, A., Bennewitz, M., Stachniss, C., and Burgard, W. (2010). OctoMap: A probabilistic, flexible, and compact 3D map representation for robotic systems. In *Proceedings of the ICRA 2010 Workshop on Best Practice in 3D Perception and Modeling for Mobile Manipulation*.

[Xue et al., 2009] Xue, Z., Kasper, A., Zoellner, M. J., and Dillmann, R. (2009). An automatic grasp planning system for service robots. In *14th International Conference on Advanced Robotics*.

[Yamauchi, 1997] Yamauchi, B. (1997). A frontier-based approach for autonomous exploration. In *Proceedings of the IEEE International Symposium on Computational Intelligence in Robotics and Automation (CIRA)*, page 146, Monterey, California.

[Yu and Malik, 1998] Yu, Y. and Malik, J. (1998). Recovering photometric properties of architectural scenes from photographs. In *Proceedings of the 25th annual conference on Computer graphics and interactive techniques (SIGGRAPH)*, pages 207–217, New York, NY, USA. ACM.

[Zhang, 1994] Zhang, Z. (1994). Iterative point matching for registration of free-form curves and surfaces. *International Journal of Computer Vision*, 13(2):119–152.

[Zhang, 1999] Zhang, Z. (1999). Flexible camera calibration by viewing a plane from unknown orientations. *IEEE International Conference on Computer Vision*, 1:666.

[Zhao and Shibasaki, 2001] Zhao, H. and Shibasaki, R. (2001). Reconstructing textured CAD model of urban environment using vehicle-borne laser range scanners and line cameras. In *Proceedings of the Second International Workshop on Computer Vision Systems (ICVS)*, pages 284–297, London, UK. Springer-Verlag.

[Ziegler and Pitzer, 2008] Ziegler, J. and Pitzer, B. (2008). Bahnplanung für das autonome Fahrzeug AnnieWAY. In *5. Workshop Fahrerassistenzsysteme*, Walting, Germany.

Schriftenreihe
Institut für Mess- und Regelungstechnik
Karlsruher Institut für Technologie
(1613-4214)

Die Bände sind unter www.ksp.kit.edu als PDF frei verfügbar oder als Druckausgabe bestellbar.

Band 001 Hans, Annegret
Entwicklung eines Inline-Viskosimeters auf Basis eines magnetisch-induktiven Durchflussmessers. 2004
ISBN 3-937300-02-3

Band 002 Heizmann, Michael
Auswertung von forensischen Riefenspuren mittels automatischer Sichtprüfung. 2004
ISBN 3-937300-05-8

Band 003 Herbst, Jürgen
Zerstörungsfreie Prüfung von Abwasserkanälen mit Klopfschall. 2004
ISBN 3-937300-23-6

Band 004 Kammel, Sören
Deflektometrische Untersuchung spiegelnd reflektierender Freiformflächen. 2005
ISBN 3-937300-28-7

Band 005 Geistler, Alexander
Bordautonome Ortung von Schienenfahrzeugen mit Wirbelstrom-Sensoren. 2007
ISBN 978-3-86644-123-1

Band 006 Horn, Jan
Zweidimensionale Geschwindigkeitsmessung texturierter Oberflächen mit flächenhaften bildgebenden Sensoren. 2007
ISBN 978-3-86644-076-0

Band 007 Hoffmann, Christian
Fahrzeugdetektion durch Fusion monoskopischer Videomerkmale. 2007
ISBN 978-3-86644-139-2

Band 008 Dang, Thao
Kontinuierliche Selbstkalibrierung von Stereokameras. 2007
ISBN 978-3-86644-164-4

Band 009 Kapp, Andreas
Ein Beitrag zur Verbesserung und Erweiterung der Lidar-Signalverarbeitung für Fahrzeuge. 2007
ISBN 978-3-86644-174-3

Band 010 Horbach, Jan
Verfahren zur optischen 3D-Vermessung spiegelnder Oberflächen. 2008
ISBN 978-3-86644-202-3

Band 011 Böhringer, Frank
Gleisselektive Ortung von Schienenfahrzeugen mit bordautonomer Sensorik. 2008
ISBN 978-3-86644-196-5

Band 012 Xin, Binjian
Auswertung und Charakterisierung dreidimensionaler Messdaten technischer Oberflächen mit Riefentexturen. 2009
ISBN 978-3-86644-326-6

Band 013 Cech, Markus
Fahrspurschätzung aus monokularen Bildfolgen für innerstädtische Fahrerassistenzanwendungen. 2009
ISBN 978-3-86644-351-8

Band 014 Speck, Christoph
Automatisierte Auswertung forensischer Spuren auf Patronenhülsen. 2009
ISBN 978-3-86644-365-5

Band 015 Bachmann, Alexander
Dichte Objektsegmentierung in Stereobildfolgen. 2010
ISBN 978-3-86644-541-3

Band 016 Duchow, Christian
Videobasierte Wahrnehmung markierter Kreuzungen mit lokalem Markierungstest und Bayes'scher Modellierung. 2011
ISBN 978-3-86644-630-4

Band 017 Pink, Oliver
Bildbasierte Selbstlokalisierung von Straßenfahrzeugen. 2011
ISBN 978-3-86644-708-0

Band 018 Hensel, Stefan
Wirbelstromsensorbasierte Lokalisierung von Schienenfahrzeugen in topologischen Karten. 2011
ISBN 978-3-86644-749-3

Band 019 Carsten Hasberg
Simultane Lokalisierung und Kartierung spurgeführter Systeme. 2012
ISBN 978-3-86644-831-5

Band 020 Pitzer, Benjamin
Automatic Reconstruction of Textured 3D Models. 2014
ISBN 978-3-86644-805-6